SEDUCED BY DEATH

SEDUCED BY DEATH

Doctors, Patients, and Assisted Suicide

Revised and Updated

Herbert Hendin, M.D.

W. W. NORTON & COMPANY
New York   London

Copyright © 1998, 1997 by Herbert Hendin, M.D.

Previous edition published as *Seduced by Death: Doctors, Patients, and the Dutch Cure*

The text of this book is composed in Bembo
Composition and manufacturing by the Haddon Craftsmen Inc.

Library of Congress Cataloging-in-Publication Data

Hendin. Herbert.
    Seduced by death : doctors, patients, and assisted suicide / Herbert Hendin. —
Rev. and updated.
        p.   cm.
    First ed. subtitled: Doctors, patients, and the Dutch cure.
    Includes bibliographical references and index.
    ISBN 0-393-31791-9 (pbk.)
    1. Euthanasia.   2. Assisted suicide.   3. Terminal care—Moral and ethical aspects.
4. Euthanasia—Netherlands.   5. Assisted suicide—Netherlands.   6. Euthanasia—
United States.   7. Assisted suicide—United States.   I. Title.
R726.H46   1998
179'.7—dc21
                                                                            98-10372
                                                                            CIP

W. W. Norton & Company, Inc., 500 Fifth Avenue, New York, N.Y. 10110
                    http://www.wwnorton.com

W. W. Norton & Company Ltd., 10 Coptic Street, London WC1A 1PU

1 2 3 4 5 6 7 8 9 0

To Jo

CONTENTS

Acknowledgments 9

Preface: A Victory for Patients 11

Introduction 23

1. Suicide, Assisted Suicide, and Medical Illness 31

2. Selling Suicide 39

3. Seduced by Death 63

4. The Politics of Euthanasia 111

5. A Cure for Suicide 151

6. Why the Netherlands?
Why the United States? 163

7. Theory and Practice 183

8. Who Should Decide?
Coma and Dementia 215

9. Caring Beyond Cure 229

Afterword: The Culture of Euthanasia 257

References 269

Index 295

ACKNOWLEDGMENTS

I am grateful to everyone whom I interviewed in the Netherlands—physicians and patients, academics and laypeople, euthanasia advocates and opponents—for providing me with the material that made my work possible. Who they are and the roles they played will become evident in the course of this book.

No one could have been more fortunate than I in having colleagues who read the book in manuscript, generously shared their knowledge with me, and suggested additional reading that was helpful. I will always be grateful to Yale Kamisar, Clarence Darrow Distinguished Professor of Law at the University of Michigan; Thomas Marzen of the National Legal Center for the Medically Dependent and Disabled; Barry Bostrum, Editor of *Issues in Law and Medicine;* Daniel Callahan, President of The Hastings Center; Carlos Gomez, Director of the Palliative Care Center at the University of Virginia; and Derek Phillips, Professor of Sociology at the University of Amsterdam.

Danuta Wasserman, Director of the Center for Suicide Research and Prevention and Professor of Psychiatry and Suicidology at the Karolinska Institute in Sweden, and Gunnar

Ekland, Professor Emeritus of Epidemiology at the Karolinska Institute, made helpful suggestions for dealing with the Dutch statistical data on suicide.

Alan Lipschitz, a member of the Scientific Council of the American Foundation for Suicide Prevention, read all of the versions of the manuscript. His suggestions were a constant challenge to explain and clarify what was unclear.

Bette-Jane Crigger, Editor of the *Hastings Center Report,* not only improved the manuscript by editing it prior to my submitting it for publication, but made valuable suggestions for reorganizing some of the chapters.

Drake McFeely, President at W. W. Norton, and Donald Lamm, the Chairman, made suggestions that helped sharpen and focus this book. I am also grateful to Carol Houck Smith, my editor at W. W. Norton for over a decade, for her help.

Hanny Veenendaal, Janneke Lam-Hesseling, Valentin Byvack, and Maria Verheij translated Dutch articles and book chapters for me.

Matthew Nock provided research assistance for this project.

The *Journal of the American Medical Association,* the *American Journal of Psychiatry, Issues in Law and Medicine,* the *Journal of Suicide and Life-Threatening Behavior,* the *Hastings Center Report,* the *Duquesne Law Review,* the *Journal of Forensic Psychiatry,* the *New York Times,* and *Newsday* permitted me to use material from articles of mine on assisted suicide and euthanasia that they had published.

I am grateful to The Rockefeller Foundation for permitting me to work on this project as a scholar in residence at the Rockefeller Study Center in Bellagio, Italy.

My wife, Josephine Hendin, Professor and Chair of the Department of English at New York University, has been intimately involved with this study of assisted suicide and euthanasia over the past five years and with all of my work for the past thirty years.

PREFACE:
A VICTORY FOR PATIENTS

In the spring of 1996, legalization of physician-assisted suicide seemed to be inevitable. In the space of a month, two appellate courts had declared there to be a constitutional right to physician-assisted suicide, overturning longstanding state laws in New York and Washington that prohibited the practice. Many observers expected the U.S. Supreme Court to follow suit. Earlier, Oregon had become the first state to legalize physician-assisted suicide; although that decision was still being contested in the courts, had the Supreme Court recognized and accepted a constitutional right to physician-assisted suicide, Oregon was ready to become the first state in which it was practiced.

When Laurence Tribe, a distinguished Harvard law professor skilled in presenting cases to the Supreme Court, agreed to argue the New York case *(Vacco v. Quill)*[1] for the plaintiffs, euthanasia advocates were elated and opponents were dismayed. Although advocates understandably wished to create an atmosphere that would discourage opposition, there seemed a substantial basis for their optimism.

Oral arguments held before the Court in January 1997 showed, however, that the outcome was not inevitable. The

Justices indicated that they were considering the realities of medicine in ways that the appellate courts had not. They asked how it was possible to recognize the right to physician-assisted suicide only for terminally ill patients—requested by the plaintiffs—and not for chronically ill patients who have longer to suffer, or for those who suffer emotional pain unaccompanied by physical illness. Similarly, they did not seem to see it possible to end such a right with assisted suicide in which a patient takes a lethal dose of medication prescribed by a doctor and to forbid physicians to give lethal injections (euthanasia) to those patients who were unable to swallow drugs, or otherwise effect their own deaths.

The decision handed down by the Court on June 26, 1997, was first and foremost a victory for patients. The importance of what the Court rejected—a federal constitutional right to assisted suicide—was at least equaled by the medical importance of what the majority of Justices embraced: the right of terminally ill patients not to suffer. The decision thus made a substantial contribution to the practice of medicine and the care of patients at the end of life.

For example, the briefs arguing against the New York and Washington laws prohibiting assisting in suicide had equated the right to withdraw from treatment that would hasten death with physician-assisted suicide, maintaining that since one was permissible the other should be also. The appellate courts supported this contention.

But a patient's right to withdraw from any treatment is no different from his or her right not to initiate any treatment—no matter how life-saving it may be. It has nothing to do with a "right to hasten death" and everything to do with the fact that medical practice depends on the principle of informed consent. Insulin cannot be forced on a patient with diabetes. Nor can a young patient be required to live with a respirator, even if he or she will die without it. All patients—not only those who are terminally ill—can exercise the right to withdraw from treatment even if the decision ends their lives. If treatment is withdrawn and the patient does not die, neither the doctor nor the family kills the patient. This is different from assisted suicide, whose intention is always to end life; when it fails, as it frequently does, families and physicians intervene more actively—families with plastic bags and physicians with lethal injections.

The Supreme Court reaffirmed that the legal foundation for informed consent and the right to refuse treatment was not based on an abstract right to hasten death, but on traditional common-law rights to protection from unwanted invasion of one's body. The Court recognized differences in intent between withdrawal of treatment—where the doctor and the patient may not intend death but merely freedom from unwanted technology, medicine, or drugs—and physician-assisted suicide, where both doctor and patient have death as their specific goal. In addition, the Court recognized causative differences between a patient dying from an underlying disease after treatment withdrawal and a patient dying from a lethal dose of drugs after physician-assisted suicide.

The Court's firm recognition of the difference between withdrawal of treatment and assisted suicide will be of help to doctors and patients. Both need to understand when it is appropriate to withdraw treatment that only prolongs suffering. Confusion created by the contention that withdrawal of treatment is the same as physician-assisted suicide has made some physicians reluctant to withdraw such treatments. The Court's decision will help relieve their concern.

In the brief filed by Laurence Tribe in the New York case, there were disturbing descriptions of the condition of patients who chose sedation when they were close to death because their suffering could not be relieved in any other way. They were described as being in a "deathlike" state, in the "monstrous" condition of having "their minds chemically shut down" while they were "imprisoned in their decaying bodies." If they had chosen to forgo medically administered nutrition, the brief described them as being "deliberately starved to death." In fact, most such patients die peacefully without suffering. Had the Court accepted the frightening picture of sedation presented in the brief, it would have been hard for physicians to recommend and patients to seek what is at times necessary. The Court furthered hospice and palliative care by accepting such sedation as an essential and beneficial aspect of the medical care that may be needed to help dying patients.

The Justices were also sensitive, in ways that the appellate courts were not, to the likelihood of deaths that were not requested or coerced if assisted suicide were legalized. The Ninth Circuit Court of Appeals took any such danger to be minimal declaring in the Washington case, "Should an error actually occur it is likely to benefit the individual by permitting a victim of pain and suffering to end his life peacefully and with dignity . . ." The detachment that considers that even a wrongful death would be a benefit to any person who is terminally ill is removed from medical reality. The overwhelming majority of terminally ill patients do not want to hasten death and virtually never want to do so when their suffering is addressed properly.

By contrast, the Supreme Court Justices were concerned with the voluntariness of decisions about assisted suicide. They referred several times to the experience of the Netherlands, where assisted suicide and euthanasia have long been sanctioned, noting that Dutch patients are often coerced or not consulted about the decision to end their lives.

Justice Breyer wondered whether the relative absence of

palliative care centers in the Netherlands is related to the sanction given to assisted suicide and euthanasia. The evidence suggests that it is. The Dutch began giving legal sanction to assisted suicide and euthanasia before the advances in palliative care of the last fifteen years, at a time when there were few resources for suffering patients. Assisted suicide and euthanasia, intended originally for the exceptional case, have increasingly become accepted and almost routine ways of dealing with serious or terminal illness in the Netherlands. The easier solution of euthanasia seems to have contributed to the failure of palliative care and hospice care to develop in that country; both could be said to be among the casualties of euthanasia.

The Court also recognized the state's legitimate concern with preventing suicide. The Justices understood that people who become suicidal in response to medical illness are not so different from those who otherwise become suicidal: they are usually frightened and depressed. The Court cited my work to say that suicidal, terminally ill patients "usually respond well to treatment for pain medication and depressive illness and are grateful to be alive." Chief Justice Rehnquist articulated the concern that "legal physician-assisted suicide could make it more difficult for the state to protect depressed or mentally ill persons, or those who are suffering from untreated pain, from suicidal impulses."

The Supreme Court went on to support the state's "interest in protecting other vulnerable groups—the poor, the elderly and disabled persons—from abuse, neglect, and mistakes." The Court of Appeals in the Washington case had dismissed the concern that people might be pressured into physician-assisted suicide as "ludicrous on its face."

In fact, Compassion in Dying, a group that champions assisted suicide and brought the Washington case to court, had presented to the public a model case of assisted suicide that turned out on closer examination to reflect such coercion. The cover story of a *New York Times Magazine* article described the assisted suicide of Louise, a Seattle woman whose death was arranged by her doctor and the Reverend Ralph Mero, head of Compassion in Dying. That story, discussed in detail in Chapter 2, reveals a woman expressing conflicting wishes about living and dying but finding support only for death. Everyone around Louise, including her doctor, contributes to the pressure for Louise to stick to a decision about which she is clearly hesitant. To no avail a terrified Louise finally tells her mother, "I just feel as if everyone is ganging up on me, pressuring me. I just want some time." There is not much dignity or compassion in the way Louise was helped to die.

The Supreme Court opinion was an implicit challenge to every state to prevent tragedies of neglect, care that only prolongs suffering, and abuses of assisted suicide by providing to all the good palliative care now received by a few. The fact that the patients involved in the New York and Washington cases could have received such care was a key factor in the Court's decision. Five concurring opinions also contained a warning: if the states did not meet their obligations to relieve suffering, the Supreme Court would revisit the issue.

Although the decision did not preclude the states from considering the possibility of assisted suicide in their effort to care for terminally ill patients, most of the Justices seemed to regard it as not necessary. In addition, the array of legal and medical reasons they gave for ruling in favor of the New York and Washington prohibitions against assisted suicide is having an influence on state deliberation about the practice.

Most states—Oregon is a notable exception—will not become involved in a struggle over legalization, but all will need to address what must be done if the Court's challenge is to be met: improving education of physicians in palliative care, removing regulations that restrict the ways in which physicians can treat pain, widening the availability of hospice care, fostering proper reimbursement for end-of-life care, and passing better-crafted surrogacy laws that both protect incompetent patients and permit proxies to see to it that inappropriate treatments are withdrawn.

Even before the Supreme Court decision the climate had begun to change. Legalization initiatives for assisted suicide in most state legislatures have not gone forward; instead more states have passed laws prohibiting assisted suicide. And Congress passed its own law ensuring that no federal funds would be used to support physician-assisted suicide. Some leading proponents of assisted suicide have changed their mind. Full-blown legalization, while possible, now seems less likely.

Most attention is shifting to the larger and more difficult question of providing good care for those who are terminally ill. Our failure to provide this care created the understandable but unwise belief that legalization of assisted suicide would make things better and permitted Jack Kevorkian to be seen as the champion of those who are terminally ill.

If we are successful in avoiding legalization and in providing adequate care for terminally ill patients, then euthanasia advocates like Jack Kevorkian may be given some credit for issuing a wake-up call to the medical community. For it was partly to avoid this bugler's becoming the Pied Piper that American medicine has undertaken a major campaign to educate physicians on the care of those who are dying.

Doctors, patients, and all of us should be grateful that the Supreme Court decision has given us an opportunity to focus on end-of-life care. As we meet that challenge, the question of physician-assisted suicide should no longer be relevant.

―――

Changing the situation in the Netherlands will be more difficult for a number of reasons: the Dutch medical establishment has a stake in defending their euthanasia policies, the authority of that establishment is less apt to be questioned in the Netherlands than it would be in the United States, doctors have become educated to euthanasia rather than to palliative care, and the public is unaware that when terminally ill they should have more options than suffering or hastening death.

A glimpse of both the promise and the frustration of the Dutch situation is evident in the experience of Dr. Zbigniew Zylicz, whom I met while visiting some of the few Dutch hospices after the original publication of this book. Zylicz, who came to the Netherlands from Poland eighteen years ago, is one of the few recognized palliative care experts in the country. He runs the Hospice Rozenhuyvel in Rozendaal while serving as a consultant to several hundred doctors responsible for caring for several hundred thousand patients in his part of the Netherlands. In this role he makes about 500 house calls a year seeing the terminally ill patients of other doctors and advising these doctors on how to relieve their patients' suffering. In addition, he conducts year-round classes to train doctors in palliative care. His knowledge of palliative care and his enthusiasm for caring for his patients were so great that I came away almost persuaded that if there were fifty doctors like Zylicz in the Netherlands, euthanasia would disappear.

Zylicz confirmed for me that it was harder to engage Dutch doctors in palliative care because of the easier option of euthanasia, that the Dutch government-sanctioned study of the issue was largely political research designed to defend and justify euthanasia practices, and that the pressure on Dutch doctors not to point out abuses or criticize the system was great.

He told me of a Dutch woman he had been treating at a

hospital before he came to Rosendaal. She was dying of breast cancer but had made it clear that she did not want euthanasia. He left her after a weekend in which he had been able to stabilize her condition and make her relatively comfortable. He learned from the nurse the next morning that this patient had died and that it appeared that another doctor had ended her life without her consent. The other doctor confirmed that he had done so because she was not dying quickly enough and he needed space for another patient. At that time Zylicz feared revealing publicly what had occurred so instead resigned from the hospital.

I had been given similar accounts by several other Dutch doctors, but because all were afraid of the consequences of being identified by the Dutch medical establishment I did not refer to them in the earlier version of this book. Zylicz told me that my work had emboldened him and other Dutch doctors to be more forthright in their criticism of Dutch euthanasia practices.

In June of 1997 the *Journal of the American Medical Association* published an article I wrote together with Dr. Zylicz and Chris Rutenfrans, a political scientist working in the Dutch Department of Justice, that evaluated the Dutch experience and included a critique of recent Dutch-government-sanctioned research on the subject that had been published in two articles in the *New England Journal of Medicine*. The articles purported to show that physician-assisted suicide and euthanasia were working well in the Netherlands. The *Journal,* which has been a strong euthanasia advocate, editorially supported the authors' claims that fears of a "slippery slope" in the Netherlands were false alarms. Our article demonstrated that a careful reading of even the authors' own research indicated that the picture in the Netherlands was not nearly so sanguine as the editorial and the Dutch articles maintained.

For example, more than half of Dutch physicians feel free to suggest assisted suicide or euthanasia to their patients, which compromises the voluntariness of the process. Sixty percent of cases are not reported, which makes regulation impossible. About a quarter of physicians admit to ending the lives of patients who did not give their consent, which is, at least in theory, illegal in the Netherlands as it is elsewhere.

A few examples may be helpful. A wife who no longer wished to care for her sick husband gave him a choice between euthanasia and admission to a home for the chronically ill. The man, afraid of being left to the mercy of strangers in an unfamiliar place, chose to be killed; the doctor, although aware of the coercion, ended the man's life. A physician ended the life of a nun a few days before she would have died because she was in excruciating pain but her religious convictions did not permit her to ask for death.

An earlier 1990 study sanctioned by the Dutch government, while intended to relieve alarm over Dutch euthanasia practices, only aggravated it. The recently published research, which largely replicated the 1990 study, is proving to have the same effect partly because the percentage of cases in which doctors gave medications with the explicit intention of ending patients' lives without the consent of the patients has gone up considerably.

So much has happened in the past year that it has been necessary to revise this book. I consider myself fortunate to have had the opportunity to contribute to these events, to the effort to improve care for those who are terminally ill, and to help educate the public and the medical profession as to why legalization of assisted suicide would make that goal harder to achieve.

. . . in subjecting moribund patients to treatments that are painful and disfiguring . . . doctors play not God, but Satan.

—Kenneth Praeger, M.D.

A medical science that is in need of euthanasia has to be changed as soon as possible to a medicine that cares beyond cure.

—D. J. Bakker, M.D.

INTRODUCTION

Most of us have seen times when it may seem right for a doctor to help a terminally ill person die. Partly because of such experiences, when people are asked, "Are you in favor of euthanasia?" most reply that they are, meaning little more than that they would rather die painlessly than painfully. When people are asked, "If terminally ill, would you rather be given treatment to make you comfortable or have your life ended by a physician?" their responses are different.

Physicians and the public often come to the question of euthanasia with their minds made up. They seldom look further than seeing physician-assisted suicide and euthanasia as an optional service or a right. But the more we know about the practice of assisted suicide and euthanasia, the more evident it becomes that we need to take a closer look.

Some twenty years ago, people in the Netherlands, well-intentioned physicians among them, began a process that has made physician-assisted suicide and euthanasia common practice there today. What the Dutch experience can teach us is, in part, the subject of this book.

Although philosophical and political arguments about the morality of assisted death are important, they have distracted us from considering the evidence accumulated both in the Netherlands and in our own country of the actual human experience of assisted suicide and euthanasia for those who are seriously or terminally ill, their families, and their doctors. Moreover, the question of legalizing such practices has so commanded our attention as to have diverted us from fully considering how to manage the final phase of living and to care for those we cannot cure. I have tried in this book to address the actual experience and practice of euthanasia and assisted suicide and to explore how we can meet the needs of those who are terminally ill.

For most of my professional life as a psychiatrist I have studied and treated people who wanted to end their lives, some of whom were terminally ill. In the past decade that work led to a concern for those whose suffering led them to want medical help with suicide.

Ten years ago, when I helped to organize the American Foundation for Suicide Prevention, an organization that funds research and education designed to prevent suicide, assisted suicide and euthanasia were not our concern. In the past few years, public activism for assisted suicide and euthanasia has changed that. While acknowledging that there are cases where helping a terminally ill patient to die in the final weeks of illness may seem humane, we were troubled by hasty efforts to legalize assisted suicide and euthanasia before the public had a chance to understand the implications of legalization and its potential impact on the care of people who are depressed or become so in response to serious or terminal illness. This study of assisted suicide and euthanasia in this country and the Netherlands grew out of that concern.

Euthanasia and assisted suicide have been advocated as giving patients greater control over their death and improving the circumstances under which they die. Is this actually the case? How much is the choice for euthanasia made by the patient and how much is it influenced by the doctor? What is the effect of legalizing assisted suicide on patients who are suicidal? What do assisted suicide and euthanasia tell us about what we need to do to provide appropriate care for those who are terminally ill?

Anyone trying to answer such questions will be led to the Netherlands, the only country where euthanasia is accepted practice. When I first came to the country, my Dutch colleagues knew that, despite my reservations, I had no fixed position on what social policy toward assisted suicide and euthanasia should be. They accepted my uncertainty; if anything it seemed to make them more receptive to discussing cases frankly with me.

Few Americans have been given an opportunity to see the Dutch system firsthand and to hear the details of cases from its strongest advocates and practitioners. The Dutch seemed certain that the more I learned, the more I would be persuaded of the virtues of euthanasia as practiced in the Netherlands. It turned out quite the opposite. The more I heard, the more I saw, and the more I was told by euthanasia advocates, the more shocked I was not only at the number of what could only be called wrongful deaths but at the Dutch insistence on defending what seemed indefensible.

I am certain that if given the opportunity to see assisted suicide and euthanasia in operation, most Americans—including many euthanasia advocates—would react as I have. I have never felt more urgently the need to communicate to others what I have learned.

Before looking at assisted suicide in this country and the Netherlands, it is necessary to understand the relationship of suicide, assisted suicide, and medical illness. Chapter 1 looks at the nature of this relationship, illustrating it with the story of Tim, a relatively young man dying of leukemia who at first wanted help in ending his life but who came to feel differently once he could discuss the sources of his desperation.

In the United States, assisted suicide and euthanasia are now marketed aggressively as a compelling and compassionate response to serious illness. Does closer examination bear out such a claim? Chapter 2 looks at the cases and the individuals in the United States that have figured prominently in efforts to promote legalizing assisted suicide and euthanasia. The situation is a good deal more complex and troubled than advocates have been willing to acknowledge.

The discussion of the Dutch experience in Chapter 3 provides an opportunity to see assisted suicide and euthanasia in practice, to see who is helped and who harmed, and how and why. It draws on extensive interviews with leading practitioners of euthanasia in the Netherlands; with officials of the Royal Dutch Medical Association; with the investigator who led the Dutch-government-sanctioned study of euthanasia; with the psychologist who helped introduce assisted suicide to the country; and with the psychiatrist whose assistance in the suicide of his patient, a mother mourning the loss of her son to cancer, set a legal precedent allowing assisted suicide as a "treatment" for mental suffering. The chapter also focuses on the doctor's role in influencing or determining the decision for euthanasia and on the tendency for doctors in the Netherlands to make such decisions without consulting even competent patients.

The interview material in Chapter 3 was initially published in a professional journal. Before publication I sent the material to key people involved in the interviews and revisited them in the Netherlands. Some wished to soften what they had said, and I permitted them to do so. Some wished me to change my conclusions, which of course I could not do. Their responses to my criticism of Dutch euthanasia policies are included in Chapter 3 and are as revealing as the original interviews of Dutch attitudes toward the subject.

The doctors who help set Dutch euthanasia policies are aware that euthanasia is basically out of control in the Netherlands. They admitted this to me privately. Yet in their public statements and articles they maintain there are no serious problems. They not only attempt to suppress dissent from domestic critics, but actively work to promote and normalize euthanasia. How they do this and what motivates their actions—the politics of euthanasia—are treated in Chapter 4. This chapter concludes with an analysis of a filming of the actual death of a man by euthanasia. Shown first on Dutch television and then worldwide, the film celebrates the doctor's role and presents euthanasia as an ordinary event.

What happens to our ability to treat depressed and suicidal patients when assisted suicide and euthanasia become easily available options? The consequences of Dutch acceptance of assisted suicide and euthanasia on individual and social efforts to deal with the problem of suicide suggest that the title for Chapter 5, "A Cure for Suicide," is more than ironic.

Chapter 6, "Why the Netherlands? Why the United States?" seeks first to understand historically, socially, and politically why the Netherlands is the only country that has embraced euthanasia. Second, it addresses why there is such strong pressure to legalize assisted suicide and euthanasia in the United States when there is not such pressure in most of the rest of the world.

Much that is written about euthanasia is derived from well-reasoned social, ethical, medical, or legal arguments that often seem speculative and far removed from life or death. Political rhetoric about individual rights further removes the issue of dying from the complex context of human relationships in which we live. In Chapter 7, "Theory and Practice," with the experience of the Netherlands in mind, I address the social, ethical, medical, and legal issues involved in euthanasia and attempt to locate the discussion of assisted suicide and euthanasia in the actual context of illness and dying.

In cases of persistent coma or dementia where patients cannot participate in decisions to continue or withdraw treatment, should treatment decisions be ultimately or primarily the province of doctors? What weight should be given to the prior expressed wishes of patients or those expressed now by their families? Chapter 8, "Who Should Decide? Coma and Dementia," addresses the current dilemmas we face in dealing with these situations.

Chapter 9, "Caring Beyond Cure," responds to an elderly woman who asked me what she should do to protect herself when terminally ill so that euthanasia does not seem necessary. The chapter also addresses what society needs to do to avoid the Scylla of either excessive or neglectful medical care and the Charybdis of euthanasia.

An Afterword summarizes the reasons for my opposition to legalization, addresses some of the misinformation about assisted suicide and euthanasia that needs to be corrected if we are to have informed public debate, and discusses the kind of experiences that draw some patients and some doctors so strongly to euthanasia. The book concludes with a description of what happens to doctors and patients in a Dutch nursing home in a culture that has accepted euthanasia.

SEDUCED BY DEATH

Chapter 1

SUICIDE, ASSISTED SUICIDE, AND MEDICAL ILLNESS

A few years ago, a young professional in his early thirties who had acute myelocytic leukemia was referred to me for consultation. With medical treatment, Tim was given a 25 percent chance of survival; without it, he was told, he would die in a few months. Tim, an ambitious executive whose focus on career success had led him to neglect his relationships with his wife and family, was stunned. His immediate reaction was a desperate, angry preoccupation with suicide and a request for support in carrying it out. He was worried about becoming dependent and feared both the symptoms of his disease and the side effects of treatment.

Tim's request speaks directly to the question at the heart of assisted suicide and euthanasia: Does our need to care for people who are terminally ill and to reduce their suffering require us to give physicians the right to end their lives?

Asking this question, however, helps make us aware that neither legalizing nor forbidding euthanasia addresses the much larger problem of providing humane care for those who are terminally ill. To some degree the call for legalization is a symptom of our failure to develop a better response to the problems of dying and the fear of unbearable pain or artificial prolongation of life in intolerable circumstances.

People are apt to assume that seriously or terminally ill people who wish to end their lives are different from those who are otherwise suicidal. Yet the first reaction of many patients, like Tim, to the knowledge of serious illness and possible death is anxiety, depression, and a wish to die. Such patients are not significantly different from patients who react to other crises with the desire to end the crisis by ending their lives.

Patients rarely cite the fear of death itself as their reason for requesting assisted suicide or euthanasia, but clinicians often see such patients displace anxieties about death onto the circumstances of dying: pain, dependence, loss of dignity, and the unpleasant side effects of medical treatments. Focusing one's fear or rage onto these palpable events distracts from the fear of death itself. Tim's anxieties about the painful circumstances that would surround his death were not irrational, but all his fears about dying amplified them.

Once Tim and I could talk about the possibility or likelihood of his dying—what separation from his family and the destruction of his body meant to him—his desperation subsided. He accepted medical treatment and used the remaining months of his life to become closer to his wife and parents. At first, he would not talk to his wife about his illness because of his resentment that she was going on with her life while he would likely not be going on with his. A session with the two of them cleared the air and made it possible for them to talk openly with each other. Two days before he died, Tim talked about what he would have missed without the opportunity for a loving parting.[1]

The last days of most patients can be given such meaning if those treating them know how to engage them. Tim's need for communication with his wife, communication that was not possible until he voiced his envy and resentment over her going on with her life while he was probably not going to be doing so, finds parallels in the lives of most dying patients.

In a twist on conventional wisdom, the English palliative care specialist Robert Twycross has written, "where there is hope there is life," referring not to hope of a cure, but hope of doing something that gives meaning to life as long as it lasts.[2] Virtually everyone who is dying has unfinished business, even if only the need to share their life and their death with friends, family, a doctor, or a hospice worker. Without such purpose, terminally ill patients who are not in great physical distress may be tortured by the feeling that they are only waiting to die and may want to die at once.

If assisted suicide were legal, Tim probably would have asked a doctor's help in taking his own life. Because he was mentally competent, he would have qualified for assisted suicide and would surely have found a doctor who would agree to his request.

Since the Oregon law and similar laws being considered in other states do not require an independently referred doctor for a second opinion, Tim would likely have been referred by a physician supportive of assisted suicide to a colleague who was equally supportive; the evaluation would have been pro forma. He could have been put to death in an unrecognized state of terror, unable to give himself the chance of getting well or of dying in the dignified way he did. The Oregon law is the latest example of how public frustration can lead to action that only compounds the problem; in the rush to legislate, advocates have failed to understand the problem they are claiming to solve.

Long before today's movement to legalize assisted suicide of patients who are seriously or terminally ill, we knew that physical illness contributes significantly to the motivation for suicide. Medical illness plays an important role in 25 percent of suicides, and this percentage rises with age: from 50 percent in suicides who are over fifty years old, to over 70 percent in suicides older than sixty.[3]

Most suicide attempts reflect a patient's ambivalence about dying, and those requesting assisted suicide show an equal ambivalence. The desire for death waxes and wanes in terminally ill patients, even among those who express a persistent wish to die.[4] Some patients may voice suicidal thoughts in response to transient depression or severe pain, but these patients usually find relief with treatment of their depressive illness or pain and are grateful to be alive.[5] Strikingly, the overwhelming majority of the patients who are terminally ill fight for life until the end; only 2 to 4 percent of suicides occur in the context of terminal illness.[6]

Like Tim, the vast majority of those who request assisted suicide or euthanasia are motivated primarily by dread of what will happen to them rather than by current pain or suffering.[7] Similarly, in several studies, more individuals, particularly elderly individuals, killed themselves because they feared or *mistakenly* believed they had cancer than killed themselves and actually had cancer.[8] In the same way, preoccupation with suicide is greater in those awaiting the results of tests for HIV antibodies than in those who know that they are HIV positive.[9]

Patients do not know what to expect and cannot foresee how their conditions will unfold as they decline toward death. Facing this ignorance, they fill the vacuum with their fantasies and fears. When these fears are dealt with by a caring and knowledgeable physician, the request for death usually disappears.

Mental illness raises the suicide risk even more than physical illness. Nearly 95 percent of those who kill themselves have been shown to have a diagnosable psychiatric illness in the months preceding suicide.[10] The majority suffer from depression that can be treated. This is particularly true of those over fifty, who are more prone than younger victims to take their lives during the type of acute depressive episode that responds most effectively to treatment.

Like other suicidal individuals, patients who desire an early death during a serious or terminal illness are usually suffering from a treatable depressive condition.[11] Although pain and other factors such as lack of family support contribute to the wish for death, recent research has confirmed that none is as significant as the presence of depression, which researchers have found to be the only predictor of the desire for death.[12]

Both patients who attempt suicide and those who request assisted suicide often test the affection and care of others, confiding feelings like "I don't want to be a burden to my family" or "My family would be better off without me." Such statements are classic indicators of suicidal depression.

Expressions of being a burden usually reflect depressed feelings of worthlessness or guilt, and may be pleas for reassurance. Whether physically healthy or terminally ill, these patients need assurance that they are still wanted; they also need treatment for depression. If the doctor does not recognize the ambivalence, anxiety, and depression that underlie a patient's request for death, the patient becomes trapped by that request and can die in a state of unrecognized terror.

In recent years we have become aware that in depressed patients anxiety, panic, or terror are symptoms that most strongly predict short-term risk for suicide.[13] Desperation, which Tim exemplified in his initial interviews, best describes their affective state.[14]

Unfortunately, depression itself is commonly underdiagnosed and often inadequately treated.[15] Although most people who kill themselves are under medical care at the time of death, their physicians often fail to recognize the symptoms of depressive illness or, even if they do, fail to give adequate treatment.[16]

The fact that a patient finds relief in the prospect of death is not a sign that the decision is appropriate. Patients who are depressed and suicidal may appear calm and less depressed after deciding to end their lives, whether by themselves or with the help of a doctor. It is coping with the uncertainties of life that agitate and depress them.[17]

Depression, often precipitated by discovering one has a serious illness, also exaggerates the tendency toward seeing problems in black-or-white terms, overlooking solutions and alternative possibilities. Suicidal individuals are especially prone to put conditions on life: "I won't live without my husband," ". . . if I lose my looks, power, prestige, or health," or ". . . if I am to die soon." They are afflicted by the need to make demands on life that cannot be fulfilled. Determining the time, place, and circumstances of their death is the most dramatic expression of their need for control. When a patient finds a doctor who shares the view that life is worth living only if certain conditions are met, the patient's rigidity is reinforced.[18]

An aspect of the depressed individual's need for control is the attempt to try to treat life as an intellectual balancing act. In drawing on the concept of *bilanz Selbstmord,* or "balanced suicide," promoted by German philosophers in the early part of this century,[19] proponents of what is called "rational suicide" seem to be doing something similar. Balanced suicide is said to result when individuals assumed to be mentally unimpaired dispassionately took stock of their life situation, found it unacceptable, and foreseeing no significant change for the better, decided to end their lives.

Contemporary advocates see a close analogy between a rational decision for suicide and the decision of the directors of a firm to declare bankruptcy and go out of business. Yet the idea that life can be measured on a balance scale is itself a characteristic of suicidal people. Some of the most depressed suicidal patients spend years making elaborate lists of reasons why they should go on living to counter the many reasons they can think of for dying.

Patients are not alone in their inability to tolerate situations they cannot control. Lewis Thomas has written insightfully about the sense of failure and helplessness that doctors may experience in the face of death;[20] such feelings may explain why doctors have such difficulty discussing terminal illness with patients. A majority of doctors avoid such discussions, while most patients would prefer frank talk.[21] These feelings might also explain both doctors' tendency to use excessive measures to maintain life and their need to make death a physician's decision. By deciding when patients die, by making death a medical decision, the physician preserves the illusion of mastery over the disease and the accompanying feelings of helplessness. The physician, not the illness, is responsible for the death. Assisting suicide and euthanasia become ways of dealing with the frustration of not being able to cure the disease.

Chapter 2

SELLING SUICIDE

Euthanasia advocates have advanced their cause with the dramatic presentation of suffering patients whose lives they have helped to end. These model cases have been marketed to the American people to persuade them that legalization of euthanasia is necessary. The advocates' own role in determining the outcome when patients approach them—often with an ambivalent request to die—is one of the least-understood aspects of the problem. In this context it will be useful to study these model cases and to examine the role of three three people who have done most to popularize euthanasia in this country: Timothy Quill, Jack Kevorkian, and Derek Humphry.

Quill and Diane

The doctor assisting a suicide is not simply a dispassionate observer responding to the patient's needs and wishes. This is illustrated by the best-known case of assisted suicide in this country—Dr. Timothy Quill and Diane, his patient of eight years. In the *New England Journal of Medicine*[1] and in a subsequent book, *Death and Dignity: Making Choices and Taking*

Charge.[2] Quill, an associate professor at the University of Rochester School of Medicine, presented a seemingly reasonable case for assisting in her suicide.

Quill, Diane's internist, tells us that she came from an alcoholic family and suffered from depression and alcoholism through much of her adult life. At the time of her death, she was a recovered alcoholic who had recently been diagnosed with acute leukemia, the same condition suffered by Tim, the patient mentioned earlier. Like Tim, she was given a 1-in-4 chance of surviving painful chemotherapy and radiation. Diane told Quill that "she talked to a psychologist she had seen in the past"[3] and implied that the psychologist supported her decision to end her life. After Quill helped implement her decision, he published his account to persuade the medical community to approve such actions.

Quill's account aroused considerable controversy among physicians, many of whom responded with letters to the *New England Journal of Medicine* for or against ending the life of a terminally ill patient. It was left to psychiatrists, most notably Dr. Patricia Wesley of Yale, to challenge both Quill's role in Diane's decision and his self-portrait as a compassionate figure responding in a disinterested way to a patient's needs.[4]

Quill tells us that once the suspicion of leukemia was confirmed by bone marrow biopsy, the hospital oncologist, believing that delay was dangerous, "broke the news to Diane" and began plans for chemotherapy. When Quill saw her shortly thereafter "she was enraged at his [the oncologist's] presumption that she would want treatment, and devastated by the finality of the diagnosis."[5] She informed Quill that she wanted no treatment and wished to go home to be with her family. Instead of exploring with her what had occurred with the oncologist or the wisdom of making a hasty decision in anger, Quill tells us that "together we lamented her tragedy and the unfairness of life."[6]

Diane justified her refusal of treatment and her demand for suicide by her need to be in control and by her conviction that she would die during the treatment for leukemia. Quill never questioned Diane's insistence on total control—an impossible demand in the face of serious illness—nor does he see this insistence as a sign of depression.

Quill also did not challenge Diane's certainty that treatment would fail, which she had no way of knowing. It is not surprising, given Quill's responses, that Diane went one step further than refusing treatment, to ask for his help in dying. Although he initially told her he could not take part in her suicide, he tells us—and appears to have conveyed to her—that her request "made perfect sense."[7] Wesley points out that "it is frighteningly naive to assume that when our guide to medical practice is 'doing what the patient wants,' we will escape the imposition of the physician's values on the clinical encounter. Personal values can be sequestered in the questions not asked, or the gentle challenge not posed, when both should have been."[8]

Quill responded to Diane's wish for assisted suicide by referring her to the Hemlock Society, describing it as "helpful" and implicitly confirming her attitude that "if you cannot be fully independent, you are better off dead." Wesley adds: "In making this referral and describing it as 'helpful,' Quill once again powerfully shaped the clinical interaction between himself and his patient. It is not a neutral act to refer a patient contemplating suicide to the Hemlock Society. . . . It renders utterly incoherent to us, as possibly it did to Diane, Dr. Quill's claim that he had left the door open for her to change her mind."[9] Wesley questions whether the result would have been different if Quill had recommended a support group for cancer patients.[10]

Diane returned to Quill requesting barbiturates, which were the Hemlock Society's recommended method of suicide, and he prescribed them while assuring himself that she knew the lethal amount. He explains that he decided to help her because he feared "the effects of a violent death on her family" or "the consequences of an ineffective suicide."[11] He does not tell us whether these were his own fantasies or whether he was succumbing to the emotional blackmail of an explicit suicide threat.

Diane came to say goodbye to Quill shortly before her death and promised a reunion at her favorite spot on the edge of Lake Geneva, with dragons shining in the sunset. Quill concludes his account by regretting that legal obstacles prevented his presence at her deathbed and wondering whether he "will see Diane again, on the shore of Lake Geneva at sunset, with dragons swimming on the horizon."[12]

Fantasies of reunion in a magical netherworld after death are common among suicidal people. That both doctor and patient shared them suggests that neither really came to grips with Diane's death.

Quill's account, with its shared fantasy of reunion on Lake Geneva, reinforces our sense that Quill permitted his own needs and attitudes to intrude into the decision to assist with Diane's suicide. When the dynamics of patients contemplating suicide or requesting assisted suicide are not explored and understood, the patient's death is likely to result. Quill made no effort to explore Diane's attitudes or to understand what was shaping them. He determined what transpired more than he realizes while persuading himself that he simply followed his patient' wishes.

Although Diane's case is not a persuasive argument for assisted suicide or euthanasia, one might expect to find more-convincing cases in Quill's book, *Death and Dignity*. Yet one does not. Quill makes the strongest argument for euthanasia with a patient who killed himself because he did not want to involve his family and friends in the illegal act of assisting in his suicide. This is not Quill's case, though; the story was related to him by a member of the Hemlock Society who was prepared to assist in the suicide before the patient decided to act alone.

The book, which could have been a convincing demonstration of the need to withhold or withdraw unwise treatments, seems aimed at blurring the distinction between such accepted withholding or withdrawal and physician-assisted suicide. The effectiveness of the book's illustrations is marred by Quill's need to keep reinvoking Diane to continue justifying having assisted in her suicide. Diane reappears in virtually every chapter. Apart from defending his decision to assist her, Quill laments the fact that the need to avoid prosecution made it impossible for him to be with her when she took the pills he prescribed. But, with or without legalized assisted suicide, most people would want to die in the company of their families, not their family doctors; it would seem to be one of the advantages of assisted suicide over euthanasia. Quill's lament reenforces our sense that his emotional involvement with Diane, and an even stronger involvement with promoting assisted suicide and euthanasia, clouded his judgment.

Kevorkian and Humphry

If Timothy Quill raised the issue of assisted suicide primarily for physicians, the general public has encountered assisted suicide and euthanasia largely through the publicity afforded Jack Kevorkian, Michigan's "suicide doctor," and Derek Humphry, founder of the Hemlock Society. In some of Kevorkian's cases the push for the patient's death came from relatives, in others no medical pathology was found on autopsy, and in virtutally no case were any alternatives to assisted suicide adequately explored.

Many patients drawn to Kevorkian have been, like Diane,

people whose terror of illness has persuaded them that quick death is the best solution: Janet Adkins, his first patient, was a woman in the early stages of Alzheimer's disease who feared the later progress of the disease. Adkins consulted Kevorkian, a retired Michigan pathologist passionately committed to promoting assisted suicide and the use of his "suicide machine." After a brief conversation, Kevorkian decided she was a suitable candidate and used the machine to help Adkins kill herself.[13] Clearly Kevorkian's lack of knowledge of her and his investment in promoting assisted suicide disqualified him from making such a determination. At the time, no Michigan law prohibited assisted suicide (most states have such laws), but Kevorkian was admonished by the Oakland County Circuit Court not to repeat the practice.[14] Disregarding the admonition, Kevorkian subsequently helped to end the lives of many others, some of whom were seriously ill but not near death.[15] One such patient, Marjorie Wantz, had a history of suicide attempts; she complained of pelvic pain, but an autopsy done after Kevorkian assisted in her suicide showed no evidence of physical disease.

Kevorkian sees as euthanasia candidates not only those suffering from disease, deformity, or trauma, but people with "intense anxiety or psychic torture inflicted by self or others."[16] The latter could have been the justification for assisting in the suicide of Judith Curren, a woman with chronic fatigue syndrome and fibromyalgia, a nonlethal muscular disorder.[17] Three weeks before her death her husband, who played an active role in the arrangements with Kevorkian, had been arrested on a domestic assault charge. Curren was addicted to painkillers and had complained of depression as well as spousal abuse. When Kevorkian's attorney Geoffrey Feiger was asked if Kevorkian knew of her history, he replied that it was irrelevant.

Although Kevorkian has employed a psychiatrist and fellow euthanasia advocate, Dr. George Reding, as a "consultant" in some of his cases, it is not clear whether he did so with Curren. Like Kevorkian, Reding was drawn to euthanasia early in his career. He writes that, while a medical intern assisting his father who was a clinical oncologist, he practiced active euthanasia on some of his father's patients.[18] He does not tell us whether he had their consent or even that of his father. He lists a series of brief quotes taken from Kevorkian's patients, without telling us a single other fact about these patients, as evidence that Kevorkian made the right decision in helping to end their lives. Reding presents no evidence of any exploration of these patients' feelings. How could he when he tells us, "I found myself apologizing to each one of these patients for having subjected them to a psychiatric examination."[19]

Moreover, as Michael Betzold, who has intensively studied the files of the Kevorkian cases, points out, "Kevorkian has helped people die after they have expressed doubts." One patient wrote her daughter after meeting Kevorkian of being "aware that I am in a volatile state. Easily swayed. . . . I may be susceptible to being used for publicity." Another had been diagnosed with multiple sclerosis when Kevorkian helped her die; on autopsy there was no evidence of the disease. She was said by her friend and her daughter to have been in doubt to the end.[20]

Kevorkian admits no doubts, and his vision goes far beyond legalization of assisted suicide. He advocates creating a board-certified medical specialty, "obitiatry," based on a four-year medical residency that would train physicians in the practice of "medicide." A grandfather clause would permit pioneers like himself to be certified to develop the program. Kevorkian presents a detailed model plan for the state of Michigan, dividing it into eleven geographic zones, each with its own obitiatry headquarters and death clinic. He walks us through the process by which Wanda Endittal, a hypothetical patient with multiple sclerosis, seeks help to end her life. Her physician, Dr. Frieda Blame, refers her to an obitiatrist, Dr. Will B. Reddy. After an elaborate consultation process with other obitiatrists, including psychiatrist Dr. Lotte Goode, Wanda's case is referred to the "action obitiatrists." One of them, Dr. Dewey Ledder, makes a last review of her file, and the other, Dr. Shelby Donne, performs the medicide. The account reads much like a Swiftian satire on the world we would create if Kevorkian's vision were to be followed, and indeed Kevorkian recognizes that his plan "may sound overblown, overly grandiose or impractical."[21]

Kevorkian's fascination with death, which is also expressed in his paintings of dismembered bodies, has a long and strange history. He was first called "Dr. Death" during his medical residency in 1956 because of his interest in photographing the retinal blood vessels of patients at the moment of their death in the hope of using the information to distinguish between death and coma, shock, or fainting.[22] He achieved notoriety a few years later with papers suggesting that death row inmates be anesthetized at execution time so that their living bodies could be used for experiments lasting hours or even months, after which they would be given a lethal dose of the anesthetic.[23] He noted that human experiments on criminals would save the lives of innocent animals killed in the name of science. He first used the word "obitiatry" in connection with these experiments.

His persistent interest in such experimentation made him a pariah among physicians and caused the loss of an academic appointment at the University of Michigan. "The medical profession made a mistake when they ostracized me," he told *U.S. News & World Report* in 1990. "I have no career anymore. This is the substitute."[24]

Kevorkian's license to practice medicine was eventually suspended by the Michigan medical society,[25] but a Michigan judge ruled that he could not be prosecuted for murder in the absence of a state law prohibiting assisting a suicide.[26] In 1993, Michigan passed such a law on a temporary basis, which Kevorkian violated with the avowed intention of testing whether the law was constitutional;[27] that law was upheld by the Michigan Supreme Court. Moreover, the court ruled that even in the absence of such a law—and the temporary statute eventually expired—assisting in a suicide could still be prosecuted as a felony.

Kevorkian was then tried and acquitted three times for his participation in assisted suicide. In one case his attorney, Geoffrey Feiger, argued successfully that Kevorkian's intention was to relieve pain and not to cause death. This argument has been compared to that of a son ending the life of an elderly parent and claiming his intention was not to kill but merely to accelerate his inheritance. Ridicule of Kevorkian, Feiger, or the Michigan juries should not prevent our recognizing how much juries' unwillingness to convict Kevorkian reflects people's terror at the prospect of a painful death and their unawareness of solutions beyond Kevorkian's.

Derek Humphry, another prominent euthanasia proponent, assisted in the suicide of his first wife, wrote a book about it (*Jean's Way*),[28] and with his second wife, Ann Wickett, formed the Hemlock Society to support the right to assisted suicide. Humphry, like Kevorkian and Quill, tapped into deeply felt anxieties concerning dying in intolerable circumstances, anxieties that led some to support his efforts without regard for the consequences. Initially he claimed he would never distribute information to the general public on how to commit suicide because the information might be used by depressed and suicidal young people.[29] Then he published *Final Exit,* a how-to-kill-yourself manual, and promoted its sale to the general public.[30] When asked about the contradiction between his original statement and his how-to-do-it book, he replied, "I simply changed my mind." Since the publication of *Final Exit* there has been a significant rise in the number of people—some of them young people found dead with the book nearby—who asphyxiated themselves with a plastic bag, a method recommended by Humphry.[31]

Humphry's participation in the suicide pact of his second wife's parents also raised questions. In her book, *Double Exit*,[32] her letters, conversations with friends, and her own taped suicide "note," Humphry's second wife, Ann Wickett, made clear that she was tormented by having actively participated with Humphry in the suicide pact of her parents.[33] Although her ninety-two-year-old father may have been ready to die, she knew that her seventy-eight-year-old mother was not. Such pacts have been romanticized and considered rational suicides, but published case reports confirm my own clinical experience that in most such pacts a man who wishes to end his life coerces a woman into joining him.

Even after death, euthanasia and assisted suicide can be a tool serving the idiosyncratic needs for power and control of its practitioners. Ann Wickett blamed Humphry for her death, accusing him of first abandoning and then divorcing her when she developed breast cancer.[34] At one point he left a message on her answering machine threatening to reveal her involvement in the death of her mother if she did not stop attacking him and the Hemlock Society. She had found it necessary to physically restrain her mother while assisting in her death, which made her legally vulnerable in a way that Humphry, who had no such difficulty with her father, was not. Confronted during a national television interview with the taped threat to Ann Wickett, Humphry responded, "I did it in the heat of anger and I have my flaws and errors, just like everybody else."[35]

Selling Death and Dignity

Dying is hard to market. Voters, many repelled by the image of doctors giving their patients lethal injections, rejected euthanasia initiatives in Washington and California. Learning from those defeats, Oregon sponsors of a similar measure limited it to assisted suicide, in which the physician supplies the means but does not directly perform the act. The patient assumes a role now familiar in euthanasia promotion: the noble individualist fighting to exercise the right to die.

Both assisted suicide and euthanasia have been presented as empowering patients by giving them control over their death; assisted suicide has been seen as less problematic, however, in that it offers protection against potential medical abuse, since the final act is in the patient's hands. Neither advocates nor opponents believe that it is possible morally or legally to permit assisted suicide but to deny its "benefits" to those too enfeebled to induce their own death.[36] Most advocates, such as Kevorkian, Humphry, and Quill, admit that assisted suicide is but a first step toward euthanasia, a step for which it is easier to win public acceptance.[37] Opponents see little protection in assisted suicide: people who are helpless or seriously ill are vulnerable to influence or coercion by physicians or relatives who can achieve the same results whether directly administering the lethal dose or not.

Proponents have found the ultimate marketing technique to promote the normalization of assisted suicide and euthanasia: the presentation of a case history designed to show the rightness of hastening death. Such examples exploit nightmarish images of unnecessarily prolonged disability and dying. These extraordinary cases—where most would agree it was desirable to end life—are represented as typical. Those who participate in the death (the relatives, the euthanasia advocates,

---

and the physician) are celebrated as enhancing the dignity of the patient, who is usually presented as a heroic, fully independent figure.

How much truth is there in this presentation? Does this accurately describe what happens? Even in cases advocates believe best illustrate the desirability of legalizing assisted suicide, there is ample room to question whether the death expressed the patient's wishes and met his or her needs. To dramatize these model cases, advocates present them in some detail—and this creates the opportunity to see the discrepancy between the theory and the practice of assisted suicide and euthanasia.

How a death can be orchestrated and publicized to promote assisted suicide—at the expense of the patient—was illustrated by an article featured on the cover of the *New York Times Magazine* in the fall of 1993.[38] The article described the assisted suicide of Louise, a Seattle woman whose death was arranged by her doctor and by the Reverend Ralph Mero, head of Compassion in Dying, a group that champions assisted suicide. Members of the group counsel people who are terminally ill, advise on lethal doses, convince cautious doctors to become involved, and remain present during the death. Mero and his followers do not provide the means for suicide (which the patients obtain from their doctors) and purport not to encourage the patients to seek suicide.

Mero arranged for a *Times* reporter to interview Louise in the last weeks of her life, offering Louise's death as an illustration of the beneficial effects of the organization's work. Yet the account rather serves to illustrate how life and death were both rendered miserable for Louise.

Louise, who was referred to Mero by her doctor, had been ill with an unnamed degenerative neurological disease. The reporter tells us, "Louise had mentioned suicide periodically during her six years of illness, but the subject came into sud-

den focus in May during a somber visit to her doctor's office."
As Louise recounted it, "I really wasn't having any different
symptoms, I just knew something had changed. I looked the
doctor right in the eye and said, 'I'm starting to die.' And she
said, 'I've had the same impression for a couple of days.' " A
magnetic resonance image (MRI) confirmed early deterioration of the frontal lobes of Louise's brain, which led her doctor to warn her that she had at most a few months to live.
Louise said her doctor explained that "she didn't want to scare
me. . . . She just wanted to be honest. She told me that once
the disease becomes active, it progresses very fast, that I would
become mentally incapacitated and wouldn't be myself,
couldn't care for myself anymore. She would have to look into
hospice care, or the hospital, or some other facility where I
would stay until I died."

We are told that Louise did not hesitate with her answer.
"I can't do that. . . . I don't want that." The reporter continues, "Her doctor, Louise thought, looked both sad and relieved. 'I know, I know,' the doctor said. 'But it has to come
from you.' " Louise made sure that they were both talking
about suicide and then said, "That's what I'd like to do, go
for as long as I can and then end it."

What happened between Louise and her doctor? The doctor's quick affirmation even before the MRI scan had confirmed Louise's decline is somewhat disturbing. She prefaced
a grim description of Louise's prognosis with assurance that
she did not want to scare her. The doctor's relief when Louise
chose suicide betrays the doctor's attitude toward a patient in
Louise's condition.

As the account continues, the doctor indicates that she
would be willing to help, had recently helped another patient
whom Louise knew, and would prescribe enough barbiturates
to kill Louise. To avoid legal trouble, she would not be there

when Louise committed suicide. They exchanged several hugs and Louise went home.

The doctor was concerned that a friend and patient whom she had advised about assisted suicide had not died from medication he had taken; his friends had had to suffocate him with a plastic bag. The doctor called Compassion in Dying for advice. The reporter quotes the doctor as saying about contacting Mero, "I was ecstatic to find someone who's doing what he's doing. . . . I loved the fact that there were guidelines."

On the phone, Mero advised the doctor on the medication to prescribe before visiting Louise, suggesting that he was prepared to help Louise die before knowing her, meeting her, or in any way determining for himself whether she met any guidelines. When he did meet Louise, she asked him at once if he would help with her suicide and be there when she did it and she was almost tearfully grateful when he said yes. He repeated many times that it had to be her choice. Louise affirmed that it was, saying that all she wanted "these next few weeks is to live as peacefully as possible." Louise seemed concerned with being close to others during her final time and with transforming her remaining days into a loving leave-taking.

The doctor was concerned that Louise's judgment might soon become impaired: "The question is, at what point is her will going to be affected, and, if suicide is what she wants, does she have the right to do it when she still has the will?" The doctor, like Mero, said she did not want to influence the patient but was worried that Louise might not act in time. "If she loses her mind and doesn't do this, she's going into the hospital. But the last thing I want to do is pressure her to do this."

The closeness before dying that Louise seemed to want was lost in the flurry of activity and planning for her death as those involved with her dying pursued their own agendas. At a subsequent meeting of Mero and Louise, with Louise's mother and Louise's doctor also present, Mero gave Louise a checklist of the steps to be taken during the suicide, from the food to be eaten to how the doctor would call the medical examiner.

The doctor indicated that she would be out of town for the next week, but that she had told her partner of Louise's plans. "You don't have to wait for me to get back," she told Louise, hinting, the reporter tells us, that it might be best to not await her return. The doctor was more direct when alone with Louise's mother, telling her that she was afraid that Louise might not be coherent enough to act if she waited past the coming weekend.

The doctor and Mero discussed how blunt they could be with Louise, wanting her to make an informed decision without frightening her into acting sooner than she was ready. They hoped "she would read between the lines." Mero assured the reporter that he always wanted to err on the side of caution. Mero is described by the reporter as "a cautious, deliberate man who is not necessarily joking when he says: 'I was spontaneous. Once. When I was nine years old.' " When discussing *Compassion in Dying*, Mero "talks so slowly that a listener sometimes wonders if the next word will ever come."

A few days after the meeting, Mero called the reporter in New York and asked her to come to Seattle as soon as possible. He knew she was planning to come the following week, but he warned her not to wait that long.

The reporter left immediately for Seattle and found Louise in a debilitated condition. She was in pain, getting weaker, and spoke of wanting to end her life while she could still be in control. She said she was almost ready but not quite. She needed about a week, mainly to relax and be with her mother.

The reporter "blurted out" to Louise, "Your doctor feels that if you don't act by this weekend you may not be able to." Her words were met with a "wrenching silence" and Louise, looking sharply at her mother, indicated that she hadn't been told that. Her mother said gently that this is what the doctor had told her. Louise looked terrified, and her mother told her that it was okay to be afraid. "I'm not afraid. I just feel as if everyone is ganging up on me, pressuring me," Louise said. "I just want some time."

Louise's mother was growing less certain that Louise would actually take her own life. When she tried to ask her directly, Louise replied, "I feel like it's all we ever talk about." A friend who had agreed to be with Louise during the suicide was also uncomfortable with Louise's ambivalence but was inclined to attribute her irritability and uncertainty to her mental decline. When Louise indicated that she would wait for Mero to return from a trip and ask his opinion on her holding on for a few days, the friend suggested that this was a bad idea since Mero did not know her well and might not understand the change in her mood.

Like many people in extreme situations, Louise expressed two conflicting wishes—to live and to die—but only for death did she find support. The anxiety of her doctor, Mero, her mother, and her friend that Louise might change her mind or lose her "will" may have originated in their desire to honor Louise's wishes, or even in their own view of what kind of life is worth living, but eventually it overpowered Louise's ambivalence, and their agenda, more than Louise's wishes, drove the pace of events. Louise began to lose her own death, while those around her acted in the name of supporting her autonomy.

Confounding predictions, Louise made it through the weekend. Over the next days she was in touch with Mero by phone, but, he told the reporter, he kept the conversations short because he was uncomfortable with her growing dependence on his opinion. Nevertheless, after a few such conversations, the contents of which are not revealed, Louise indicated she was ready, and that evening Mero came and the assisted suicide was performed. A detailed description of the death scene provides the beginning, the end, and the drama of the published story. When, six and one-half hours after taking the sleeping pills, Louise did not die, her friend considered calling the doctor for advice, but Mero advised waiting. Had she not died from the pills, Mero subsequently implied to the reporter, he would have used a plastic bag to suffocate her.

After seven hours the end came. The doctor was called; the death was not listed as a suicide.

Everyone—Mero, the friend, the mother, the doctor, and the reporter—became part of a network pressuring Louise to stick to her decision and execute it on their schedule. The death seems to have been clocked by their anxiety that she might want to live. Mero and the doctor influenced the feelings of the mother and the friend so that the issue was not their warm leave-taking and the affection they had for Louise, but whether they could get her to die according to the time requirements of Mero, the doctor (who probably could not stay away indefinitely), the reporter (who was working with Mero to construct a story on an actual assisted suicide), and the disease, which obeyed a more flexible schedule than previously thought. Louise was explicit that all of them had become instruments of pressure in moving her along. Mero appeared to act more subtly and indirectly through his effect on the others involved with Louise.

Lisa Belkin, the *Times* reporter, describes in detail what happened, including her own role. Her account shows Compassion in Dying and Mero violating the limits they themselves set. The organization's guidelines state that its representatives evaluate the patient prior to making the decision to assist suicide, do not encourage patients to choose assisted suicide, and are never actively the agent for suicide. Belkin indicates that Mero agreed to help assist in the suicide even before meeting Louise, he advised her to act quickly, and he was prepared to be the agent for death if the pills did not work. The failure is not simply of adherence to Mero's own guidelines, but of the illusion that such guidelines truly operate to protect patients. Belkin's misgivings, evident throughout the piece, are perhaps even suggested by her title, "There's No Simple Suicide."

Without a death there would be, of course, no story, and Mero and Belkin had a stake in the story, although Mero had criticized Kevorkian to the reporter for wanting publicity. The doctor developed a time frame for Louise to act, conveniently coinciding with her own absence, although it would be medically impossible to predict with such precision when Louise would be unable to make a decision and, in fact, the doctor's prediction was wrong. Her own past troubled experience with a patient who was a friend seems to have colored the doctor's need to have Louise's suicide over with quickly and in her absence if possible. Louise was clearly frustrated by not having someone to talk to who had no stake in persuading her.

Individually and collectively, those involved engendered a terror that Louise bore alone while they reassured each other that they were gratifying her last wishes. The end of her life does not seem like death with dignity; nor is there much compassion conveyed in the way Louise was helped to die. Compassion is not an easy emotion to express in the context of an imminent loss. It requires that we look beyond our own pain to convey the power and meaning of all that has gone before in our life with another. Although the mother, the friend, Mero, and the physician may have acted out of good intentions in assisting the suicide, none appears to have honored Louise's need for a "peaceful" parting. None seems to have been able to accept the difficult emotions involved in loving someone who is dying and knowing there is little one can do but convey love and respect for the life that has been lived. The effort to deal with the discomfort of Louise's situation seems to have driven the others to "do something" to eliminate the situation.

Watching someone die can be intolerably painful for those who care for the patient. Their wish to have it over with can become a form of pressure on the patient that must be distinguished from the patient's own wants. The patient who wants to live until the end but senses her family cannot tolerate watching her die is familiar to those who care for people who are terminally ill. Once those close to the patient decide to assist in the suicide, their haste can make the pressure on the patient many times greater. The mood of those assisting is reflected in Macbeth's famous line, "If it were done when 'tis done, then 'twere well it were done quickly."[39]

Certainly assisted suicide—the fact that she took the lethal medication herself—offered no protection to Louise. It is hard to see how her doctor, Mero, her mother, her friend, and the reporter could have done more to rush her toward death.[40]

Euthanasia advocates like Mero protest that they behave responsibly because they repeatedly ask patients, "Are you sure you want to die?" or they say, "You don't have to go through with this." This becomes a shared ritual reaffirming the practitioners' willingness to act and the patient's desire to protect the practitioner, affirmed when the patient responds with the obligatory "Yes, I want to" answer. The patient's interests would be better served by a willingness to hear what the patient is really feeling about her situation and how illness has affected her view of her own past and of her present relationships.

In addition to marketing their cases, leading euthanasia advocates like Kevorkian, Humphry, and Quill have marketed their own personalities to promote their cause: Humphry used assisting in his wife's death to present himself as the enlightened pioneer; Quill used Diane's death to present himself as the compassionate physician; Kevorkian used his willingness to end the lives of so many who came to him to present himself as an anti–medical establishment visionary.

Although George Delury, a Manhattan editor, served four months in jail for his role in encouraging and facilitating the suicide of his wife, Myrna Lebov, it has helped to make him a celebrity spokesman for the cause of assisted suicide. Delury entered into a plea bargain acknowledging his guilt;[41] he was said by his attorney to have feared a jury's reaction to his diary entries that reveal that his desire to be relieved of the burden of caring for a wife suffering with multiple sclerosis was a major influence on her decision to let him assist in her suicide.

When Delury wrote, "You are sucking my life out of me like a vampire and nobody cares,"[42]—a passage he later admitted showing to his wife[43]—he made explicit a message that he communicated to his wife in dozens of less direct ways. In the four months preceding her death, the period recorded in his diary, he makes clear that the driving force in his life had become his desire to persuade Myrna that it was time for her to die.

In a recently published book, *But What If She Wants to Die?*[44] Delury reveals that Myrna Lebov, who was fifty-two, was not terminally ill, was not in pain, and probably had many years to live. She enjoyed the company of friends and the swimming she did with her physical therapist. Although Delury had daily help in caring for Myrna from a health aide provided by Medicaid, and Myrna had a family that cared about her, Delury was weary of his wife's dependency and despaired over the drudgery of attending to her bodily functions and emotional needs. He seems to have wanted to be free of the burden of his wife's existence even if care could be provided for her by her sister or by a nursing home.

If Delury was unable to cope with a wife with a deteriorating medical condition, he seems to have been a caring husband before then. He and Myrna learned of her illness a month before their marriage. Despite the recurring symptoms of her disease it does not appear to have stopped them from having a loving and supportive relationship for two decades.

The last years of Myrna's life were another matter. While others could still enjoy her company, Delury could not. He became obsessed with persuading her to die. When Myrna grew more cheerful, Delury became discouraged. He says that Myrna did not want to take medication for her depression, a decision he clearly supported. When describing in his diary a therapist who had encouraged Myrna to engage in activities she found pleasurable, he complains bitterly that the therapist did not understand that the goal of this therapy should be to help Myrna to accept that her life was over.

Delury's frankness has won him praise. He admits freely that Myrna told him that only he wanted her dead. He concedes that Myrna may have been motivated to die by a desire to please him but says that should be seen as noble on her part. He says he wants the whole truth known and sees that as proof that he has no reason for guilt. He seems completely unaware of how cruel his behavior is in constantly reminding Myrna of how unpleasant he finds her existence.

Under Delury's unrelenting pressure, Myrna eventually gives up. DeLury wonders why, when taking pills to end her life, she did not say good-bye. It is not easy to say good-bye to someone so eager to be rid of you.

Delury had been planning to write a book about his participation in Myrna's death. When he writes of contemplating ending her life without her consent he worries that New York's "Son of Sam" law, designed to prevent a felon from profiting from a crime, would be invoked. In his book he also reveals for the first time that the medication he prepared for Myrna did not kill her; he had to eventually use a plastic bag to suffocate her. He kept this a secret because he feared being brought up on a murder charge. Although he cannot be re-tried, Myrna's sister and brother have brought a wrongful death suit against Delury, invoking the "Son of Sam" law.

Delury's case continues to generate ironies. On the basis of the notoriety afforded the case, he was invited to participate in an American Psychiatric Association panel discussion on assisted suicide. He was also invited to contribute an article to an issue of the *Journal of Forensic Psychiatry* devoted to the role of the psychiatrist in assisted suicide, an even more dubious assignment given what he thought the attitude of his wife's therapist should have been in pushing Myrna toward death.

Delury joined the Hemlock Society and is proud that a past president of the society called him an inspiration to the group. The society may be having second thoughts. Although the publication of his book made him a sought after TV guest, his revelations seem to alienate most readers and viewers. Many readers will respond to *But What If She Wanted To Die?* by thinking that she didn't.

In contrast to the detailed account presented by Lisa Belkin or provided by George Delury, most case reports are vignettes limited to one or two paragraphs describing the patient's medical symptoms; they usually leave out the social context in which euthanasia is being considered, obscuring the complex and often subtle pressures on patients' "autonomous" decisions to seek death. The opening chapter of *Choosing Death,* a book of essays about euthanasia, describes four cases in which euthanasia is presented as indicated or warranted.[45] Although the authors do not point it out, in every case the detailed narrative makes clear that the motives and personality of another person, who could not stand to see the condition of the patient, intruded upon what was happening. In one case a patient's homosexual lover cannot bear to watch him suffering; in another, a doctor is considering strangling his father, also a doctor, because he cannot endure his father's growing dementia; in a third case a husband whose wife is a stroke victim cannot wait the few days of her lingering death because the situation recalls his mother's attending for years to his father who was also a stroke victim; and in another, nurses who cannot stand the suffering of a patient contemplate ending her life, although she has given no indication of wanting assistance in dying.

In the selling of assisted suicide and euthanasia, words like "empowerment" and "dignity" are associated only with the choice for dying. But who is being empowered? The more one knows about individual cases, the more apparent it becomes that needs other than those of the patient often prevail. "Empowerment" flows toward the relatives, the doctor who offers a speedy way out if he or she cannot offer a cure, or the activists who find in death a cause that gives meaning to their own lives. The patient, who may have asked to die in the hope of receiving emotional reassurance that all around her want her to live, may find that like Myrna and Louise she has set in motion a process whose momentum she cannot control. If death with dignity is to be a fact and not a selling slogan, surely what is required is a loving parting that acknowledges the value of the life lived and affirms its continuing meaning.

Euthanasia advocates try to use the individual case to demonstrate that there are some instances of rational or justifiable assisted suicide or euthanasia. If they can demonstrate that there are *some* such cases, they believe that would justify legalizing euthanasia.

Their argument recalls Abraham's approach in persuading God not to carry out his intention to destroy everyone in Sodom. Abraham asks if it would be right for God to destroy Sodom if there are fifty who are righteous within the city. When God agrees to spare Sodom if there are fifty who are righteous, Abraham asks what about forty-five, gradually reduces the number to ten, and gets God to spare the city for the time being for the sake of the ten.[46]

Abraham is arguing, however, in favor of saving life; we want him to succeed and are relieved that he does. God is concerned with not seeming to be unreasonable, although there is something comical in Abraham's using this to manipulate Him. Euthanasia advocates are arguing that if there are ten cases where euthanasia might be appropriate, we should legalize a practice that is likely wrongly to kill thousands.

Assisted suicide and euthanasia are being marketed as the only ways to achieve both dignity and release from pain. On a life-or-death "purchase," people need to know more about what they are buying and how payment will be extracted. Death ought to be hard to sell.

It does not seem possible to study assisted suicide and euthanasia without looking at the Netherlands, where doctors can with impunity and with public acceptance practice euthanasia and assisted suicide provided they follow certain guidelines. Is the Netherlands the place where Jack Kevorkian's vision has come to pass? Are Dutch doctors any more alert than those in the United States to the physician's role in determining the outcome when a patient requests assistance in dying? How much can the Dutch experience with euthanasia help to guide or caution us?

Chapter 3

SEDUCED BY DEATH

In the Dutch city of Assen in the spring of 1993, a court of three judges acquitted a psychiatrist who had assisted in the suicide of his patient, a physically healthy fifty-year-old woman who had lost her two sons and had recently divorced her husband. The court ruled that the psychiatrist, Dr. Boudewijn Chabot, was justified in his actions because his patient was competent to make the decision to die freely, her suffering was irremediable, and the doctor met the Dutch criterion for *force majeure,* meaning he was compelled by an overpowering force to put the welfare of his patient above the law, which formally prohibits assisted suicide and euthanasia.[1]

The Assen case joins the handful of internationally known Dutch court trials of assisted suicide and euthanasia, each referred to by the name of the city where it was tried. The court's landmark decision in the Assen case gave legal sanction for assisted suicide and euthanasia for patients who were not physically ill.

Assisted suicide and euthanasia are not yet advocated in the United States for physically healthy patients regarded as having purely psychiatric ailments. But the ruling in the Assen case seems to justify warnings of a "slippery slope" that descends inexorably from assisted suicide to euthanasia, from those who are terminally ill to those who are chronically ill, from those who are physically ill to those who are mentally ill, and from those who request euthanasia to those whose lives are ended at the doctor's discretion.

The rationale for such extensions has been that it is a form of discrimination to deny assisted death to chronically ill people who will suffer longer than those who are terminally ill; and that it is bias to force endurance of psychological pain when it is not associated with physical illness. The next step, involuntary euthanasia, while not legally sanctioned by the Dutch, is increasingly justified as necessary to care for patients who are not competent to choose for themselves.[2]

De facto legalization of euthanasia and assisted suicide exists in the Netherlands.[3] Although the criminal law provides punishment for euthanasia and a lesser punishment for assisted suicide, the same code stipulates circumstances for exceptions to the law.[4] In a series of cases over the last twenty years, the Dutch courts have ruled that *force majeure* is such a special circumstance;[5] euthanasia is thus permitted when a doctor faces an unresolvable conflict between the law, which makes euthanasia illegal, and his responsibility to help a patient whose irremediable suffering makes euthanasia necessary.[6]

The Dutch courts and the Royal Dutch Medical Association (KNMG) have established guidelines for physicians to follow in selecting patients for either assisted suicide or euthanasia: (1) voluntariness—the patient's request must be freely made, well considered, and persistent; (2) unbearable suffering—the patient's suffering cannot be relieved by other means (i.e., other alternatives must have been considered); and (3) consultation—the attending physician should consult with a colleague.[7] Doctors are expected to report cases of euthanasia as deaths due to "unnatural causes" with the understanding that they will not be prosecuted if the guidelines have been followed. In 1993, these guidelines were incorporated into a statute which stipulates that a physician following them will not be prosecuted.[8]

Despite Dutch acceptance of euthanasia, hard facts about it have not been easy to come by. Estimates of the number of euthanasia cases range from 5,000 to 20,000 of the 130,000 deaths in the Netherlands each year.[9] Charges of widespread involuntary euthanasia have been made.[10]

To ascertain actual Dutch medical practice regarding euthanasia, a government commission,[11] headed by Professor Jan Remmelink, attorney general of the Dutch Supreme Court, arranged for a remarkable study of the problem by investigators at Erasmus University. Physician participants were granted anonymity and immunity from prosecution for candid information about euthanasia.[12] The Remmelink study, published in Dutch in 1991 and in English the following year, found that 49,000 of the yearly deaths in the Netherlands involve a medical decision at the end of life (MDEL). Ninety-five percent of these MDEL cases involve, in equal numbers, either withholding or discontinuing life support, or the alleviation of pain and symptoms through medication that might hasten death. Frank euthanasia was the cause of death in 2,300 cases, that is, in 2 percent of all Dutch deaths. Assisted suicide was relatively uncommon, occurring some four hundred times per year. Over 50 percent of Dutch physicians admitted to practicing euthanasia; cancer patients were the majority of their cases. Only 60 percent of doctors kept a written record of their cases, and only 29 percent filled out the death certificates honestly in euthanasia cases.[13]

The Euthanasia Doctors

Dr. Herbert Cohen, one of the best-known practitioners of euthanasia in the Netherlands, provided a human dimension to these figures. Originally a family practitioner, he is now the director of a palliative care unit at the Daniel Den Hoed Clinic in Rotterdam. Foreign journalists and physicians, including Jack Kevorkian, have visited the Netherlands to talk with him. Cohen says he is too well known as a euthanasia advocate to perform it at the hospital, although he serves as a consultant in euthanasia cases.

Cohen does not like to say how many times he has performed euthanasia because people take the figure out of context, but he said it was more than 50 and less than 100. The number was so high because cases had been referred to him by colleagues who felt he was more qualified than they to deal with patients who asked to die.

"Have you noticed," he asked me, "that all of the cases that had broken new ground in Dutch law involved women, although there are as many total cases of euthanasia among men?" He speculated it was "because women can make an appeal to a doctor that is stronger, more existential."

His own involvement with euthanasia began fifteen years earlier while treating a woman patient for cardiac myopathy. She became more and more handicapped, unable to walk, and plagued by chest pains even when at rest. Cohen lived nearby and visited her each midnight to inject a diuretic and a painkiller so she could sleep. One day she told him, "This is an important day. It is the hundredth day you have come, and that's enough." The woman had talked it over with her husband and had decided she wanted to end her life. Cohen had called the Dutch Voluntary Euthanasia Society (NVVE) about how best to perform euthanasia, but the society was young then and had no idea. They found him a sympathetic anesthesiologist, and two months later he performed the euthanasia.

Asked why he became so involved with euthanasia, Cohen said, "There is satisfaction in being involved in the terminal phase of life. You become part of a family, although I have a family. There is a special warmth and intimacy and harmony. It is true for them as well; it improves relations among the family. My absolution is the Christmas cards I receive from relatives." He knows it would seem strange to some, but sometimes when he went to perform euthanasia he brought flowers.

He said he had been interested in the end of life for a long time, implying that his interest predated his involvement with euthanasia. He went on to say that he had lost half of his relatives, but not his parents, in the concentration camps during World War II; they had been deported from the Netherlands.

Cohen told me also of being asked to consult about euthanasia for an elderly woman (Mrs. A) who had a concentration camp syndrome. She had been tortured in the camp during World War II and as she became older was increasingly unable to suppress the memories. Although he agreed that euthanasia was warranted in her case, since her death he sometimes thinks of his life as before and after Mrs. A.

He spoke of a beautiful young woman of thirty-five with a rapidly progressing multiple sclerosis who had a "methodical determination" to die. Her arms and legs were paralyzed; she was able to move only one finger. She had had a number of episodes of breathing difficulty. Cohen said he was called in by her nursing home and discussed the matter with her for six months before her suffering and persistence persuaded him to go ahead with euthanasia. He said, "In the discussions the patient has to convince the devil's advocate—me—that it is okay. The idea that each case gets easier and easier is just rubbish." In this case the nursing home did not want euthanasia performed there, so the woman's parents offered to let her die in their home.

Cohen went on to say that

in the first five or six years I did not notify the authorities. Then I had another multiple sclerosis case, also in consultation, where the patient was receiving supportive help from thirty-five volunteers, with all of whom she had discussed her desire for euthanasia. My colleague and I felt that in such a case the authorities had to be notified. It couldn't be kept secret. I met with such understanding from the police that I became a fan of the law.

I asked Cohen if he had paid a price for his involvement, thinking of the exhaustion that a few years earlier had impelled him to give up his family practice after twenty-five years. Since giving up his practice he had served only in his capacity at the palliative care unit and as a consultant for, not practitioner of, euthanasia. He said, "The price of any dubious act is doubt. I am not avoiding your question, though it sounds like it," adding, "I don't sleep for the week after." He said he didn't drive to the home or back when he performed euthanasia because he was so focused that he could have had an accident.

We discussed the finding in the Remmelink study that the doctor was often the person who first raised the subject of euthanasia with the patient. Cohen was in favor of the doctor doing so and quoted a Dutch saying that an important happening casts a shadow before it. Raising the subject of euthanasia, he said, has an emancipating effect; he saw no danger that such initiation by the doctor might unduly influence or even compromise the voluntary nature of the patient's decision.

He and most Dutch physicians, as well as most patients, prefer euthanasia to assisted suicide. Cohen explained that there are personal reasons behind the preference.

The first time you do it, euthanasia is difficult, like climbing a mountain. You think it would be easier to write a prescription. I found out it's not easier. The guidelines are the same as for euthanasia. When you write a prescription, you are responsible for the effect when it's taken. You have to be present or available on the phone, ready to terminate the life if something goes wrong. Drugs may take three or four hours with relatives phoning, thinking the patient is dead, when it is not so. After you do it once, you do it again only if the patient strongly prefers it.

Although Cohen pictured death as liberating patients from debilitating illness, tormenting memories, or a life of disability, he was also drawn to euthanasia by a special close bonding he developed with a dying patient whose life he would end, a closeness that seemed unlike anything else he had encountered. One suspected he had been more troubled by his participation in euthanasia than he realized or admitted; expressions like "dubious act" and the need for "absolution" are suggestive. That he felt his life had been changed by participating in the death of the woman tormented by memories of the concentration camp suggested that he might now be afflicted by disturbing memories of her and others whose lives he had ended. Closeness to his patients through participation in their deaths, identification with them, and guilt seemed mingled. As intense as the experience had been for him, he seemed pleased if not relieved to be talking about euthanasia or consulting about it rather than still performing it.

At the influential NVVE, I waited for its president, Dr. Lide Jannink-Kapelle, an ex-coroner whose interest in assisted suicide and euthanasia had been sparked by her contact with the families of those who committed suicide. While waiting I was shown an English-language film, *An Appointment with Death,* which well illustrated that the character, needs, and limitations of the physician are as critical as those of the patient in determining the choice of euthanasia.[14]

One of the cases presented involved a man of about sixty who is diagnosed with cancer and told he has a year to live. He arranges for his doctor to help end his life when his symptoms become intolerable, discussing it with his wife and grown children and securing their agreement. He feels that the peace of mind his decision has given him leaves him free to fight the disease. Several years later he is still active, pleased that he has lived longer than predicted, and satisfied with how he has handled matters. His case is surely as reasonable an argument for euthanasia as one could make. The man had no suicidal intention to begin with, was not trying to end his life prematurely, and used the knowledge that he could die comfortably to live as long as he could without anxiety.

Another case involved a forty-one-year-old artist who is diagnosed as HIV-positive. He has no physical symptoms but has seen others suffer and wants his physician's assistance in suicide. The doctor compassionately explains to him that he might live for some years symptom-free. Over time the man repeats his request for assisted suicide; eventually the doctor accedes to it. The patient seems to need the doctor, perhaps this particular doctor with whom he has some relationship, to accept and to assist in the suicide, so the doctor is present as the patient takes the medicine the doctor prescribed. Yet we cannot see any good reason why the doctor consents to the suicide when he does, since it seems evident that the patient would wait longer to obtain the doctor's agreement. The patient does not threaten to go elsewhere or to kill himself if the doctor continues to put him off. The doctor tells an interviewer that some patients chose to die sooner and some later than he would think appropriate, implying that this patient is in the former group. We are left with the question of why the doctor would assist a death he considered premature.

Even more striking is the degree to which the patient is overwhelmed at learning that he is HIV-positive and the doctor's inability to deal with this. The doctor keeps establishing that his patient was persistent in his request, but he does not address the terror that lies beneath it. With a psychologically sensitive physician looking for more than repeated requests to die, more likely in a culture not so accepting of euthanasia, this man would probably not need to die when he does.

After viewing the film, I met with Jannink-Kapelle, the president of the NVVE, and Martine Cornelisse-Claassen, a psychology coordinator on her staff. The NVVE has over 66,000 members; it receives all of its budget of 1 million guilders per year (well over half a million dollars) from members and private contributions.

I questioned them about the differences in approach to assisted suicide and euthanasia of the Dutch physicians represented by the KNMG and the NVVE. Jannink-Kapelle told me the KNMG wanted to medicalize euthanasia. The NVVE believes that a minister or a friend can be the primary person involved in advising the person, while the KNMG and the Dutch courts consider only a physician to be an appropriate helper. The NVVE stresses the patient's autonomy in all situations, preferring assisted suicide to euthanasia whenever possible and seeing the KNMG as more willing to place decisions in the physician's hands when the patient's will is in doubt. Cornelisse-Claassen showed me the euthanasia "passport" she and thousands of other NVVE members carry as a means of ensuring patient control in decision making. It lists the variety of situations in which they do not want medical treatment or would want their lives terminated painlessly.

Professor René Diekstra believes assisted suicide, as opposed to euthanasia, helps ensure that death will be voluntary, but his own experiences indicate how hard it is to achieve that goal. In 1980, at the age of thirty-four, with his mentor and friend, professor of social psychiatry Nicholas Speijer, Diekstra coauthored a book on suicide and assisted suicide that made Diekstra a leading Dutch authority on the subject.[15] At forty-nine, he was then professor of psychology at the renowned University of Leiden and dean of the university's social science faculty.

When we spoke, Diekstra was disappointed that assisted suicide was underutilized and euthanasia overutilized. He gave examples of patients in physical or mental distress who were told they would be helped with assisted suicide if they persisted in feeling it was necessary, but who delayed for months or years committing suicide and in many cases did not do it at all. He felt that general practitioners seeing such patients and performing euthanasia were often killing people who did not have to die.

Both Diekstra and Speijer believed, however, that the therapist has an obligation to assist a depressed patient who wants suicide if treatment has not succeeded. Diekstra told me of several patients that he had been able to involve in psychotherapy on the promise that if treatment did not work he would assist in their suicide. I replied that most therapists involve comparable patients in therapy without such a promise by making clear that they accept the suicidal feelings as part of the therapy, they are not uncomfortable or frightened by such feelings, and they will not go to extreme lengths to stop the patient's suicide, conveying that ultimately the patient is responsible for being alive.

I pointed out that many patients come into therapy with

sometimes conscious but more often unconscious fantasies that cast the therapist in the role of their executioner. A commitment on the therapist's part to become executioner if treatment fails plays into and reinforces these fantasies. It may also play into the therapist's illusion that if he cannot cure the patient, no one else can either.

Apart from the fact that a patient may make no progress with one therapist but succeed with another, I could see how some patients would use such an agreement to go through the motions of treatment until they could declare a failure and demand the promised assisted suicide. Diekstra replied that then they would be breaking the contract, which would be evident by their not doing their therapeutic homework (he was a cognitive therapist), and he would have to break off the treatment.

From 1982 to 1988, Diekstra served as the clinical psychologist on a committee that consulted with health practitioners who were considering assisted suicide for their patients. The committee included a lawyer, a psychiatrist, a professor of ethics, a pain treatment specialist, and a citizen representing the community at large. The consulting health professionals completed a questionnaire, discussed the case with the group, which often recommended additional consultation, and made their recommendations at a final meeting. The opportunity to consult with the committee often had a preventive effect. This was particularly true of patients with mental disorders—about 30 percent of all cases the committee saw. In an article reviewing the committee's work, Diekstra wrote that without such consultation the professionals would often have assisted in a suicide despite viable treatment alternatives. As the result of an emotional involvement with the patients, the professionals had often "prematurely transferred their own feelings of powerlessness or helplessness with regard to the patient's condition onto the rationality or even the inevitability of the patient's suicide."[16]

I asked if he felt that similar patients were now being put to death under the present Dutch system, which did not provide or require such thorough consultation. He replied, "Of course."

Diekstra was troubled that his vision of providing relief from irremediable suffering while preserving autonomy was lost in the realities of euthanasia in the Netherlands. He was disturbed that a system he had helped to father wrongly put to death more people than the relatively small number who met the Dutch criteria for appropriate euthanasia or assisted suicide. He thought there would be a backlash when the public eventually realized what was actually happening. He also thought it possible that world opinion would force the Netherlands to regulate the procedures more carefully.

Diekstra had been involved in a case that meant a good deal to him personally and to which he had referred in published articles.[17] His mentor, Nicholas Speijer, when dying of cancer at seventy-six, made a pact with his wife, who was seventy-four and not ill, to join him in suicide. Diekstra wrote admiringly of Speijer as being true to his belief in dying with dignity in circumstances of his own choosing. That his wife "went with him" is mentioned almost parenthetically.[18]

Diekstra's first response to my asking what happened with the Speijers was to tell me that Mrs. Speijer's first name was René, the same as his. He then said that two weeks after her death, when a colleague had suggested to him that Speijer had made her do it, he became enraged and demanded that the colleague never repeat what he had said to anyone. With the passage of time, however, Diekstra had come to feel there was some truth in the suggestion. He told me that Speijer "was the dominant person in the relationship and he wanted her to join him. Had she been more independent, it probably wouldn't have happened."

Diekstra had been asked by the Speijers to discuss their decision with them. The Speijers told him that before Speijer became ill with cancer a year earlier, they had talked of dying a beautiful death together. Mrs. Speijer had made the point that they had no children and that there was no one who needed her or would miss her. Although she was not sick and did not claim to be irremediably depressed, her suicide was assisted. Perhaps given his relationship with Speijer, Diekstra did not feel free to suggest alternatives or seriously to question their decision regarding Mrs. Speijer. His initial response that he and Mrs. Speijer shared the same first name suggests an identification with her perhaps centered around their both having played a subordinate role in relationship to Speijer. His earlier rage at the implication of coercion suggested that he was more troubled by what had occurred and by his participation than he was able to acknowledge.

Guidelines and agreements do not always encompass the emotional complexity of the relationships between doctors and patients, which can involve death anxieties for both. Even Speijer, who wrote the guidelines for assisted suicide, violated them himself in promoting and arranging his wife's suicide. Diekstra was proud of the fact that no health professional who had followed the rules of conduct that he and Speijer had outlined for assisted suicide—voluntariness, long-standing request, unbearable suffering, no prospect for improvement, consultation with a colleague, and documentation of what took place—had ever been prosecuted. I could understand his pride that prosecutors accepted these criteria, but asked if he was not disappointed that practitioners who violated them were rarely prosecuted and never punished.[19] He surprised me by agreeing completely.

Perhaps Diekstra's experience with Speijer and his wife made him acutely aware of the importance of independent consultants to guard against unnecessary deaths. About the Assen case, Diekstra was clear: "Chabot shouldn't have done it. Chabot had an earlier case that he consulted us about. We got the patient into treatment and the wish for suicide disappeared. He shouldn't have done this case on his own." He had declined to be an expert witness in the Chabot case, but was vague about the reasons for his refusal.

The Slippery Slope

There was nothing vague about the effects of the landmark trial and acquittal of Dr. Boudewijn Chabot. The decision established a legal basis for assisting in the suicide of Dutch patients who were in psychological distress but had no physical illness. Chabot believed his patient was not clinically depressed and had no psychiatric illness but was suffering and wanted to die.

The controversy and international interest aroused by the case seemed remote when I met Chabot on a Sunday morning in Haarlem, a small, beautiful Dutch city not far from Amsterdam. We met in his boyhood home, where he now kept a room for use on weekends. He was kind, considerate, and responsive, and I could understand why Herbert Cohen had described him as sweet and gentle.

We spoke first about his background in psychiatry. He received his medical training in Amsterdam in the 1960s, undergoing a personal psychoanalysis during that period. During his medical studies, Chabot had been involved in neurophysiological brain research. He studied in England for a year with Isaac Marks researching treatments for phobias and "sexual perversions." When he returned to the Netherlands, he trained psychology students in psychotherapy and practiced Masters and Johnson therapy for couples with sexual problems.

In 1989, a personal experience interested Chabot in euthanasia. A young woman he knew who was not ill medically or psychiatrically wanted to die. He referred her to Diekstra's department in Leiden so she could consider the matter in a "balanced way." A woman colleague of Diekstra who took the patient's wish to die seriously was of tremendous help. She was able to transform the young woman's wish to die into a wish to change her life. Although she made one suicide attempt during psychotherapy, she did not kill herself. If the patient is told in advance that the doctor will never assist suicide, Chabot added, there is no reason for the patient to talk. He was impressed by Diekstra's and his colleague's approach to the case and wanted to implement their techniques, while agreeing that the therapist will provide death if treatment fails.

Chabot made himself available to the NVVE for referrals. In July 1991 he was called about "Netty Boomsma"—the fictional name he has given to his Assen patient—who had lost her second son, aged twenty, to cancer in May 1991. Her first son had died by suicide some years earlier, also at the age of twenty. Netty was now interested only in suicide. Chabot told his caller that Netty was in a state of bereavement and needed time to complete the process. Try to convince her, his caller urged.

Since she had to travel a long distance, Chabot saw Netty for three hours on her first visit and again the next day. She told Chabot that the suicide of her first son had been completely unexpected. He was on military duty in Germany, involved in his first serious love affair, when the young woman left him for another young man. While home on a visit, Netty's son was sad but never spoke of suicide, and he returned to Germany for the last weeks of his tour. While carrying a loaded gun on guard duty, he shot himself in the heart. He left a note for his mother, brother, and father saying that they were the best but he could not live without his girlfriend. On the day her second son died of cancer, after her friends left and she was alone, Netty took pills in a suicide attempt. She wanted a funeral together with her younger boy. She then had her first son reburied next to the second and bought the space in between for herself.

Chabot told me that since Netty was a social worker who was trained to be introspective and knew the sort of information he wanted to hear, they could go into issues quickly. At the end of the first day she asked for Vesparax, a mixture of barbiturates sometimes used in assisted suicide. "You are not the first person I have been to," she said. Her general practitioner, a psychologist, and a psychiatric social worker all refused to assist in her suicide. She showed him letters she had received in response to her requests for help; all the replies advised her to see a psychiatrist. One wrote, "If there is really no possibility for you, the psychiatrist will soon know."

Chabot told her he needed time. "There may be alternatives," he said. "I don't know." He assured her that he would not drag on the interviews. She told him that every day was awful for her. She was not a "believer," but felt she was "pulled to her boys." Chabot made a commitment to help her with her suicide if she would truly explore her life in their sessions and still felt she wanted to die. He told me there was no trace of the psychotic in her.

Chabot saw Netty a total of thirty hours from August 3, 1991, when he saw her for the first time, to September 7, when the decision to go ahead with assisted suicide was made. Her sister and brother-in-law attended some sessions, Chabot said, since they all were close to Netty, loved her, and supported her decision. Her sister said Netty had wanted to die since the death of her first son, her favorite, but had felt she could not do it because of her second boy, who was dyslexic, had difficulties in school, and should not be left with his alcoholic father.

Netty's marriage was a disaster from the beginning. She was twenty-two and her husband was twenty-eight. She was not really in love but married to get away from an unpleasant relationship with a domineering mother and a father who went along with whatever her mother wanted. Her husband believed a woman should stay at home, which she did for a while, but she felt as if she were in a cage. She decided to work and earn her own money. Netty told Chabot she started to live the day her first child was born. The child made it possible for her to be something apart from her disapproving mother. Six years later she had her second son. When her children were small she went to social work school at night while she held a job, which she enjoyed, during the day. Netty continued to work until her son's chemotherapy started in January 1990.

Netty's husband blamed her for their first son's death, implying she was responsible for his education and so was responsible for his suicide. Her husband would beat Netty when he was drunk. She would leave him, but then would return because of her second son. At one point she planned to kill herself and her child by driving into a canal, but felt she could not take his life.

At the end of 1988, two weeks after her father died, Netty left her husband, and her son went with her. By then her son had become a comfort for her. He understood her grief and tried to console her. Over the years he became more important to her.

Netty felt guilty that she had not divorced her husband earlier. She thought children would improve her marriage, and then felt she could not separate her children from their father. She realized she had used the children as an excuse not to divorce. Remaining in the marriage was the main failure of her life, she said. If she had left, perhaps things would have been different and her son would not have killed himself.

By the summer of 1989, both her sister and her brother-in-law felt she was almost her old self, but her former energy never returned. Before her first son's suicide, Netty was involved in many activities, particularly painting. Those interests ceased with his death.

In November 1990 her second son went to the hospital for injuries sustained when his moped was hit by a truck. While he was there, doctors discovered that he had a teratoma of the lung, which had become malignant and inoperable. The only possible treatment was chemotherapy. The boy died as a consequence of the chemotherapy, which destroyed his white blood cells. At the end he was on a respirator, which Netty agreed to have disconnected.

On August 25, Netty told Chabot that they had gone into all the details of her life and that she had not come for bereavement therapy (she had gone through that briefly after the first son's death), nor did she want any medication. She needed an answer to her question: Was he going to help her with her suicide? While the process might be going too quickly for him, she was not coming back unless he agreed to help her. If he did not help her, she might take her life herself.

Chabot told Netty that he needed to have the opinion of experts regarding the case. He made a complete written summary of her case as he knew it. He asked a number of experts for their opinion, two of whom—including Joost Schudel, professor and chair of the Department of Psychiatry at Erasmus University and chair of the Committee on Ethics of the KNMG—recommended that Chabot not go forward. Schudel believed Netty needed bereavement therapy, not assisted suicide. He felt her condition was not irremediable; thus if Netty refused treatment, suicide should not be permitted. Chabot, though, compared Netty to a patient who can refuse chemotherapy for cancer and request euthanasia if the chances for treatment to succeed are small. The other experts agreed with him, seeing Netty's suffering as unbearable with little prospect that therapy would help. Among those who approved Chabot's assisting in the suicide was Carlo Mittendorf, a clinical psychologist specializing in bereavement.

Chabot asked only Dr. Frank van Ree, one of the few Dutch psychiatrists publishing on assisted suicide, to see the patient, but van Ree felt it was not necessary. Since the majority of the consultants agreed with Chabot, and particularly since the expert in bereavement therapy thought the chances for improvement were slight, Chabot went ahead.

Chabot had one more session with Netty, her sister, and her brother-in-law during which he still tried to get Netty to postpone the decision. She persisted in saying she did not want bereavement therapy. Her sister was emotional in saying goodbye. She said she and Netty had cared for their father when he was dying and now she and her husband would be with Netty till the end. Chabot said he needed them to come back one more time, since he had not received all the replies to his letters requesting consultation.

Netty's last visit to Chabot's office was on September 20. She brought a friend, a married woman, along with her. Chabot said he would get her the pills by October 1, promising rapidly lethal compounds recommended to physicians by the Royal Dutch Association for the Advancement of Pharmacy.

Chabot said the week prior to Netty's death was the most difficult time for him. She had been so grateful and so considerate of his feelings, saying to him, "I feel so good, but I know you are having a hard time."

Prior to September 27, Netty's final day, Chabot said he had much to do. He typed up a report of all his interviews so that they would be available for the public prosecutor after her death. Her former husband did not accept Netty's decision. He had said he would call the police and that she would be put in a hospital. He told Netty he would report Chabot to the police if he assisted her. Since her ex-husband could drop in at her house at any time and could be violent, her car was moved to another place so that it would not show that she was home. Chabot said he felt as if he were in a detective film.

Netty's sister and brother-in-law changed their minds about being with Netty at the end. Her sister said they did not want to be there because their children would then ask for details. Netty's friend would be there, however. At the last minute, Chabot invited a colleague who was a general practitioner to witness the death so that he could testify in court how Chabot behaved. Chabot complained that his friend is now in trouble and may have to appear before a medical tribunal to explain his participation in the case.

Chabot, his friend, Netty, and her friend sat around a table at Netty's home. Chabot said to Netty, "I hope you don't feel pressed to go on just because we are here." She said she wanted to go ahead. She asked to die in what had been her younger son's room and on his bed. They all went upstairs, and Chabot gave her a liquid as well as some capsules that a pharmacist had prepared for him. She opened the capsules as she had been advised and put the contents in some custard. Jokingly she asked him if he could not have given her some capsules before to practice. She sat down on the bed and asked them to turn on the record player, which played the Bach flute sonata that was played at both her sons' funerals. She took the glass and drank the liquid, saying that it was not too bad. While the music was playing, Netty kissed a photograph of her two sons that was next to the bed. She asked her friend to sit next to her. Her friend was stroking her hair. Netty said she had made a great effort to fix her hair and her friend was messing it up. The friend replied she would make it beautiful later. To Chabot, Netty said, "Why do young kids want suicide?" thinking of her son. He recalled saying to her after five minutes, "Think of your boys." In seven minutes she lost consciousness while being held by her friend. Then she slept. Her heart stopped in half an hour.

Chabot followed the approved procedure for officially reporting an unnatural death. In the summer of 1992 there was a police investigation. He said, "They spoke to her friend, her sister, her former husband, her former psychiatrist, me, everybody." It was a long, difficult period for Chabot until he was told in December 1992 that he would have to go to court.

The court case was heard in Assen in April 1993. The trial took an entire day. In Dutch courts there is no jury; decisions are made by three judges. The defendant gets to speak first and last if he so chooses. The judges had all the written reports solicited by Chabot, including the two negative ones. An ethicist whom Chabot had later asked for an opinion also sided with Chabot. Only Dries van Dantzig, a professor of psychotherapy who had agreed with Chabot, was asked to appear in person. Even the prosecutor's expert witness, Robert Giel, a professor of social psychology at the University of Groningen, wrote an opinion that the assisted suicide was justified. The prosecutor asked for a one-year conditional sentence, which would mean that if found guilty Chabot would go to prison for a year only if he repeated the offense.

After the prosecutor and Eugene Sutorius, Chabot's defense attorney, delivered their summations, Chabot made the concluding remarks. He asked the court to judge him, not Netty. He read from her letters to him in which she wrote of their growing close through sharing the experience of her impending death; she expressed her gratitude to Chabot for being willing to reunite her peacefully with her boys. Chabot said she was not a patient, but a woman who did not want to live.

In April, Chabot learned that he was acquitted. The court

said he was guilty of assisting in her suicide but that he had followed the guidelines and had good reasons for his actions: he had an overpowering conflict of duties, and there was only a small chance of success with bereavement therapy. The court felt that Netty had been suffering irremediably and that the psychological as opposed to physical source of the suffering was not relevant.

The Ministry of Justice took the case to an appeals court in Leeuwarden. There van Ree, the psychiatrist Chabot had asked to see Netty, was asked to testify as to why he had not done so. Van Ree explained that he felt he understood the case and that it would only cause the patient pain to be seen again. This explanation was not challenged.

At the end of September 1993, Chabot learned that he was exonerated by the appeals court. As is common in the Netherlands, the Leeuwarden court modified the Assen court's opinion in the matter. The appeals court felt that, because the source of the suffering was not somatic and the competence of the person was at stake, it was relevant to look into psychiatric pathology. Since all the experts agreed the patient was competent, the court upheld the decision, adding to Dutch case law the precedent that a patient a physician claims is not suffering from either psychiatric or physical illness can receive assisted suicide simply because he or she is unhappy. The Ministry of Justice appealed the case to the Dutch Supreme Court.

The Dutch Supreme Court, which ruled on the Assen case in June 1994, affirmed the lower court's decision that mental suffering can be grounds for assisted suicide, but it found Chabot guilty of not having had a psychiatric consultant see the patient. Although the court expressed the belief that such consultation was particularly necessary in the absence of physical illness, since it felt that in all other regards Chabot had behaved responsibly, it imposed no punishment. The case was seen as a triumph by euthanasia advocates, since it legally established mental suffering as a basis for euthanasia.[20]

Netty Boomsma's relationship with Chabot seems to illustrate what I suggested to Diekstra: that some suicidal patients would use the agreement to assist in their suicide to mark time until the therapist felt obliged to fulfill his promise. This type of contract seems to me psychologically unsound, much as the one often made in the United States with suicidal patients requiring them not to kill themselves before calling the therapist.

Chabot insisted that Netty was not depressed, was not really a patient, but was simply a grieving woman who wanted to die. Although Netty had not exhibited the sad affect associated with depression, patients obsessively bent on suicide often do not. In the loss of pleasure in activities that she previously enjoyed, Netty surely met that criterion established for the diagnosis of depression. Any therapy would have required challenging the premises under which Netty came, and would probably have included some trial on medication. In this sense no therapy could be said to have been undertaken with Netty, so one can understand why Chabot insists she was not a patient.

Chabot stated that if he had not agreed to Netty's terms, she would never have come back. I asked why, if she did not follow his prescription for treatment, he would feel obliged to follow hers. Certainly at the end he was succumbing to blackmail.

Yet Chabot's critics were probably also right in believing that Chabot wanted to assist in Netty's suicide and needed her insistence and determination to justify his actions. He seemed to want to pioneer the acceptance of assisted suicide for psychiatric patients; his need to play such a role dovetailed with Netty's need to sacrifice her life on an altar of atonement.

Clearly she was a patient seeking her executioner. Both she and Chabot experienced a closeness in her death; there seems to be some feeling on Chabot's part, as on Diekstra's, of needing to be included in the patient's death if you are unable to help the patient live.

Like others who assist in suicide, Chabot seems to have entered into the patient's fantasy of death as a reunion. Just as Quill joined Diane's fantasy of meeting again on the shores of Lake Geneva, so Chabot's comment to Netty right before her death that she should think about her boys suggests that he too saw her death as a return to her lost children. To create metaphors that portray death as something other than death makes dying seem an attractive, fairy-tale-like option. But like fairy tales, beneath the surface such metaphors contain some tormented and savage emotions. By treating Netty not as a patient but as a devoted mother whose desire to join her boys in death was not a sign of illness but a legitimate and realizable goal, Chabot made it impossible to explore her guilt toward her children and her need for punishment.

From what Chabot elicited in sessions with Netty, it was clear that bereavement counseling would likely have failed, but less narrowly focused psychotherapy might have succeeded. Netty's personality problems far antedated her bereavement. She said she became a person only when her first son was born, and she stayed alive only for the sake of her second son. She was not about to grant Chabot's request that she give him more time, that she stay alive for his sake as she had done for her second son.

Netty seemed to need someone who could tell her in a firm but kind way that she had never really lived for herself and that it was not too late to try. She could always kill herself, but she ought to give life a chance first. Netty's guilt over her first son's suicide had sources that were deeper than her failure to divorce. Caring for her second son seems to have had an expiatory quality. One suspects that a therapy that gave her the opportunity to explore her relationship to her sons might have engaged her.

No one should underestimate the grief of a mother who has lost a beloved child, but neither should one ignore the many ways life offers to deal with the feelings of loss, guilt, and pain of a child's death. The Dutch like to present patients with concrete alternatives. For Netty, it might have been possible to utilize her skills as a social worker and involve her in a facility or project devoted to youth suicide prevention. Her last words to Chabot—"Why do young kids want suicide?"—suggest that work which permitted her to deal with that question might have meaningfully engaged her in a way that would have been more positive for her as well as for those she might have helped.

Does Dutch law provide a forum for determining whether assisted suicide or euthanasia is right in an individual case? In the Netherlands the legal system is consensual, that is, it aims at a decision that tries to meet the needs of all concerned, including the community at large, rather than adversarial, where one side wins and the other loses. The implications of a consensual approach became clear in discussing the Assen case with Sutorius, who defended Chabot. The most prominent attorney in the Netherlands defending physicians in assisted suicide and euthanasia cases, Sutorius is often invited to serve as a judge on the court of appeals, an honor which in the Dutch system can be given to distinguished attorneys. "Euthanasia, which started with terminal illness, has moved to a different plane," Sutorius said proudly of the outcome of the Assen case.

Defending Boudewijn Chabot's role in Netty Boomsma's assisted suicide was, for Sutorius, the culmination of a long involvement with euthanasia that began with his representing people who committed acts of civil disobedience in the 1960s and 1970s—strikes, occupation of buildings, and conscientious objection. Sutorius had defended doctors performing euthanasia since 1982 and felt the Assen court ruling that psychic suffering could not be separated from physical suffering was particularly important. Concern for his patient's mental anguish was held to legally qualify as creating for Chabot the *force majeure* that demanded resolution through assisted suicide.

To American eyes accustomed to an adversarial judicial system, in which both sides try to win, the trial in the Assen case seems strange. There were reasons for the prosecution to question Chabot's action if only because one would be hard pressed to claim Netty's condition was incurable or that a patient's refusal of therapy is sufficient justification for helping her die. Time alone was likely to have altered her mood. None of Chabot's consultants had actually seen Netty, and they were not unanimous in their support. Yet experts like Schudel who had written an opinion disapproving of the action were not called. The only expert witness called testified for the defense. The only expert witness consulted by the prosecutor wrote an opinion justifying Chabot's actions. I asked Herman Feber, a prosecutor in the Dutch appeals court who specializes in euthanasia cases, if the prosecutor was reluctant to pursue the case. Feber, who is himself an advocate of euthanasia, knew the prosecutor and said he was, but he had been ordered to try the case by the Ministry of Justice, something which Sutorius also confirmed for me.

Feber is a close friend of Schudel; of their discussions of the Assen case he said, "We would give Chabot a rating of 5 on a scale of 1 to 10 for his handling of the case. Chabot was just too ready to give her the pills." Feber noted that if the doctor wants, he can assist in suicide secretly. If he reports the case and the conditions are not fulfilled, he will be prosecuted. He thought Chabot had wanted a public discussion of his case. He added, "There were also questions about his not providing treatment and not having the consultants see the patient."

I told Feber I thought the consultants bore some of the responsibility for not seeing Chabot's patient. Responsible people will ask to see in person the son or daughter of a colleague before writing a letter of recommendation for him or her, so it seemed hard to understand how an expert could make a decision about whether Netty Boomsma would live or die without insisting on seeing her. The notion that it would be too distressing for her to see a consultant seemed a little thin. Feber shrugged his shoulders in a way that indicated he thought that was perhaps true.

Like the Dutch in general, most lawyers, judges, and prosecutors are supporters of assisted suicide and euthanasia, and are concerned with protecting it as a right; as a result they seem more supportive of doctors who practice it than protective of patients. Feber himself reluctantly prosecuted a recent case involving a psychiatrist whom Sutorius defended. Both he and Sutorius agreed that too many years had passed since the patient's death to prosecute the case, but Feber had been ordered to prosecute and did so. The psychiatrist was acquitted.

Supporting the physician even in the most questionable cases in order to protect euthanasia policy extends beyond the courtroom. Sutorius had been involved in still another case concerning assisted suicide by a psychiatrist, and together with Schudel had been among the coauthors of a paper about it entitled "The Case of the Overzealous Inspector."[21] Although the case had not been brought to trial, an inspector in the Health Department had brought the matter before a medical tribunal, which has disciplinary rather than legal status. The patient had been chronically depressed with major depressive episodes during which he was psychotic. The justification for acceding to the patient's request for suicide had been that he had not responded to treatment, that his suffering was unbearable, and that in between his major depressive, psychotic episodes he was competent.

The article seems intended to intimidate inspectors, nurses, and other staff who question assisted suicide. Sutorius and his psychiatrist coauthors were critical of the inspector for bringing the case to a Dutch medical tribunal and for appealing to a higher tribunal when the physician was not censured. They were critical of the hospital's nurses for opposing the assisted suicide and critical of the medical tribunal for paying too much attention to the nurses' opinion.

Yet the case was not so cut-and-dried. The psychiatrist had hidden his intention to assist in the patient's suicide when he sought to have the patient legally committed. The hospital had refused to permit the assisted suicide on its grounds, though it had not challenged the psychiatrist's right to prescribe the pills that would be used in the suicide or the use of its pharmacy to fill the prescription. The health inspector had raised the point that medication then being developed might have helped the patient. Combined with the implausibility that in between psychotic episodes the judgment of this depressed patient was not distorted by his residual depression and he was reasonably able to request his own death, all of these circumstances invited further questions. None were asked, however, and nothing stopped the death; in its aftermath, attention focused on justifying what had already happened. Despite its distinguished defenders, the case suggests that inspectors and nurses must be vigilant if there are to be adequate safeguards in the Dutch system.

If this case could be called "The Case of the Overzealous Inspector," it seemed the Assen case could be called "The Case of the Reluctant Prosecutor." In euthanasia cases, reluctant prosecutors would seem to be more common in the Netherlands than overzealous inspectors.

Involuntary Euthanasia

That it is often the doctor and not the patient who determines the choice for death was underlined by the Remmelink study's documentation of "involuntary euthanasia," a term that is disturbing to the Dutch. The Dutch define euthanasia as the ending of the life of one person by another at the first person's request. If life is ended without request, they do not consider it to be euthanasia.[22] "Nonvoluntary euthanasia" is a term often used, although not by the Dutch, to describe a physician's ending the life of a patient incapable of giving or refusing consent.[23] The Remmelink study uses the more troubling expression "termination of the patient without explicit request" to refer to euthanasia performed without consent on competent, partially competent, and incompetent patients.

The study revealed that in over 1,000 cases, physicians admitted they actively caused or hastened death without any request from the patient.[24] The impossibility of treating pain effectively was the reason given for killing the patient in about 30 percent of these cases. The remaining 70 percent were killed with a variety of different justifications ranging from "low quality of life" to "all treatment was withdrawn but the patient did not die."[25] The Remmelink Commission considered these cases not to be morally troublesome because the suffering of the patients involved had become "unbearable" and they would usually have died soon anyhow.[26] Twenty-seven percent of physicians indicated that they had terminated the lives of patients without a request from the patient to do so; another 32 percent could conceive of doing so.[27]

According to the study, other forms of hastening death without the patient's consent are common practice in the Netherlands as well. In half of the 49,000 MDEL cases, decisions that might or were intended to end the life of the patient were made without consulting the patient.[28] In nearly 20,000 cases (about 80 percent), physicians gave the patient's impaired ability to communicate as their justification for not seeking consent.[29] This left about 5,000 cases in which physicians made decisions that might or were intended to end the lives of competent patients without consulting them.[30]

Involuntary euthanasia—that is, terminating the life of competent patients without their explicit consent—raised such large questions that the study's principal investigator seemed the best person to address them. Dr. Paul van der Maas of the Dijkzicht Hospital in Rotterdam, where he is also chair of the Department of Public Health and Social Medicine of Erasmus University, had led the investigative effort. Van der Maas, his colleague Loes Pijnenborg, and I talked first about borderline cases that are not classified as euthanasia nor as termination of the patient without request, but probably should be. When a doctor gives a patient medication with the primary intention of shortening life (done in 1,350 cases according to the study) and the patient consents, why is that not euthanasia? The only real difference, van der Maas pointed out, is that in ordinary euthanasia cases, death is immediate, whereas in these cases, death may take much longer. If, as in most such cases, a patient is given medication to end his life and does not know it, the case would seem to fall into the category of termination of the patient without request. Yet these cases are not so classified. Van der Maas was willing to concede that given such ambiguities, the actual number of cases of (voluntary) euthanasia was higher than the official figure, but was reluctant to admit that this was true of nonvoluntary or involuntary euthanasia cases as well.

The alarming statistics in the Remmelink study indicate that in thousands of cases, decisions that might or were intended to end a fully competent patient's life were made without consulting the patient. Why, I asked van der Maas, did the report not include a recommendation that doctors discuss their plans with competent patients? Van der Maas answered that although he would make such a point in other contexts, it was understood that the report was not a policy document and would put forward as few recommendations as possible. This was necessary to secure and retain the cooperation of the KNMG and the participating doctors.

This political climate seemed to have important consequences for the study. In the interests of maintaining harmony, virtually all of the explanations of the physicians in the study appear to have been accepted at face value even when follow-up questions seemed necessary. For example, physicians who did not communicate with competent patients concerning decisions that might or were intended to end their lives most often gave as a reason for not doing so that they had previously had some discussion of the subject with the patient.[31] Yet it seems incomprehensible that a physician would terminate the life of a competent patient on the basis of some prior discussion without checking to see whether the patient still felt the same way. One cannot help but conjecture that physicians who did so felt it appropriate to end the patient's life and did not wish to risk a negative reply, since ending life then would amount to murder. It is also possible that physicians justified the death by stretching the patient's prior statement, which may, according to the replies of doctors interviewed in the study, have been no more than an urgent request for relief from pain. Challenging such explanations could have clarified the doctors' rationale for ending patients' lives without first ascertaining their wishes.

Other responses warranted further inquiry as well. Failure

to obtain consultation, not providing alternative treatment plans, claiming that in almost all cases life was only shortened a few hours or days—all these were accepted without challenge. Van der Maas seemed concerned that to do otherwise would compromise the neutrality of the investigation. I had the impression that the study's interviewers, who were primarily physicians themselves, questioned their peers in perhaps too collegial a manner.

The Remmelink Commission accepted the study with one major addition: they felt that even if the termination of patients' lives without explicit request is appropriate, such cases should also be reported to the authorities. Subsequent legislation incorporated what had previously been case law; i.e., if *force majeure* applies and guidelines are followed, the physician will not be prosecuted for performing assisted suicide or euthanasia (although both still remain illegal); the legislation also includes the requirement that physicians report all cases in which life was terminated without explicit request.[32] The KNMG is opposed to this broadening of the notification procedure, particularly since the new legislative protection does not extend to such cases but leaves them to be decided individually. The new law, however, also included "mental duress" as an exceptional circumstance that could exempt a physician from prosecution, so it could conceivably be used in a defense of nonvoluntary euthanasia given that the consent of the patient killed is irrelevant to such a defense.[33]

In his private comments van der Maas seemed concerned about terminations of life without request, but in his public utterances he was more restrained in his criticism. He wrote an article subsequent to the study demonstrating that in many of the cases in which patients' lives were ended without their consent, doctors were required to make emergency decisions with patients who were not competent or not fully competent. Nonetheless, he indicated that cases involving acts that terminated life without request should be avoided whenever possible.[34] In contrast to the response of the KNMG, van der Maas himself said it was right to broaden the notification procedure to include such cases. That seemed to say more than anything else that he saw the problem as serious.

I was curious how Eugene Sutorius would respond when confronted by the fact that thousands of both competent and incompetent patients were put to death without their consent. When I raised this question with him, he pointed out that there were times when doctors felt they had to act because patients or families could not. He knew of one case where a doctor had terminated the life of a nun a few days before she otherwise would have died because she was in excruciating pain, but her religious convictions did not permit her to ask for death. Sutorius did not argue, however, when I asked why she should not have been permitted to die in the way she wanted. I said I had known terminally ill patients who were not religious, but for whom the need to struggle to the end was terribly important. Their right not to go quietly would seem to merit respect as much as the rights of those who wish a painless death. He agreed.

"The Doctor Decides"

Who should decide whether a patient who cannot speak for himself should live or die? Professor Joost Schudel, chair of a KNMG subcommittee on medical decisions at the end of life, which addresses physicians' life-ending decisions for patients who are not mentally competent, declared unambiguously: "The doctor decides."

Professor Schudel explained that the cardinal principle that a doctor should follow with such patients is to ask himself if he would accept life if he were in the patient's position. I asked if the relatives of such a patient could decide they wished the patient to be kept alive and Schudel repeated no, "the doctor decides," adding that the Netherlands was not like America, where relatives have more say in medical decisions. In the Dutch context the relationship between doctor and patient seemed to be reaching new dimensions in which the wishes of the doctor were presumed identical to those of the patient.

To bring the conversation down to earth, I asked Schudel about my mother, who was then ninety-two. She was unable to communicate intelligibly but was in relatively good health and in no evident physical or emotional distress. I told him that since my mother had never given me instructions that she would not want to live in such a situation, I felt some responsibility for her well-being. I had read that in the Netherlands and under KNMG guidelines, doctors would not treat demented patients for infectious diseases. A leading Dutch advocate of euthanasia frequently cites the remark "Pneumonia is an old person's best friend." Schudel did not answer directly at first, but told me that KNMG policies do not include operating on demented people, since you cannot explain to them the discomfort you are going to cause, and you have to ask yourself what kind of life you are giving them. Demented patients who refused to eat, Schudel told me, would not be urged to do so or given IV feeding. By not eating, he explained, these patients were coming as close as they could to indicating their wish to die.

He seemed reluctant, at first, perhaps out of consideration for my feelings, to state what Dutch policy would be in treating pneumonia in a person like my mother, preferring to talk about such patients in general when I would refer to her. Finally he said that such patients would be given symptomatic relief for difficulties in breathing, but the underlying infection would not be treated, since one had to ask what quality of life the patient would be returned to. I said it seemed to me that she would be returned to the same quality of life she had immediately before she developed pneumonia. I thought but did not say that it sounded as though the pneumonia provided an excuse to get rid of someone who doctors decided did not have a life of sufficient quality to preserve. Schudel suggested that I get further clarification from Robert Dillmann, secretary for medical affairs of the KNMG, who drafted their position papers on medical ethics and their recent report on dementia and whom he knew I was scheduled to meet.

Dillmann explained that while the KNMG position did reflect what Schudel said, it also gave the physician a great deal of latitude. He pointed out that in cases where relatives were pressing to end the patient's life, having the doctor decide could be a form of protection. He believed nonetheless that most doctors would be influenced by a relative's wishes in such cases. Yet this leaves the patients dependent on a flexible physician and a caring relative.

The Dutch are divided on the issue of treating infectious diseases in patients with dementia when the decision would mean life or death. Without stating his own position, Sutorius said he did not think there would be a consensus in the Netherlands for withholding antibiotics from dementia patients. Jannink-Kappelle, president of the NVVE, supported nontreatment of such cases. René Diekstra, on the other hand, thought nontreatment of pneumonia in dementia patients "would be an outrage, a violation of human rights that devalues all people with dementia. Our system is not careful in distinguishing the appropriate from the inappropriate."

The Dutch are in something of a bind with regard to demented patients. By their definition, euthanasia is possible only with competent patients, so they cannot sanction it for people who are demented. Patients suffering the early signs of Alzheimer's disease but fearful of its progression could, while still competent, request and receive euthanasia. They could not, however, make a request that would be honored for euthanasia to be performed at some subsequent date when they were demented. Such individuals might have to end their lives months or years before they would otherwise have considered it necessary. One Dutch psychiatrist who feared the burden of his possible dementia on his family indicated to me his intention of doing just that.

The KNMG has modified this position somewhat in declaring that if severe dementia is accompanied by severe physical suffering, and the patient has made an advance request to be put to death if demented, such a request can be implemented.[35] Led by Els Borst-Eilers, Dutch minister of health, some Dutch euthanasia advocates would like such requests honored even if there is no physical suffering.[36] So far the KNMG and a Dutch commission on life-terminating decisions have only recommended public discussion of the matter. More alarmingly, they have also called for public discussion of ending the lives of patients with dementia who have made no such advance request.[37] Since euthanasia can take place only on a voluntary basis with competent patients, ending the life of any demented patients would simply not to be called euthanasia.

When I raised with Herbert Cohen the many thousands of cases in the Remmelink study in which doctors make decisions that may be or are intended to end life without consulting competent patients, he said, "There is a certain paternalism built into our system." Like most physicians, Herbert Cohen was against the new legislation that required doctors to report all cases in which patients' lives had been terminated without their request. He thought it a silly idea as long as such practices are illegal, saying, "You can't expect someone to turn himself in for a crime." He went on to note that "death is influenced by a doctor's decision in almost all nontraumatic cases. Death is an orchestrated happening."

That the doctor is clearly the conductor of the orchestra controlling the tempo and pitch of patients' deaths has aroused the concern even of avid supporters of assisted suicide and euthanasia. Dr. Johanna Groen-Prakken, a psychoanalyst and euthanasia advocate who is a member of the NVVE, told me of her concern that too many physicians were unaware of how a patient's moods can fluctuate in the course of their treatment. After a colostomy necessitated by colon cancer, her own uncle, a retired physician, had been acutely depressed, stopped eating, and asked her to assist in his suicide. She told him he could always end his life but should get healthy first, and arranged to have him discharged from the hospital into a more cheerful setting in a nursing home. When she visited him in the home a few days later he was smoking a cigar and no longer talking of suicide. Two years later his cancer had metastasized. But now her uncle, no longer wanting an assisted suicide, feared involuntary euthanasia. He was afraid his family would give him pills to hasten his death in order to collect their inheritance. His relatives assured him that they all wanted him to live. In the course of his treatment, this man had gone from wanting an immediate death to fearing that he would be deprived of the chance to die naturally.

Groen-Prakken was particularly concerned for those patients whose families were unable or unwilling to act as mediators with doctors who might be unaware of patients' fears of involuntary euthanasia. Her mother, demented and in a nursing home, told Groen-Prakken not to throw away some violets in her room because "you don't throw away living things." Groen-Prakken thought that doctors were not trained to understand such statements as metaphorical expressions of the patient's own will to live, even with reduced capacities. She saw a terrible danger here and believed that many younger doctors were too casual about helping people die. She would like the doctors to have two consultants with at least twenty-five years of experience as doctors so that they could understand how patients' moods vary at different stages in their treatment and lives.

Dutch Postscript

A little less than a year after my original visit, I returned to the Netherlands. I had sent advance copies of an article I had written dealing with euthanasia in the Netherlands to some of those in the country who had been major sources of information, including Paul van der Maas, Herbert Cohen, Boudewijn Chabot, Robert Dillmann, and René Diekstra. I was able to see Chabot, Dillmann, and Cohen in person, as well as a number of others significantly involved in euthanasia in the Netherlands.

Ten months after our original interview, Chabot and I met again in Haarlem. He had written to me detailing his strong objections to certain aspects of my account.

Chabot was most concerned that my description of the Assen case reflected on his ability as a psychotherapist. He was vehement in his feeling that his decision to assist in Netty's suicide was not based on pressure from her, citing as proof that the courts had agreed he had not been pressured. He also stated that when Netty said she would leave if he would not help her right away, she added that she knew it was not easy for him and would understand if he could not help her.

He insisted that he had not simply agreed to assist in her suicide if she continued to want it, although my notes show that he said this several times in different ways. He felt the case note he wrote on August 2, 1991, more accurately reflected his words:

> I believe what you've told me (i.e., that she wanted to re-
> peat her attempted suicide and wanted to see me only to
> receive barbiturates to end her life effectively and with dig-
> nity). And I take it seriously. But I am not at all convinced
> there is no other way out. Tell me in detail everything that
> has happened, how your life developed right from the start
> up to the point you have reached now. I can never help
> anyone with what you are asking from me unless I am con-
> vinced there is no other way out. That conviction I haven't
> gotten at all from what you've told me.[38]

Chabot also felt that he had explored with Netty all of the suggestions I made regarding her psychotherapy. Finally, he was insistent that Netty suffered from no psychiatric disorder of any kind, that she was not a psychiatric patient but a woman having a normal grief reaction, seeing a doctor because she wanted assistance with her suicide.

I suggested to Chabot that Netty essentially called the tune in their relationship. The time frame was dictated by her. Even in this second interview he had told me that he would have liked more time to "seduce her into psychotherapy" but she did not give it to him. He said he could understand, but did not agree, that his submitting to her time frame in the context of her threatening to kill herself or to stop seeing him might be seen by me as blackmail. His present elaboration of what occurred confirmed for me that Netty did not deal with him in an openly coercive way—which was not likely to have been effective—but got what she wanted in a subtler manner.

I pointed out to Chabot that he seemed to want to have it both ways: maintaining on the one hand that Netty was not a psychiatric patient, which justified his responding to her request for assisted suicide, and on the other that he had a therapeutic relationship with her in which he made interpretations of her feelings and behavior. Treatment, however, would have required an engagement on Netty's part, not simply her coming to meet the conditions necessary to receive assisted suicide. It would have required Chabot to insist on that engagement for him to continue to see her.

Chabot asked me if I couldn't conceive of a grieving patient who was not depressed and had no psychiatric problem. I replied that such patients may have suicidal thoughts but seldom act on them, and when they do, more is usually at work.

He insisted that Netty did not meet the formal psychiatric criteria for depression and had no personality disorder. Yet the years of persistent, pervasive loss of pleasure in life she had experienced from the time of her first son's death (after which she had been hospitalized) suggested that she had a mood disorder with severe depressive episodes after each child's death. In addition, I pointed out that in patients like Netty a fixed obsessional desire for suicide often masks other depressive symptoms, although characteristically not the loss of pleasure in previously pleasurable activities.

Chabot said if I was right about the case, then he belonged in prison. I told him that I believed the Dutch system encouraged what happened to Netty Boomsma and that there was a shared responsibility for what occurred.

Dr. Robert Dillmann was pleased with the Dutch Supreme Court's opinion in the Assen case for reasons apart from Chabot's guilt or innocence. He considered it important that the court had ruled that *force majeure* could apply even when patients were not terminally ill. He hoped this would lead to the dropping of prosecution in a number of recent cases where the absence of terminal illness was the basis for the prosecution.

Dillmann was pleased that the Dutch Supreme Court had ruled that a psychiatric patient could be competent and therefore capable of receiving euthanasia. He thought it reasonable that the courts should insist on having a consultant personally see patients in psychiatric cases, although he felt it unfair that Chabot should be found guilty on this issue since previous medical cases would not have led him to believe such consultation was necessary.

Dillmann reminded me that the Dutch Supreme Court could not review evidence but only made rulings based on the law, using facts adduced by the lower court cases. Since the lower courts had accepted the evaluation of the experts that Netty Boomsma was mentally competent to end her life, the supreme court simply treated that as fact.

Dillmann agreed with the court that *force majeure* could apply only if no effective treatment was possible. The supreme court also did not review the question of whether treatment was possible in the Assen case, since the lower courts had decided on the basis of expert testimony that it was not. Netty Boomsma's own refusal of treatment, however, played a part in the determination by the experts and by the lower courts that treatment was impossible. Her refusal, however, must be seen in the context of her having the possibility if she was persistent in persuading Chabot to assist in her suicide. For some who are suicidal, legitimizing assisted suicide both creates a demand for it and encourages refusal of other alternatives.

Dillmann pointed out that in a published article he expressed concern over euthanasia cases not being reported by physicians, as well as patients being terminated without explicit request; an article by van der Maas had expressed the hope that the number of cases terminated without explicit request be reduced. In the light of these articles, Dillmann felt it was unfair to imply "a conspiracy of silence" regarding problems with euthanasia. When I later read the Dillmann article, I discovered that his proposed solution to the problem was to *not* require *either* group of cases to be reported to the authorities.[39] Not requiring reporting would seem to cure nonreporting in much the same way as euthanasia cures suicidal depression. Of course, Dillmann and the KNMG maintain that leaving the problem in medical hands will resolve it, and greater use of advance directives will make it unnecessary for physicians to exercise their own judgment.

Van der Maas noted in his article that the 1,000 patients referred to in the Remmelink study whose lives were terminated without explicit request really could be reduced to a few hundred, since a third were "already in the dying phase" and another third died as the result of treatment for pain.[40] Focusing on the thousand cases, however, does not address the more than another thousand cases where the primary intention in giving painkilling medication was to end the life of the patient. Nor does it address the 5,000 cases in which medical decisions that could or were intended to end the life of the patient were taken without consulting competent patients.[41]

The Remmelink Commission lumped all of these cases together by saying that in the overwhelming majority of instances of termination of life without explicit request, patients were in the "dying phase," and therefore ending their lives was normal medical practice. Dillmann did agree that it was not right for the commission to group all these cases together.

The issue of patients in the "dying phase" was raised as well by Paul van der Maas. He was understandably concerned that I should distinguish the data presented in the study he directed from a supplement written by the Remmelink Commission. In the supplement the commission concluded that the termination of life without explicit request should be regarded as acceptable medical practice and ought to be defined as "medical help in dying," despite the inclusion in this group of large

numbers of competent patients. Although separating himself
from the language of the supplemental report, van der Maas
justified its conclusion, pointing out in a letter to me, "These
cases include nontreatment decisions, such as not giving antibiotics to dying cancer patients. This can also be described
as not prolonging suffering without hope of improvement. In
the majority of cases this would be considered good medical
treatment anywhere."[42]

In practice, however, this means that in a deeply troubling
number of instances the criterion of voluntariness, that is, respect for the patient's autonomy, lapses when the patient has
entered the dying phase of life—determined when the doctor
decides that the patient has only a few days, weeks, or months
to live. At that point the doctor is justified in speeding up the
process without consultation even with fully competent patients. This is not seen as problematic, since the patient is
dying anyhow and may be in pain.

Here the logic, or at least the consistency, of the Dutch
criteria seems to break down. The patient's autonomy is
abandoned, and the only available rationale for ending the
patient's life becomes compassion for the patient's pain and
suffering. Yet since the KNMG and the courts have agreed
that suffering is subjective, how could death be justified without consulting the recipient of this compassion? In these cases
the patient has no autonomy because the doctor has decided
that the quality of the patient's life is such that it is time for
the patient to die.

How can anyone decide for a competent patient that because he or she has only a few weeks left to live this time is
not valuable? One could just as soon argue that each of those
days becomes infinitely more valuable. And even accepting the
devaluation of the final days or weeks of life that seems to underlie the Dutch system does not diminish the obligation to

discuss with a fully competent patient a decision that might or was intended to end his or her life. That the Remmelink Commission would choose not even to distinguish competent from incompetent patients in justifying doctors' practices suggests again the bias toward protecting doctors rather than patients that runs through the Dutch system.

Van der Maas also took exception to my characterization of the relationship between the physicians doing the interviewing and those providing the information as perhaps too collegial. He felt that this description undermined the credibility of Dutch physicians and thus, indirectly, of his study. In response I stressed that I consider the study a groundbreaking effort, one on which further investigations can build in an effort to understand euthanasia in the Netherlands. Neverthless, there are limitations to a study when physician–interviewers do not challenge even incredible explanations provided by their physician-subjects, and "collegial" does not seem too strong a word to describe what took place.

A few days before another meeting I had with Dillmann, a new coalition government had been organized that excluded the Christian Democrats, who have traditionally opposed assisted suicide and euthanasia. Dr. Els Borst-Eilers, an ardent euthanasia advocate, had been appointed minister of health. Dillmann was somewhat more hopeful during this talk that the new government would decriminalize euthanasia so that doctors would not have to report euthanasia cases. I indicated that my reservation about exclusive medical supervision of euthanasia cases stemmed from the fact that doctors who worked with euthanasia often talked as if the guidelines were an unpleasant necessity to be followed in order to avoid criticism or difficulty with the law, rather than safeguards necessary to protect patients. Indeed, Dr. Herbert Cohen, with whom I had recently met again, had told me that the concept of patients needing protection from doctors would be incomprehensibly foreign to Dutch readers. Dillmann replied that since in the overwhelming number of cases there was no problem, he could understand Cohen's viewpoint. He had retreated from his acknowledgment ten months earlier that there were large numbers of patients in the Netherlands whose lives were ended by physicians who ignored the established guidelines.

I discussed with Dillmann the need for a follow-up on the Remmelink Commission study and my concern that doctors were not enthusiastic about having one. Dillmann said that in any case there would be a follow-up; the Ministry of Justice had announced that in two years there would be an evaluation of the current procedures specifically regarding reported and unreported cases.

Herbert Cohen objected to the publication in my article of much of what he had told me in our original meeting. As we spoke, he went down a list of euthanasia advocates mentioned in my article and put a check next to those with whom I had been in touch. The next day I received a call from the NVVE (whom Cohen had called) on behalf of its president, Dr. Jannink-Kappelle, with whom I had not spoken or corresponded since preparing my article, requesting a copy of that part of the piece dealing with the interview I had with her. I faxed the material to her with a request that I be able to talk with her about her reactions to it.

Jannink-Kappelle had two major objections to my description of our interview. First, she denied there were any differences between the NVVE and the KNMG in their attitudes toward assisted suicide and euthanasia, although a major part of our discussion had dealt with those differences. Second, she denied there was anything inappropriate in helping to end the life of the man who, although asymptomatic, tested positive for HIV. She repeated several times that the doctor who assisted in the death was one of "our finest doctors." Then she said that the AIDS virus probably affected the young man's brain, although the point made in the film was that the man had no such symptoms. It would seem more accurate to say that the doctor who helped the man die did so reluctantly out of his inability to cope with the man's terror.

The Dutch seem reluctant to acknowledge that the doctor's role in euthanasia is more than that of a neutral observer responding to a patient's needs. This is particularly evident when families pressure patients to request euthanasia.

In a study of euthanasia done in Dutch hospitals prior to the Remmelink study, doctors and nurses told Professor H. W. Hilhorst, a sociologist at the Catholic Theological University in Utrecht, that more requests for euthanasia came from families than from patients themselves. He concluded that the family, the doctors, and the nurses often pressured the patient to request euthanasia.[43]

The Remmelink study provided little information about the extent to which patients might feel pressure to die apart from the finding that more than half of Dutch physicians considered it appropriate to introduce the subject of euthanasia to their patients. Virtually all the medical advocates of euthanasia that I spoke with in the Netherlands saw this as enabling the patient to consider an option that he or she may have felt inhibited about bringing up, rather than a form of coercion. They seemed not to recognize that the doctor was also telling the patient that his or her life was not worth living, a message that would have a powerful effect on the patient's outlook and decision.

The Dutch courts have implicitly encouraged physicians to make such value decisions. Originally the courts interpreted *force majeure* as applying if virtually anyone in the doctor's situation would have acted as he did, essentially saying that basic human decency and compassion compelled such action. Subsequently the courts have interpreted it as applying if merely any other member of the medical profession would have acted as did the doctor, which is quite a different standard. Jos Welie, an ethicist formerly at the University of Nijmegen, points out that this ruling elevates physicians to a superior moral status, making their judgments on life and death always just.[44] When combined with court rulings that have made the use of another physician as a consultant not necessary for a *force majeure* acquittal in medical cases, there is an increasing tendency to free the physician from oversight even within his own profession.[45]

Euthanasia, advocated and instituted to foster patient autonomy and self-determination, has actually increased the paternalistic power of the medical profession. Physicians' organizations protect the interests of their members like guilds or unions everywhere. Physicians are especially unaccustomed to explaining their decisions to nonphysicians. American medicine has reluctantly accepted that in matters of what we call "quality assurance," the input of nurses, social workers, psychologists, and even lay administrators, the tension between disciplines, and the different perspectives they bring can be invaluable. In cases like that of the nun, the doctor may be best qualified to know how long she is likely to live, but someone on an interdisciplinary team would have recognized that it was her right to die as she wished, even in pain. Moreover, considering the appalling frequency with which physicians end the lives of patients without their consent, more than one Dutch euthanasia advocate has conceded that the general acceptance of euthanasia has probably encouraged doctors to feel they can decide for patients what is an acceptable quality of life.

My primary aim in going to the Netherlands was to learn what might be applicable to the United States. The people I met on both sides of the question in the Netherlands were intelligent and caring. If they were not, their experience would have less relevance for us. Yet in the name of humanitarian goals, bright and compassionate people were wrongly ending other people's lives.

Chapter 4

THE POLITICS OF
EUTHANASIA

Why do the Dutch minimize the overwhelming evidence—including that of their own government-sponsored report—that in thousands of cases medical decisions are made that may or are intended to end the lives of competent patients without their knowledge or consent? It had been suggested to me that political considerations were perhaps a determining factor, and I pursued this question with the KNMG's Robert Dillmann. He said they were. The KNMG (Royal Dutch Medical Association) and the NVVE (Dutch Voluntary Euthanasia Society) saw themselves in a struggle with the then ruling Christian Democrats, whose leaders they see as fundamentally opposed to euthanasia. Conceding that cases are often handled improperly would play into the hands of the Christian Democratic opposition. In addition, physicians throughout Europe were savage in their criticism of Dutch euthanasia policies, and this forced the Dutch into a defensive position. Dillmann saw the van der Maas study as extremely valuable, but also as providing ammunition to those who took its findings out of context in order to attack euthanasia in the Netherlands.

Virtually all of those who have played a role in advancing the cause of euthanasia on humanitarian grounds were concerned about the problems in its implementation, yet they seemed disinclined to express their doubts publicly. René Diekstra, for example, had written an article on assisted suicide for an English medical journal that contradicted everything he said to me.[1] The article failed to mention the problems uncovered by the Remmelink study, and indeed even cited the study to conclude that "in almost all cases of euthanasia and assisted suicide doctors do comply with the rules of proper professional practice and conduct."[2] I told him of my conversation with Dillmann and asked if he too was motivated by political considerations in muting his criticism. He admitted that he was. He also told me that similar considerations influenced his not wanting to testify in the Assen case. Although he was critical of the way Chabot had handled the case, he thought it would hurt the cause of assisted suicide and euthanasia to say so.

Diekstra seemed to be in an untenable position. On the one hand, he seemed to hope for a backlash that would take euthanasia out of the exclusive hands of doctors. On the other hand, he did not himself wish to be critical of the system or perhaps to be perceived as being critical in a culture that demanded support for Dutch euthanasia policies.

Polls in the Netherlands estimate that opposition to assisted suicide and euthanasia is limited to 20 to 25 percent of the population. Euthanasia advocates dismiss medical and community opposition, attributing it to religious conservatives and to some who lost families in Nazi concentration camps; both groups are said by advocates to be unable to be objective about euthanasia.

Dr. Karl Gunning of Rotterdam helped found the Dutch Physicians' League, a small group of doctors who split off from the KNMG because of disagreement on abortion as well as euthanasia. He told me that the association has dwindled from 1,200 to 600 members, less than 3 percent of the KNMG's total of 25,000. Gunning believes that if the public were aware of the extent of involuntary euthanasia, support for euthanasia would not be so widespread and medical practice might change.

Concern that their lives might be ended without their consent has led some people to join the Dutch Patients Association (60,000 members), a group organized by religious Protestants opposed to both euthanasia and abortion. The association fields inquiries from people wanting to know whether a particular hospital is "safe," i.e., not likely to put them to death without consulting them. Together with the Sanctuary Foundation, a Protestant group also opposed to euthanasia, they distribute a "passport for life" that patients carry, indicating that in medical emergencies they do not want their life terminated without their consent.

Dutch euthanasia advocates are aggressively defensive about any criticism of assisted suicide or euthanasia in the Netherlands, presenting a united front in facing down public dissent. Dr. Richard Fenigsen, who lost family in the Holocaust, practiced for twenty years in the Netherlands before coming to the United States; he was a strong critic of involuntary euthanasia, which he considers to be widespread. After he published an article on the subject in the *Hastings Center Report*,[3] an American journal dealing with ethical issues, twenty-five prominent euthanasia advocates, including officials of the KNMG and the NVVE, signed a letter vehemently protesting the piece and its publication.[4] Whatever differences the twenty-five signers had among themselves were subordinated in an attempt to discredit Fenigsen. Ultimately his contentions concerning the prevalence of involuntary euthanasia, which the signers of the letter dismissed as anecdotal, were supported by the Remmelink study.

Dutch Critics of Euthanasia

Chabot, van der Maas, Dillmann, and Cohen asked for some changes in the text of the article that I sent them that had been accepted for publication by *Issues in Law and Medicine;* most of these changes seemed relatively minor, although important to them, and for the most part I was able to accommodate them. Cohen and Chabot were not satisfied, however, and indicated that they would attempt to stop publication of the article and the revised edition of my book, *Suicide in America,* in which they knew I planned to include some of the Dutch material.

By the time I got back to the United States, they had enlisted Dillmann, van der Maas, and Schudel in this effort. They wrote to the editors of *Issues in Law and Medicine,* to my publisher, W. W. Norton, and to me, stating that I had come to erroneous conclusions and that they did not want the material to be published. All who saw the correspondence and my detailed notes on the interviews felt that this was unwarranted and should not be allowed to delay publication. I wondered whether the same paternalism in the culture that leads many Dutch doctors to feel that they can decide whose life is worth living is reflected in their notion of being entitled to control the publication of material critical of their euthanasia practices.

Whatever pressure I felt from the Dutch medical establishment, however, was minimal compared with that experienced by Dutch critics of these euthanasia policies. The climate that surrounds euthanasia has a chilling effect on debate of the subject, making correcting flaws in the system difficult.

In May 1994, Dr. Frank Koerselman, a Dutch psychiatrist who had followed the Assen case and had read the book Chabot had written about it,[5] published an article in a Dutch medical journal critical of Chabot's treatment of Netty Boomsma, whom he saw as a depressed patient. He pointed out that Netty's refusal to take medication did not justify Chabot's contention that she would not have responded to the medication or that she was untreatable.[6] Since even Dutch psychiatrists who were privately critical of the Assen case were unwilling to say so publicly, I was particularly interested in talking with him. Although Koerselman was not available when I was in Amsterdam, we spoke extensively by telephone several months later; by then I was familiar with his work and he with mine.

Opposition to euthanasia in all but a few rare terminally ill patients reflected Koerselman's view of what it meant to be a doctor. Caring for a dying patient, he thought, involves more than most doctors are willing to do; it means being with and supporting the patient to the end. Yet a doctor is limited in what he can do, and those limits include ending a patient's life. He thought that doctors see the power given to them by euthanasia as enhancing their status; he agreed with my observation that euthanasia in the Netherlands, which began with the idea of diminishing the physician's power over the patient, had ironically actually enhanced it.

Since he considers assisted suicide never to be appropriate for a psychiatric patient, Koerselman was disturbed by the way in which euthanasia and assisted suicide were being accepted by psychiatrists. He told me of a well-known psychiatric colleague who had made a career of giving second opinions in euthanasia cases. Occasionally he prescribed treatment with medication or electroconvulsive therapy, but most often he supported euthanasia or assisted suicide. He saw patients for an hour and made a decision, claiming this freed him from decisions influenced by too close an involvement with the patient. Koerselman regards those who do become involved in assisting in a suicide in psychiatric cases as guilty of a "deadly form of professional naiveté."

Despite public criticism, Koerselman had received almost fifty letters from psychiatric colleagues about his article, almost all supportive of his position. None of his colleagues felt free, however, to publish anything critical of Chabot's handling of the Assen case.

Koerselman saw the Dutch legal system, exemplified by prosecutors and the courts, as unwilling to enforce the law in assisted suicide or euthanasia cases. He noted that he could confirm my description of the reluctant prosecutor in the Assen case. He had offered his services to the prosecutor in the Leeuwarden appeal of the case. Given the reluctance of psychiatrists openly to express criticism of Chabot, Koerselman thought the prosecutor might welcome such an offer, but he was not interested.

Since Koerselman regards himself as a social liberal who is not religious and not opposed to all euthanasia, one might suspect that he would be spared the attacks directed at any Dutch doctor critical of Dutch euthanasia practices. Koerselman complains, however, of how difficult it is for him to hold his views. He has been subject to severe condemnation that labels him as belonging to the reactionary right.

Dutch attitudes are reflected in the different treatment accorded Koerselman and Chabot in newspaper interviews. Koerselman, a respected academic psychiatrist, is repeatedly challenged to defend his position. Chabot, who had virtually withdrawn from psychiatric practice prior to his involvement in the Netty Boomsma case, is treated as a popular celebrity. He is asked to explain and expand rather than defend his views.

Although colleagues may not publicly support him, Koerselman was joined by four nonmedical authors in writing a book critical of Chabot.[7] A philosopher, Professor Hans Achterhuis, and a theologian, Dr. Johan Goud, criticize the Dutch Supreme Court for moving away from the consensus that euthanasia was acceptable only in cases of terminally ill patients where *force majeure* applied. Willem Jan Otten, an author familiar with the issues, is critical of Chabot for abdicating responsibility for his actions by presenting himself as the instrument of his patient's autonomous will. Otten points out that Chabot chose to be passive; he had the power to resist.

Tom Schalken, professor of law at the Free University of Amsterdam, sees the supreme court's decision in the Assen case as mistakenly focused on procedural matters, such as equalizing the treatment of the physically and mentally ill. Equal treatment, he believes, is relative, not absolute, and a procedural focus ignores intrinsic questions about the differences between physical and mental disease. The court also sets up an insupportable antithesis between the obligation to alleviate pain and the obligation to preserve life. Schalken points out that such sharp opposition exists only if alleviating pain is equated with ending life. Nor does Schalken consider the patient's will to die ever to be a fully autonomous decision. He is most concerned that the supreme court has normalized what was intended to be an exceptional medical response to an extreme situation. If a doctor decides a patient is untreatable but follows the rules while ending her life, his judgment will not be challenged.

In March 1995 an Amsterdam medical tribunal issued a *berisping,* or reprimand, to Chabot for his handling of the Netty Boomsma case.[8] Agreeing with the supreme court that while mental suffering was sufficient grounds for euthanasia Chabot should have had a consultant see Netty Boomsma, the tribunal addressed a more clinical range of issues. The tribunal believed that it was not demonstrated that Netty Boomsma's condition was incurable; that a decision made by Netty within six months of her son's death could not be regarded as autonomous; that no alternative treatment such as antidepressant medication or electric shock had seriously been proposed; and that even if Netty refused such treatment, Chabot should not have helped her to die. In addition, the tribunal felt that Chabot did not keep a proper professional distance from Netty: he saw her at his country house, had her spend nights there between sessions in his guest house, and had extensive social conversations with her.

Although the tribunal's criticisms may seem self-evident to observers not caught up in the Dutch situation, they were startling in a country in which even unusual cases of assisted suicide and euthanasia are supported by the courts and the medical tribunals. The Dutch press found it confusing that the tribunal was more critical of Chabot than the supreme court had been;[9] the public and most doctors continued to support Chabot.

Undercutting the tribunal's actual findings, the Dutch minister of justice, Winnie Sorgdrager, and the minister of health, Dr. Els Borst-Eilers, issued a statement indicating that the medical tribunal's decision was in full agreement with that of the Dutch Supreme Court. They went on to state that cases of euthanasia where there is no physical illness are so exceptional that the Chabot decision did not suggest the need for more vigilance on the part of prosecutors.[10] The ministers' statement also overlooks the many cases where it is primarily psychological issues that motivate the request for euthanasia whether or not some physical illness is also present. (Herbert Cohen's patient, haunted by her concentration camp memories, is an example.) The minister's statement minimized what the tribunal had said and attempted to ensure that it would not alter public policy.

Although Chabot criticized the Amsterdam tribunal's decision, he chose not to appeal. Euthanasia advocates did not feel he had to; the Assen case had set a legal precedent while establishing medical and public support for assisted suicide and euthanasia for solely mental distress.

Like Koerselman, Isaac van der Sluis, a dermatologist in Amsterdam, is among the small minority of nonreligious Dutch physicians who oppose legalized euthanasia in the Netherlands. Although he was an early advocate of a woman's right to choose abortion, he too has been labeled a reactionary fundamentalist for his opposition to euthanasia.

He spoke more in resignation than in bitterness of how difficult it had been for him to publish in the Netherlands anything he wrote in opposition to euthanasia. When some years earlier he wrote a critique of Dutch euthanasia practices, the editors pressured him to make the text less critical. Subsequently, he could get pieces critical of euthanasia published only abroad. His practice, which depended on referrals from general practitioners, was hurt by his attitude toward euthanasia, so he eventually ceased his open opposition. He saw euthanasia advocates as portraying themselves as on the "side of the angels" defending a "beautiful liberal ideal" while behaving as though in a war where any criticism of Dutch euthanasia policies served the cause of the enemy.

Chris Rutenfrans, a strong secular critic of euthanasia in the Netherlands, has a doctorate in law and criminology. Together with Caterina Dessaur, writer and professor of criminology at the University of Nijmegen, he wrote a book suggesting the ambivalence of most requests for euthanasia, stressing the coercion of the patient that often accompanies the decision to perform it, and indicating how frequently it takes place without the consent of patients.[11]

Rutenfrans was the target of another tactic euthanasia advocates use to stifle criticism. Eugene Sutorius and the NVVE took him to court to force retraction of a critical newspaper article in which he wrote that NVVE officials both advocated involuntary euthanasia and advised families of relatives how to go about it. The judge arranged for a compromise whereby Rutenfrans retracted his comments about advising relatives but not what he said about advocacy. When Rutenfrans subsequently repeated the charges of advocacy of involuntary euthanasia, Sutorius said he would sue him again but did not.[12]

Sutorius and the NVVE also warned Richard Fenigsen that he would be sued if he did not recant written statements that many prominent figures in the NVVE support involuntary as well as voluntary euthanasia. Fenigsen, who kept a file of published statements supporting his claim, refused to recant, and the matter was dropped.[13]

Documentation of actual cases of involuntary euthanasia is difficult since Dutch doctors who witness involuntary euthanasia avoid saying so publicly. Karl Gunning found this when he described competent patients who were put to death without their consent. Given the impact on their careers of opposing the medical establishment, none of the doctors who confided in him would bring such cases before the public. Gunning, too, felt vindicated by the Remmelink study's confirmation of the frequent occurrence of involuntary euthanasia.

Although D. J. Bakker, a surgeon at the Amsterdam Municipal Hospital, opposes euthanasia because of a religious belief in the sacredness of life, he remains on the KNMG ethics committee because he wants his views to be heard; he concedes that he may be tolerated as a token opponent whose views are dismissed on the grounds of his affiliation with the Christian Institute of Medical Ethics. His critique of euthanasia, however, is more medical and psychological than theological.

Bakker found that most patients who request euthanasia are not asking to be killed; often they hope to be reassured that they are still wanted. He believed that the dependency caused by illness makes a truly voluntary choice impossible. He felt it is necessary to fight suffering to help the patient, not sacrifice the patient because of his or her suffering. He, too, felt that legal sanction promotes euthanasia, which was intended for exceptional cases, into the "normal" treatment for terminal illness.

Bakker stressed that doctors, particularly younger ones, were afraid to express publicly any opposition to euthanasia because they would not be given good academic appointments. He felt it was easier for him as an established surgeon to make his position known.

Foreign Critics

In 1991, prior to the Remmelink study, Dr. Carlos Gomez, an American physician, published his study of euthanasia in the Netherlands.[14] Twenty-six euthanasia cases were presented to him by physicians and others who had been involved in the decision for euthanasia. Gomez found that guidelines such as "unbearable suffering" were flexibly interpreted, alternatives were often not provided so that euthanasia was not a "last resort," consultants were not always used and there was no way of assuring their independence, and cases were not routinely reported to the public prosecutor as required.

Gomez concluded that on the central concerns of "how to control the practice, how to keep it from being used on those that do not want it, how to provide for public accountability—the Dutch response has been, to date, inadequate."[15] He saw the regulatory procedures as unenforced and so ambiguous as to be unenforceable.

Since there is no way of determining what is unbearable pain and suffering, some of the ambiguity Gomez observed is inescapable. Critics as well as advocates maintain, and the Dutch courts have agreed, that only the patient can decide what is unbearable; the right to do so is an expression of the patient's autonomy. If autonomy is the guiding principle and the determination of unbearable pain and suffering is so subjective, then any competent person—visibly suffering or apparently healthy—has the right to choose euthanasia.

John Keown, an English legal scholar, agrees with Gomez in finding the Dutch imprecise and lax in the enforcement of their self-imposed guidelines.[16] He cites his own interview with Herbert Cohen in which he asked if Cohen would perform euthanasia on a patient who requested it because he felt himself to be a nuisance to his relatives, who wanted him dead so they could enjoy his estate. Cohen indicated that he would, "because that kind of influence—these children wanting their money now—is the same kind of power from the past that shaped us all." Keown points out that if a leading Dutch authority on euthanasia can interpret the guidelines requiring "an entirely free and voluntary request" and "unbearable suffering" in this way, "little more need be said about their inherent vagueness and elasticity."[17]

Keown uses the Remmelink study to support his critique, focusing on the thousands of cases in which the doctor's primary intention in giving palliative medicine or withdrawing treatment is to end the life of the patient. By narrowly defining euthanasia as referring only to "active voluntary euthanasia" rather than to all cases in which death is brought about on purpose as part of the medical care given to the patient, Keown considers that the Dutch minimize the frequency with which death is "intentionally accelerated by a doctor."

From thousands of cases in which without patient consent

doctors withdrew treatment or gave medication intended to hasten the patient's death, Keown concludes that nonvoluntary euthanasia is more common than voluntary euthanasia in the Netherlands. He is as unimpressed as I by the Remmelink Commission's defense that such cases can simply be excused as necessary "care for the dying."

The Dutch courts' continuing to justify euthanasia by citing *force majeure,* a concept ordinarily employed to justify actions necessary to defend life, has aroused criticism from foreign jurists. Alexander Capron, an American legal scholar and ethicist, points out that accepting *force majeure* as impelling a doctor on a course he or she is powerless to resist robs the action of its morality. It then becomes hard to accept euthanasia as a volitional and autonomous act for which a physician can be held responsible.[18]

The Dutch Supreme Court has also decided that the presence of *force majeure* is a medical decision to be determined by "responsible medical opinion" tested by the "prevailing standards of medical ethics." Keown asks, "If the court is effectively entrusting the determination of the lawfulness of euthanasia to the medical profession, does not that amount to an abdication of judicial responsibility?"[19]

Placing euthanasia beyond the watchful scrutiny of the law is exactly what Dutch euthanasia advocates—lawyers, prosecutors, ethicists, and doctors—would like to see. They maintain that when the threat of legal action is completely removed, control of abuse could come through medical enforcement—through the expansion of the authority of the medical tribunals. The 1993 Dutch statute defining conditions under which euthanasia will not be prosecuted largely, but not completely, removes the threat of such prosecution. As I indicated to Robert Dillmann, I am skeptical about purely medical control of the process because I sense that euthanasia advocates and practitioners view regulation—consultation, hospital review committees, notification—as a pro forma ritual to be complied with in order to avoid criticism; they did not seem to see it as something valuable to help and protect patients.

In practice, the legal application of *force majeure*—as demonstrated by the Assen case—seems even stranger than the theory. How could any court see *force majeure* applying to a case where the doctor solicited the NVVE for the case, and where the doctor insisted that the person whose suicide was assisted was not a patient but simply a woman who wanted to die? The use of *force majeure* to justify Chabot's actions seems more a legal ploy than one based on any genuine belief that an overriding duty to his "patient" made his action necessary.

"Angels of Death"

While I was in the Netherlands, two major stories illustrated the increasing pressure euthanasia advocates apply to reluctant doctors. The first story concerned new obligations for referring patients who sought euthanasia. Dr. J. Verhoef, the chief inspector of public health, supported by Borst-Eilers, declared that if a doctor did not agree to perform euthanasia on a patient who requested it and did not refer the patient to another doctor who would, he was guilty of malpractice and should be brought up on disciplinary charges.[20] Since some doctors do not believe in euthanasia on religious or ethical grounds, forcing them to make a referral coerces them and violates all prior assurances that no doctor need participate in the euthanasia process.

The second story suggested that resistant physicians could be circumvented by other means. G. J. van Dinter, a former Ministry of Justice official, charged—and Verhoef confirmed—that a team of traveling physicians was providing euthanasia to patients when family doctors were unwilling to do so.[21] The press referred to these physicians as "angels of death." The NVVE first denied and then confirmed its involvement in organizing these doctors.[22]

Dillmann knew of several physicians involved in such cases but believed the extent of the practice to be limited and overblown by the media; he conceded that in some cases the euthanasia was performed without the knowledge of the treating physician. Although the medical tribunals have ruled that ideally euthanasia should be performed by the treating physician, they have been reluctant to do more than caution or occasionally reprimand these "angels of death."

Dr. Wine Mulder-Meiss, a Rotterdam physician and euthanasia advocate, was involved in a number of these cases, three of which came to the attention of the authorities. In one case a doctor in a nursing home did not act on a patient's requests for euthanasia but persuaded her to reconsider. Neither he, the patient's family doctor, nor any other physician was consulted by Mulder-Meiss when she assisted in the death of the patient who was home on leave. Given the circumstances, and the fact that the patient was not terminally ill, the Hague Medical Tribunal did not believe that Mulder-Meiss had acted appropriately and reprimanded her, a decision that was sustained by the Central Medical Tribunal.[23]

In a second case, a patient with dementia who had earlier made a will requesting euthanasia if demented was put to death. This action is in contradiction to KNMG guidelines, which declare that only if there is suffering can an earlier will be used as justification for euthanasia with dementia patients. Dillmann defended the doctor, however, arguing the guidelines should not apply here since the euthanasia was done before their publication.

In a third case, Mulder-Meiss was given a ten-month suspended sentence by a judge in a Rotterdam court (reduced on appeal to one month) and was reprimanded by a medical tribunal for helping a man who was not terminally ill commit suicide with pills, gin, and a plastic bag.[24] None of three physicians treating the patient thought euthanasia or assisted suicide appropriate. Mulder-Meiss was criticized for not knowing well the patient or his medical condition and for encouraging the use of the plastic bag, which was considered not respectful of the dignity of the patient. In response to an interviewer's question as to whether the patient was blackmailing her, since he threatened to hang himself if she did not help him, Dr. Mulder-Meiss replied, "Let's say Mr. C was blackmailing me with hanging, then isn't it tragic that he had to do so because he was so eager to die." Mulder-Meiss described euthanasia as "dignified, beautiful, and peaceful, almost festive."[25]

The "angels of death" have aroused public concern. Many feel that when a doctor makes a decision after seeing a patient only briefly, it is difficult to make a case for *force majeure*. Others have argued that traveling doctors will become unnecessary if doctors who do not want to perform euthanasia can be obliged to refer patients to those who will.

The NVVE requested the help of the KNMG in setting up a pool of physicians who would be available to help in euthanasia cases when the treating physician was reluctant to do so. The NVVE requested specific criteria for what sort of physician would be suitable. The request presented a problem for the KNMG because it did not like to turn down the NVVE, although the medical association prefers that euthanasia be performed by a family physician who knows the patient rather than by a consultant. The question was probably moot, since the outcry against the traveling physicians led the NVVE to state that they were abandoning the practice.

The NVVE said it would now use nonmedical volunteers to consult with such patients and informally help them find a sympathetic physician.

Traveling doctors, nonmedical volunteers, mandated euthanasia referrals by reluctant doctors—all undercut one of the supposed safeguards of the Dutch system: the family doctor who knows the patient and his family. In cases where the family doctor sees euthanasia as not appropriate, the traveling teams and mandated referrals could bypass him and his objections.

Dr. Herbert Cohen referred to himself facetiously as one of the "angels of death"; he seemed to see himself, however, as an angel of mercy bringing the blessing of death to those otherwise unable to receive it. Cohen said he did not perform euthanasia himself in such cases, nor did he see the patients involved, but rather consulted with physicians to resolve their hesitation about proceeding with euthanasia. For example, a physician might fear legal repercussions for performing euthanasia on a patient who was not terminally ill, so Cohen would reassure him. Doctors frequently consulted him as to whether they should discuss euthanasia with patients when they were in pain or when they were getting relief from medication. The answer, Cohen explained, is to do so just when the pain is beginning to diminish; presumably the fear of the pain is present, but so is the awareness that relief is possible.

Death on Request

The ultimate step in normalizing euthanasia as a part of every day life was the Dutch television showing in the fall of 1994 of *Death on Request,* a film of a patient being put to death by euthanasia.[26] Maarten Nederhorst, who created the film, found an agreeable patient and doctor by contacting the Dutch Voluntary Euthanasia Society.

In June 1993, Cees van Wendel was diagnosed as having amyotrophic lateral sclerosis; one month later he requested euthanasia. Severe muscular weakness confined him to a wheelchair; his speech was barely audible. Cees and his wife, Antoinette, were initially reluctant to participate in the documentary but were persuaded by a visit from Maarten Nederhorst, who convinced them that the film would break the taboos surrounding euthanasia. He did not tell them that he intended to film the actual death until the project was underway for several weeks, at which time they seemed to take it for granted.

Almost 700,000 people saw the first showing of the film in the Netherlands. Subsequently the right to show the film has been acquired by a number of other countries. *Prime Time Live* excerpted and showed a Segment of the Dutch film to American viewers with a voice-over in English. Sam Donaldson introduced the program saying that it takes no sides on the issue but then added that "it is a story of courage and love."[27]

The doctor, Wilfred van Oijen, is the film's most significant person. His practice includes treating children, pregnant women, and administering death. Each of these is arranged so as to seem both part of the course of nature and part of his everyday experience.

The film opens with a chilly scene in winter—trees are bare of leaves, it is cold, wet, and inhospitable. In an undershirt in his bathroom, the doctor combs his hair getting ready for just another day. On this day his encounters will include treating a young girl, a baby, a pregnant woman, and bringing death to Cees. In the film we see the doctor attending patients in his office, picking up lethal drugs for Cees at the pharmacy, and interviewing and finally ending the life of Cees; the doctor is also shown in his own pleasant home, where his wife sits in the room reading, a testimony to the normalcy of his life.

Yet in the house calls van Oijen makes to Cees, the film betrays a tension between its message—that all want release from illness, the patient most of all—and the reality it shows in the relationship depicted between Van Oijen and Antoinette, the patient's wife, who has called the doctor and clearly wants her husband to die.

The wife appears repulsed by her husband's illness, never touching him during their conversation and never permitting Cees to answer any question the doctor asks directly. She "translates" for him, although Cees is still intelligible, able to communicate verbally, but slowly, and able to type out messages on his computer. The doctor asks him if he wants euthanasia, but it is his wife who replies. When Cees begins to cry, the doctor moves sympathetically toward him to touch his arm, but his wife tells the doctor to move away and says it is better to let him cry alone. As he weeps, she continues to talk to the doctor. The doctor at no time asks to speak to Cees alone; neither does he ask if anything would make it easier for him to communicate or if additional help in his care would make him want to live. There seems no real consensus here, but only the illusion of a consensus among all three. Because there is no direct communication with Cees, his wife prohibiting even the human gesture the doctor makes toward taking his arm, the agreement to end Cees's life is reached between the doctor and the wife.

Throughout the film, the wife's behavior reflects her tension and fear that Cees will refuse death. Although Cees communicates considerable emotion—love for her and weeping at their situation—no emotion seems to be permitted by the wife, who seems to need to keep his illness and death on the level of a management problem.

Virtually the entire film seems set up to avoid confronting any of the patient's feelings or how the relationship with his wife affects his agreeing to die. Cees is never seen alone. Van Oijen is obliged to obtain a second opinion from a consultant. The consultant, who practices on the same block as the doctor, also makes no attempt to communicate with Cees alone, and he too permits the wife to answer all the questions put to Cees. When the consultant asks the pro forma question whether Cees is sure he wants to go ahead, Antoinette answers for him. The consultant seems uncomfortable, asks a few more questions, and leaves. The consultation takes practically no time at all. The pharmacist who supplies the lethal medication—one shot to put Cees to sleep and another to help him die—seems only another player in this carefully orchestrated event.

Antoinette visits the doctor to ask where "we stand." She wants the euthanasia over with. Neither the doctor nor the filmmaker ask her reasons for wanting her husband to die sooner rather than later. Cees has set several dates, but keeps moving them back. Now he has settled on his birthday, and they arrange for van Oijen to do it at eight o'clock, after Cees celebrates by drinking a glass of port. Cees makes a joke that sleeping is a little death but this time his sleep will be a lot of death. Van Oijen tries to laugh warmly. Antoinette keeps her distance from the two and remarks that the day has gone slowly and it seems eight o'clock will never come.

Antoinette helps Cees into bed in preparation for van Oijen to administer the first shot. She tells her husband it will be a little prick in his skin. Van Oijen smiles, gives the injection, and explains that the medication will take a while to put Cees into a deep sleep. No one says goodbye. Only after the shot has put Cees to sleep does Antoinette kiss her husband. She then moves into the other room with the doctor to permit Cees to sink into a deeper sleep. After a few minutes, they return. After the second shot is administered, Antoinette and van

Oijen sit next to the bed, both holding the arm which has received the injections. Antoinette asks if this was good, presumably wanting to know if it was "good" to end Cees's life in this way. Van Oijen reassures her. They leave Cees alone very quickly. On the way into the next room, Antoinette takes a note Cees wrote to her about their relationship and what it meant to him and reads it to the doctor. She seems to want to convey to him that they in fact once had a relationship.

From the beginning, the loneliness and isolation of the husband haunt the film. Only because he is treated from the start as an object does his death seem inevitable. One leaves the film feeling that death with dignity requires more than efficient management. It requires being accorded a personhood, even though one's speech is slurred and one needs to point to letters on a board or to communicate through writing on one's computer. Throughout the film, Cees's wife denies him this personhood, as does the doctor, who never questions her control over all of the patient's communication, and even the doctor's communication with Cees.

Throughout the film the doctor, Wilfred van Oijen, is presented as a nonthreatening figure, one of us but one who has accepted the burden of ending life not "as a doctor" but as a human being empowered to perform euthanasia by the laws of the state. The doctor is not a loner seeking to do in patients but an ordinary human being with a pleasant and comfortable life who has taken on the burden of other people's deaths. Van Oijen tells us, "I perform euthanasia three or four times a year. It's not like I'm planning to go out with my Uzi and mow down crowds of people."

In the Dutch version of the film, van Oijen indicates that each year he is the second physician in three to four euthanasia cases in addition to the three or four he "believes" he performs himself. The viewer will not likely be aware that most

Dutch doctors who have performed euthanasia have done so relatively few times in a medical career. The average Dutch doctor in a general practice that includes small children and pregnant women is not involved with six or more cases of euthanasia a year. That van Oijen had become something of a specialist in euthanasia is suggested by the NVVE's referring Nederhorst to him. And while van Oijen is certainly not a terrorist or mass murderer with an Uzi, he is more of a professional hired for a special skill than he admits.

He has the ability to reassure Antoinette and perhaps himself that what they have done is both humane and desirable. As they sit together while Cees dies, Antoinette repeats many times how peaceful Cees looks and how beautiful it all is:

> *Antoinette:* "It's beautiful like this, to fall asleep so peacefully, deeper and deeper."
> *Van Oijen:* "It was beautiful."
> *Antoinette:* "Yes, very beautiful, very beautiful."

Patients with amyotrophic lateral sclerosis—a degenerative disease of the cervical spinal cord—are often selected as model cases for euthanasia because the public can readily empathize with their obvious muscular weakness, difficulty in talking, incapacity, and suffering. Van Oijen says he had to do what he did "because what else can I offer the man? I can give him wonderful equipment so he can make himself understood. I can give him the finest wheelchair there is, but in the end it is only a stopgap. He's going to die and he knows it."

It is worth noting that the English physicist Stephen Hawking is alive twenty-five years after he was diagnosed with amyotrophic lateral sclerosis as a graduate student at Cambridge and given only two and a half years to live. During the subsequent years, he has lived a brilliantly productive life and has had meaningful relationships with friends and family while far more incapacitated than Cees van Wendel. Hawking, however, has been surrounded by people who have wanted him to live, and who have not considered mechanical aids worthless because he was destined to die eventually.[28]

Rather than a story of courage, love, peace, and beauty, Cees van Wendel's is the story of a man who, whatever his past relationship with his wife, died alone. In an excerpt from his diary that is read to us, Cees asks himself, "How far can you go in asking your partner to make sacrifices?" Probably not too far when you sense and suffer from his realization that his end was being hastened by his wife and doctor, who needed him to go through with his death.

A spokesman for the Ikon television network, which produced the film, maintains that it was not intended to promote euthanasia but merely as an accurate documentation of the process.[29] Yet Nederhorst has stated that he omitted all but one of the frequent scenes of Cees crying because they would be disturbing to viewers.[30] Nederhorst also followed advice not to show too much footage of the doctor and wife alone for fear it would look as though they were conspiring together.[31] Given that what is shown still conveys a sense of conspiracy, one can assume that the unused footage would have reinforced that impression.

Nederhorst's own possible role in influencing what took place is notably absent from the film. Given the great amount of time Nederhorst had spent with Cees and Antoinette in the months prior to the euthanasia, a Dutch interviewer asked Nederhorst what role he might have played in their decision to pursue euthanasia.[32] Nederhorst hesitated before replying, then said that if anything the relationship Cees had with him and the film team led Cees to postpone the date of the euthanasia because he was enjoying their company.

This is not surprising since the filmmakers valued Cees and gave a meaning to his life and death that he was not finding elsewhere. If the filming could have been stretched out for several years, Cees would more than likely have been willing to wait. He also could not easily have changed his mind since doing so would have put an end to the enterprise.

Can one die with dignity while one's death is being filmed for millions to watch? While the people scripting the death are also actors conscious of their parts in a drama that could not take place if the patient changed his mind? At least in the Netherlands, the film was not accompanied by the commercials that preceded, interrupted, and followed the *Prime Time Live* segment. Continuous or interrupted, the whole film is a commercial for euthanasia, with *Prime Time Live* as a gullible participant.

The Politicization of Research

Any change in Dutch euthanasia policies would need to come from public knowledge of the nature and extent of Dutch euthanasia abuses as well as knowledge that the system does not provide adequate palliative care. Absent such knowledge most people in the Netherlands believe their choices are limited to continued suffering or hastening death. Unfortunately, the Dutch cannot rely on much of the research or information provided by the Dutch government or the Royal Dutch Medical Association to help them. Major research on the problem is sponsored by the Dutch government with guidelines and restrictions imposed by the KNMG; both the government and the KNMG seem determined to reveal nothing that is seriously critical of Dutch euthanasia policies. It is hard for foreigners to realize the degree to which this is possible in the Netherlands.

This politicization of research has been most apparent in the recent publication of a study sanctioned by the Dutch government that largely replicated the 1995 Remmelink study. In 1996 the investigators published a report of their new findings in Dutch,[33] and summarized their work in two articles in the *New England Journal of Medicine*.[34] These reports have given a favorable interpretation to evidence seeming to show little change by declaring that, since matters have not grown worse, there is no evidence that "physicians in the Netherlands are moving down a slippery slope." That conclusion is misleading.

THE SLIPPERY SLOPE

In this context, the "slippery slope" is the gradual extension of assisted suicide to widening groups of patients after it is legally permitted for patients designed as terminally ill. As we know, during the past two decades, the Netherlands has moved from considering assisted suicide (preferred over euthanasia by the Dutch Voluntary Euthanasia Society) to giving legal sanction to both physician-assisted suicide and euthanasia. The country has also moved from euthanasia for terminally ill patients to euthanasia for those who are chronically ill, from euthanasia for physical illness to euthanasia for psychological distress, and from voluntary euthanasia to nonvoluntary and involuntary euthanasia.[35] Except for the legal sanction of euthanasia for mental suffering without physical illness, all of these other expansions of the indications for euthanasia had taken place by 1990 and were documented by the 1990 study. Analysts of the 1990 data did not worry about the Dutch sliding farther; they noted how quickly they had already plummeted the slope, and expected that any Western country legalizing physician-assisted suicide for those who are terminally ill would be obliged to extend it in the same way.[36]

Comparing the 1990 and 1995 studies is revealing. From 1990 to 1995 the death rate from euthanasia increased 21 percent, from 1.9 percent to 2.3 percent of all deaths when based on interviews with 405 Dutch physicians selected from a stratified random sample. The rate increased 40 percent, from 1.7 percent to 2.4 percent when based on responses to a questionnaire completed by more than 4,600 physicians in both years (see Table 1). The increase in euthanasia deaths ranging from 21 to 40 percent would seem significant, but the investigators deny this even though they give "generational and cultural changes in patients attitudes" as a possible explanation. The investigators similarly describe the assisted suicide rate as remaining low although, based on the interview study, the actual number also increased over 40 percent.

GUIDELINES HAVE FAILED

More slippery than the extension of euthanasia to more patients is the inability to regulate the process within established rules. Virtually every guideline set up by the Dutch—a voluntary, well-considered, persistent request; intolerable suffering that cannot be relieved; consultation; and reporting of cases—has failed to protect patients or has been modified or violated.[38]

Many of the violations are evident in the officially sanctioned studies. For example, in the 1990 study 50 percent of physicians reported that they felt free to suggest euthanasia to patients. Neither the physicians nor the study's investigators seem to acknowledge how much the voluntariness of the process is compromised by such a suggestion.[39] Frightened and suffering patients, however, are inclined to listen to suggestions made to them by physicians, even when the doctor is telling them that their life is not worth living or causes them to suspect that the doctor must foresee a worse fate than they have imagined.

TABLE 1 *Estimated Incidence of Specific Medical Decisions at the End of Life★*

Medical Decision	1990 Study		1995 Study	
	Questionnaire Portion†	Interview Portion‡	Questionnaire Portion†	Interview Portion‡
Euthanasia	2,189 (1.7)	2,445 (1.9)	3,253 (2.4)	3,018 (2.2)
Physician-assisted suicide	244 (0.2)	380 (0.3)	271 (0.2)	542 (0.4)
Ending life without request§	1,030 (0.8)		948 (0.7)	
Opioids given with explicit intention of ending life‖		1,350 (1.0)		1,896 (1.3)
Estimated total deaths caused by active intervention by physicians#	4,813 (3.7)		6,368 (4.7)	

★Values are the number of deaths with percentages of all deaths in parentheses, based on 128,786 deaths in the Netherlands in 1990 and on 135,546 deaths in 1995.

†Figures are based on questionnaire portions of the study. A total of 6,942 questionnaires were mailed in 1991; 76 percent were returned. The sample was stratified to include a high percentage of cases where a decision at the end of life was likely to be made.

‡Figures were from the interview portions of the study. A total of 405 physicians were interviewed in 1991 and another 405 in 1995. They were selected from a stratified random sample of 599 in 1991 and 559 in 1995. Only 9 percent refused to participate in 1991 and 11 percent in 1995. Others were not traceable, had chronic illness, or did not meet other criteria. The sample was stratified to include physicians likely to have participated in end-of-life decisions.

§Comparative figures are available only for questionnaire portions of the study.

‖Comparative figures are available only for interview portions of the study.

#Total death estimates are based on data from both the questionnaire and interview studies.

Given the concerned reaction of those outside the Netherlands to physicians suggesting euthanasia, it is surprising that the investigators make no reference to it in their English-language articles. The Dutch report reveals, however, that the practice has continued and has actually somewhat increased.

Underreporting continues to be a serious problem. In only 18 percent of cases in 1990 had physicians reported their practice of euthanasia to the authorities as required by Dutch guidelines. To encourage more reporting of cases, a simplified notification procedure was enacted, ensuring that physicians would not be prosecuted if these guidelines were followed. The investigators credit the procedural change with contributing to an increase in the cases reported to 41 percent by 1995, while acknowledging that a 59 percent rate of unreported cases is still disturbingly high. The 1995 interviews reveal that in only 11 percent of the unreported cases was there consultation with another physician.[40]

Of forty-nine physicians who had not previously reported their most recent case of euthanasia, half gave as a reason their wish or that of the patient's family to avoid a judicial inquiry, 20 percent the fear of prosecution, 16 percent the failure to fulfill the requirements for accepted procedures, and 14 percent the belief that assistance with death should be a private matter. Between 15 and 20 percent of doctors say that they will not report their cases under any circumstances.

The doctors' responses demand further questions that are not asked. Why are the families afraid of judicial inquiry? Why are the doctors afraid of prosecution? The investigators state that the doctors' violations were not substantive but procedural, by which they mean failure to obtain written request from the patient, failure to write a written report, or failure to obtain a consultation that is questionably only procedural, and suggests the investigators have accepted the doctors' casualness toward the consultation process. Moreover, 20 percent of the doctors' most recent unreported cases involved ending of a life without the patient's consent.[41] Such cases, both the 1990 and 1995 studies reveal, were virtually never reported.[42]

DEATH WITHOUT CONSENT

The most alarming concern arises from the reports in these Dutch studies of patients whose physicians ended their lives without their consent. The 1990 study revealed that in 0.8 percent of the deaths (more than 1,000 cases) in the Netherlands each year, physicians admitted they actively caused death without the explicit consent of the patient. The 1995 figure is 0.7 percent (fewer than 1,000 cases), but the researchers while pointing to the decline concede that differences in the way this particular information was obtained make its significance uncertain. In both studies, however, about a quarter of physicians stated that they had "terminated the lives of patients without an explicit request" from the patient to do so, and a third more of the physicians could conceive of doing so. The use of the word "explicit" is somewhat inaccurate, since in 48 percent of these cases there was no request of any kind,[43] and in the others there were mainly references to patients' earlier statements of not wanting to suffer.[44]

The 1990 study revealed, and the 1995 study confirms, that cases classified as "termination of the patient without explicit request" were but a fraction of the nonvoluntary and involuntary euthanasia cases. International attention had centered on the 1,350 cases (1 percent of all Dutch deaths) in 1990 in which physicians gave pain medication with the explicit intention of ending the patient's life.[45] The investigators minimized the number of patients put to death who had not requested it by not including these 1,350 patients in that category.

By 1995 the number of deaths in which physicians gave pain medication with the explicit intention of ending the patient's life had increased from 1,350 cases (1 percent of all Dutch deaths) to almost 1,900 (1.4 percent of all Dutch deaths).[46] These are comparisons that the Dutch investigators do not present. As reported by the physicians in the 1995 study, in more than 80 percent of these cases (1,537 deaths), no request for death was made by the patient.[47]

Since researchers around the world have treated these deaths as cases of nonvoluntary, and if the patient was competent, involuntary euthanasia, they see this as a striking increase in the number of cases terminated without request and a refutation of the investigators' claim that there was perhaps a slight decrease in the number of such cases.

If one totals all the deaths from euthanasia, assisted suicide, ending the life of a patient without consent, and giving opioids with the explicit intention of ending life, the estimated number of deaths caused by active intervention by physicians increased from 4,813 (3.7 percent) of all deaths in 1990 to 6,368 (4.7 percent of all deaths) in 1995 (see Table 1). Based on data from the questionnaire study, this is an increase of 27 percent in cases in which physicians actively intervened to cause death. (The interview study documents a 20 percent increase.)

The Dutch investigators minimize the significance of the number of deaths without consent by explaining that the patients were incompetent. But in the 1995 study, 21 percent of the cases classified as "patients whose lives were ended without explicit request" were competent; in the 1990 study 37 percent of these cases were competent.[48] We are not told what percentage of patients were competent among those given pain medication intended to end their lives without discussing it with them, but analysis of the data for opioid administration indicates that it is likely to be at least 20 percent. More than 4,000 additional competent patients were given pain medication in amounts likely to end their lives by physicians who did not discuss the decision with them but whose primary intention was not to end their lives.[49] Whether the intention was to end life or whether death was simply likely, physicians usually gave as the reason for not discussing the decisions with patients that they had previously had some discussion of the subject with the patient.[50] We are left, as we were in 1990, with the disturbing idea that a physician would terminate or put at risk the life of a competent patient on the basis of a previous discussion without checking to learn what the patient felt currently.

As we have seen, at times even when there was specific knowledge from competent patients that they did not want euthanasia, it was done anyhow. An example was the nun whose physician ended her life a few days before she would have died because she was in excruciating pain but her doctor believed that her religious convictions were preventing her from asking for death. Another was the Dutch patient with disseminated breast cancer who had said she did not want euthanasia but who had her life ended because in the physician's words, "It could have taken another week before she died. I just needed this bed."[51]

INTERACTIVE DECISIONS

Since the government-sanctioned Dutch studies in 1990 and 1995 are primarily numerical and categorical, they do not examine the interactions among physicians, patients, and families that determine the decision for euthanasia. We need to look elsewhere for a fuller picture. Other studies conducted in the Netherlands have indicated how voluntariness is compromised, alternatives not presented, and the criterion of unrelievable suffering bypassed. A few examples may be help-fully illustrative.

A wife who no longer wished to care for her sick husband gave him a choice between euthanasia and admission to a home for the chronically ill. The man, afraid of being left to the mercy of strangers in an unfamiliar place, chose euthana-sia; the doctor, although aware of the coercion, performed it.[52] Netty Boomsma, the healthy fifty-year-old woman who lost her son recently to cancer, refused all treatment, and said she would accept only help in dying, was assisted in suicide by her psychiatrist within four months of her son's death. Her refusal of treatment was considered by her physician and the Dutch courts to make her suffering unrelievable. Wilfred van Oijen, the Dutch physician who was filmed ending the life of a pa-tient recently diagnosed with amyotrophic lateral sclerosis, had said of his the patient, "I can give him the finest wheel-chair there is, but in the end it is only a stopgap. He's going to die and he knows it." That death may be years away but a physician with this attitude may not be able to present alter-natives to this patient.

There appears to have been an erosion of medical standards in the care of terminally ill patients in the Netherlands. The 1990 and 1995 studies document that 60 percent of Dutch physicians do not report their cases of assisted suicide and eu-thanasia, more than 50 percent feel free to suggest euthanasia to their patients, and 25 percent admit to ending patients' lives without their consent. How is it that the Dutch researchers are so sanguine about their data?

Political considerations have admittedly influenced the stud-ies and their conclusions. Why were physicians not challenged when they offered implausible explanations for ending fully competent patients' lives without consulting them? The in-vestigators have explained that securing and retaining the cooperation of the Royal Dutch Medical Association and the participating physicians demanded that they not challenge the doctors they surveyed.

In addition, the researchers draw conclusions that exceed their evidence. The 1990 and 1995 studies accepted physicians' assertions that their patients had received the best-possible care and that there was no alternative to euthanasia. These statements are not supported by any objective data. Indeed, studies have demonstrated how inadequately physicians are trained in palliative care in the Netherlands.[53] Since the statements of responding physicians were accepted by the investigators without challenge, there was no exploration of possible alternatives to euthanasia.[54]

Both the 1990 and 1995 studies are flawed for all of the above reasons. When cases are classified and counted so as to minimize disturbing findings, when implausible explanations are accepted without challenge, and when conclusions that might offend are not stated, there is need for more objective and inclusive exploration and analysis.

That exploration and analysis will have to include a realization that notification by physicians of all euthanasia cases would not by itself diminish euthanasia abuse in the Netherlands. Nor would it help to better count and classify cases without exploring the interactive decision-making process that is at the heart of euthanasia and that is ignored in the Dutch research.

Dutch efforts at regulating assisted suicide and euthanasia have served as a model for proposed statutes in the United States[55] and other countries. Yet the Dutch experience indicates that these practices defy adequate regulation. Given legal sanction, euthanasia, intended originally for the exceptional case, has become an accepted way of dealing with serious or terminal illness in the Netherlands. In the process, palliative

care is one of the casualties, while Dutch hospice care lags behind that of other countries.[56] For the Dutch, accepting and
needing to defend the option of euthanasia seems to be cost-
ing them the opportunity to take advantage of the developments in palliative care of the past decade. For other countries,
knowledge of these developments still remains to be disseminated and implemented. We should accept that challenge
and avoid making the Dutch mistake.

Prospects for the Future

In 1993, on my first visit to the Netherlands, I was more op-
timistic about the possibility of regulating Dutch euthanasia
because I saw advocates like van der Maas, Dillmann, and
Diekstra acknowledge that the system was out of control. The
Remmelink study documented the difficulties; Paul van der
Maas and his colleague Loes Pijnenborg indicated they would
address the problems of euthanasia they admitted were extensive. Subsequently the significance of the problems the
study uncovered has been minimized; van der Maas—along
with Pijnenborg and others involved in the original study—
has written what amounts to an attempt to justify the 1,000
cases of involuntary euthanasia documented there.[57]

Pijnenborg has also published a thesis based on her participation in the Remmelink project. The thesis, which is intended to be read by practicing doctors, has a section in which
she gives her own conclusions and recommendations. There
she does not begin to discuss the abuses we discussed. She concedes that perhaps in a few cases, a long time ago, the decision-
making process could have been more extensive, meaning
euphemistically that patients should have been consulted. She
does suggest that physicians explore the motives of patients to
ascertain whether fear or uncertainty is playing a role. Of

course, the recommendation would not be necessary if such exploration were the rule rather than the exception. She also suggests that unclear statements like "Doctor, you must help me if my life becomes worthless" must be "clarified." Since physicians questioned in the report used statements such as these to justify ending patients' lives without further consultation, "clarification" hardly seems a strong-enough word.[58]

Pijnenborg's thesis includes findings of a separate study in which she polled Dutch and foreign doctors and ethicists, partly to ascertain whether euthanasia was as common elsewhere as it is in the Netherlands and whether the Dutch were simply more open about the practice. I was invited to participate. The questions asked suggested that the study hoped to demonstrate that the rest of the world was doing secretly what the Dutch were doing openly. The results gave no support to that hypothesis.[59] Of course, covert assisted suicide and euthanasia exist in the United States and other countries. There is no evidence, however, that either is performed on so large a scale as in the Netherlands.

Research sponsored and sanctioned by the Dutch government and the KNMG is not going to provide the information or the impetus to improve the situation. Nor is it possible in the Netherlands to conduct the independent research necessary to study euthanasia. What is needed is a study designed and executed by an international team of palliative care experts who were not part of the 1990 and 1995 studies. The Dutch do not seem likely to permit this.

To change their system, the Dutch press and public will have to become aware of the problems their policies cause. Following the widespread showing of a doctor putting a patient to death in the film *Death on Request,* there was sharp criticism of Dutch euthanasia policies throughout Europe and even in the Netherlands. Within the Netherlands there was a negative public reaction to the "angels of death"; the very existence of these traveling physicians suggested there was more reluctance on the part of local family physicians to perform euthanasia than had been imagined.

In August 1995, in an effort at damage control, the KNMG refined its guidelines: assisted suicide rather than euthanasia should be performed whenever possible; a second doctor, who had no professional or personal ties to the physician or the patient, should actually see the patient; physicians need not participate in euthanasia but must refer the patient to doctors who will; and physicians must report all cases of euthanasia to the authorities.[60]

The protection of the patient is usually cited as the central reason for preferring assisted suicide to euthanasia, yet the strain on the doctor is given by the KNMG as the reason for this suggested change. Robert Dillmann explained to a *New York Times* reporter that "many doctors find euthanasia a difficult and burdensome action, and the patient's participation diminishes the burden slightly."[61]

Doctors who perform euthanasia infrequently may follow the KNMG suggestion, and the guideline seems intended to encourage reluctant doctors to participate. The guidelines, however, will not deter or convert those practitioners who perform euthanasia on a regular basis, since the decision will remain between the physician and the patient. Herbert Cohen restated his reservations to the *Times* reporter:

Death by taking pills can take three hours or more. This creates a lot more tension, also among others who accompany the patient. There are risks because people are terribly sick. A patient can spill the medicine or choke or vomit or fall asleep before the full dose has been taken. It is never simple.[62]

With an injection, Cohen said, the patient lapses into a coma within about 10 seconds, and death often comes 10 minutes later. He described the method as emotionally harsher, but less open to error.

The KNMG's insistence that doctors who will not perform euthanasia refer patients to doctors who will echoed the suggestion of Verhoef and Borst-Eilers. Dillmann does not acknowledge the contradiction between saying that doctors need not participate and demanding a referral that is against their conscience. He explained that the doctor cannot "leave a patient in the cold at the last moment. He should help find alternatives."[63] Yet Dillmann does not envision alternatives other than suffering or euthanasia. Karl Gunning responded, "Refusing to kill someone is now called leaving a person out in the cold and is considered cruel. To cooperate and kill someone is seen as showing compassion."

In discussing the requirement to obtain a second opinion, Dillmann explained, "The consultant must see and examine the patient. The telephone is not enough."[64] His statement seems an inadvertent admission that consultations have been careless.

The reiteration of the guideline regarding consultants, however, is unlikely to have any real significance. Regular euthanasia practitioners are known by reputation to every doctor; such practitioners will be called, but since they are believers, their seeing the patient or their not being a friend of the referring physician is not apt to change the result.

The problem, therefore, is not only a slippery slope on which legalization of euthanasia for one group of patients inevitably leads to legalization for others. Legalization for whatever group happens to be first on the slope cannot be regulated. Only after guidelines have been stretched, ignored, or circumvented for some time does pressure develop to legalize what is already practiced.

Although Boudewijn Chabot seemed to wish to make a test case of Netty Boomsma, he was not the first psychiatrist to report assisting in the suicide of a patient who was depressed but had no physical illness. He was, however, the first psychiatrist whose case went to trial. And with the Dutch courts ruling that mental suffering can be grounds for assisted suicide or euthanasia, that depressed patients can be competent make a choice, and that psychiatrists are free to help them provided a consultant sees the patient, Chabot has helped make it possible for psychiatrists to do what he did without fearing state scrutiny. That he sees himself as a pioneer is somewhat understandable.

The political excuse euthanasia advocates give for not being willing to admit or call attention to abuses in the system—their fear of the Christian Democrats in government, some of whose leaders were opposed to euthanasia—is now obsolete. Since the law designed to protect doctors has now passed, if the medical profession is going to do anything to limit abuses, the time should be now. The refining of KNMG guidelines in an action that did not admit or address problems is not reassuring.

Most opponents of euthanasia are willing to concede that no one is going to totally undo *de facto* legalization in the Netherlands. Even if the Dutch public fully understood the contents of the difficult-to-read government-sanctioned studies or their implications, they would not want to give up what they consider their right to euthanasia, which they see as their only assurance that they will not have to endure an unnecessarily prolonged, painful death. It will be hard for palliative care to develop in a country so embedded in euthanasia. Yet unless it does, the Dutch will have no real options.

Nonetheless, it would be helpful for the Dutch to gain better control of euthanasia as they narrowly define it and of the process by which patients' lives are ended without their consent. Even without consensus on removing the criminal penalties against euthanasia and assisted suicide, which the public perceives as controlling doctors' behavior, there will not be much help from the legal system. With prosecutors, consultants, experts, attorneys, and probably judges concerned that any legal decision must protect euthanasia and euthanasia doctors; with public sympathies on the side of the doctor, who in most instances would not be on trial if he had not reported the case himself; and with the case details being primarily what the doctor chooses to reveal—the Dutch judicial review of euthanasia cases presents a ritualized drama that allows for only some subtle, minor improvisation before the inevitable acquittal. If our adversarial judicial system at times sacrifices justice on the altar of victory, in the Netherlands justice is sacrificed for what the Dutch regard as the higher goal of social harmony.

Chapter 5

A CURE FOR SUICIDE

Panic and a wish for immediate death are often patients' responses to learning they have a serious or terminal illness. Upon learning he had a probably incurable case of leukemia, Tim (Chapter 1) asked for assisted suicide. When his anxiety was relieved, he focused instead on his relationships with his wife and family and on making the final phase of his life meaningful. By contrast, the Dutch artist (Chapter 3) who was HIV-positive but physically asymptomatic was assisted in his suicide by two Dutch doctors who seemed unable to deal with his anxiety and depression. These different responses to a patient's panic over death personalize an important broader question: How does the willingness of the Dutch to respond with assisted suicide or euthanasia to patients who become suicidally depressed in response to medical illness affect the overall problem of suicide in the Netherlands?

Although the Dutch like to point out that since their acceptance of euthanasia, their suicide rate has dropped, if any significant percentage of cases of assisted suicide and euthanasia were included among the suicides, the Dutch suicide rate would rise considerably. In fact, the figures suggest that the drop in the Dutch suicide rate from a peak of 16.6 per 100,000 in 1983 to 12.8 in 1992 (see Table 2) may well be due to the availability of euthanasia.

TABLE 2 *Suicide Rates per 100,000 in the Netherlands (15 Years of Age or Older)*

Year	Sex		Total Number	Age Group							
	Male	Female		≤15	16–19	20–29	30–39	40–49	50–59	60–69	≥70
1980	18.4	10.3	14.3		2.3	12.0	12.8	14.7	17.8	21.5	22.3
1981	18.8	11.1	15.0		2.8	11.3	13.5	16.0	18.6	22.4	22.3
1982	19.3	12.3	15.8		4.6	11.4	13.4	17.5	18.8	23.1	27.3
1983	20.7	12.8	16.6		2.5	12.2	14.5	17.4	21.0	23.2	31.3
1984	20.6	12.7	16.6		3.0	12.0	15.4	18.1	21.5	22.3	27.9
1985	19.8	10.7	15.2		3.7	12.6	14.7	15.1	19.1	20.6	22.3
1986	18.7	11.1	14.8		2.8	11.5	14.3	16.6	17.8	19.7	23.1
1987	19.1	11.1	15.0		3.5	11.9	14.7	15.9	17.9	19.6	24.2
1988	17.9	9.9	13.7		2.6	10.7	13.6	14.0	17.4	17.0	23.2
1989	17.6	10.2	13.8		4.0	10.9	12.5	14.3	19.0	19.6	18.3
1990	17.1	9.7	13.3		4.5	9.6	14.1	13.9	15.0	16.2	21.3
1991	17.2	9.2	13.1		3.1	9.9	14.6	12.9	15.5	15.5	19.9
1992	17.2	8.7	12.8		3.5	9.5	13.7	13.7	14.0	14.5	19.9

Source: Central Bureau of Statistics (CBS), revised by the Central Directory for the Development of Scientific Policy, July 1994.

More significant than the drop itself is the fact that it has taken place in the older age groups. In the fifty to fifty-nine age group, the rate dropped from a peak of 21.5 in 1984 to 14 in 1992. Among those sixty to sixty-nine the rate dropped from a peak of 23.2 in 1983 to 14.5 in 1992. Among those seventy and over, the rate dropped from a peak of 31.3 in 1983 to 19.9 in 1992 (see graph in Figure 1). The decline of about 33 percent in these three groups is remarkable. Of the 1,886 Dutch suicides in 1983, 940 were in the three older age groups. Of the 1,587 suicides in 1992, 672 were in the three older age groups. The decrease of 268 suicides in the three older age groups was primarily responsible for the drop in the Dutch suicide rate. Comparing the five years 1980 to 1984 with the five years 1988 to 1992 provides evidence of a drop in the older-age groups that is not due to chance; these are the age groups containing the highest numbers of euthanasia cases (86 percent of the men and 78 percent of the women) and the greatest number of suicides.[1]

The past two decades have seen growing Dutch acceptance of euthanasia. The remarkable drop in suicide in the older age groups appears to be due to the fact that older suicidal patients are now asking to receive euthanasia. The likelihood that patients would end their lives if euthanasia were not available to them was one of the justifications given by Chabot and other Dutch doctors for providing such help.

Of course, euthanasia advocates can maintain that making suicide "unnecessary" for those over fifty who are physically ill is a benefit of legalization rather than a sign of abuse. Such an attitude depends, of course, on whether one believes that there are alternatives to assisted suicide or euthanasia for dealing with the problems of older people who become ill.

Among an older population, physical illness is common, and many who have trouble coping become suicidal. In a culture that accepts euthanasia, their distress becomes a legitimate rea-

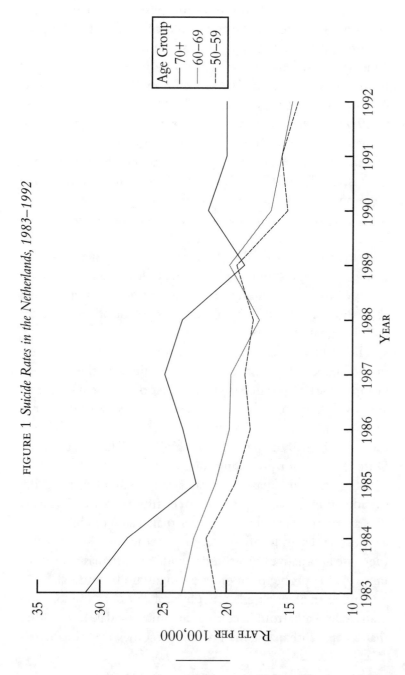

FIGURE 1 *Suicide Rates in the Netherlands, 1983–1992*

son for dying. It is perhaps not so far-fetched to describe euthanasia as the "Dutch cure for suicide."

The Psychiatrist's Role

How have Dutch psychiatrists responded to the fact that suicidally depressed patients with medical illness now appear to be receiving euthanasia in large numbers? Only 19 percent of Dutch psychiatrists thought that a psychiatric consultation was necessary when a patient with a somatic condition requested suicide.[2] Most felt that the primary caregiver should decide whether consultation was necessary. Not coincidentally, Dutch investigators found that in the Netherlands only 3 percent of the 9,720 patients a year requesting assisted suicide or euthanasia are referred for psychiatric consultation.[3]

Yet we know that patients with significant medical problems constitute a majority of older suicidal patients. And we know that primary care physicians are not reliably able to diagnose depression.

What about requests for assisted suicide made directly to Dutch psychiatrists? Of the 37 percent of psychiatrists who received at least one request for assisted suicide, 6 percent complied; the total number of such deaths a year, however, is estimated at a handful.[4] Although Chabot may have broken new ground, Dutch psychiatrists do not seem in a rush to follow him. On the other hand, 64 percent of Dutch psychiatrists felt it was acceptable to assist in the suicide of a patient purely on the basis of mental suffering.[5] Commenting on the acceptance of assisted suicide for psychiatric patients, two American physicians, Linda Ganzini and Melinda Lee, suggest that "beliefs about what is permissible expand as a result of acculturation to changes in social policy."[6]

How should a psychiatrist respond to a seriously or terminally ill patient requesting assisted suicide? The request for death ordinarily comes from patients who are desperate, whether they are medically ill or not. Supporting or denying such a request is not an adequate response. Inquiring into the source of such desperation and undertaking to relieve it is the unique contribution that the psychiatrist should be making. That inquiry must include a history of the patient's experiences with the death of those close to him or her, a history of past crises in the patient's life and how they were dealt with, and of course a past history of depression as well as any suicide attempts.

FEAR OF DEATH

Why is such an inquiry so seldom made by those responding to a patient's request for assisted suicide? Unfortunately, psychiatrists, like other physicians, are often paralyzed in the face of death and a dying patient's request to die. Their normal processes of inquiry may become suspended, leading to no real exploration of what is making the patient so desperate that he or she wants to die. Without such exploration, the psychiatrist may forget all else and simply regard the patient as a condemned person whose last wish should be granted. Although knowledgeable about counterphobic behavior, many psychiatrists have trouble recognizing and dealing with it when terrified patients embrace death.

Pieter Admiraal, a prominent Dutch practitioner of euthanasia, is one of the few Dutch doctors to recognize the important role of anxiety about death in determining the decision for euthanasia. Although he tells us that the anxiety about "spiritual and physical decay" is far more important than pain as a reason for euthanasia, he will not refer such patients for psychiatric consultation. He graphically describes the concerns of such patients:

> Anxiety about dying itself can have various causes. Dying is the loss of the world in which one has lived, worked, and loved. There is also anxiety about the moment of dying. Patients fear what comes after death. This can vary from a

vague anxiety about the unknown to a literal "deathly" fear of punishment which may be eternal. The suffering of a human being is strictly individual and is largely hidden from our objective observation. Consequently, it is difficult for one person to judge the suffering of another.[7]

Psychiatrists are trained to unearth and relieve hidden anxieties. Given his recognition of the role that anxiety about dying plays, one would think Admiraal would want psychiatric help in the cases he finds difficult.

He does not, however. Admiraal tells us that "to send a terminal patient to a psychiatrist is an insult."[8] He seems to have accepted the notion that the role of the psychiatrist is simply to determine the patient's competence, which Admiraal feels able to do on his own. A competent psychiatrist, however, can often relieve anxieties about death and in so doing obviate a patient's demand for euthanasia. Moreover, the refusal to deal with patients' fears while ending their lives subjects them to a cruel, not a merciful, death.

DEPRESSION

Psychiatrists need to be aware that in medical cases psychological issues are just as important as in cases like Netty Boomsma's, where no physical illness is present. The vast majority of requests for assisted suicide come from patients who are terrified and depressed by their anticipation of suffering and death. Studies in the Netherlands confirm the experience of palliative care specialists elsewhere that 80 percent of requests for assisted suicide and euthanasia come from patients who are not currently in significant distress from pain or other symptoms but expect that they will be.[9]

Although trained to recognize depression, many psychiatrists have little experience in treating seriously or terminally ill patients or with the depression, often covert, that frequently coexists with physical illness. The demoralizing triad of depression, anxiety, and the wish to die, seen as a response to serious illness, can be treated by a combination of empathy, psychotherapy, and medication. Such treatment usually alters a patient's attitude about living with illness.

The recent Dutch acceptance of assisted suicide for depressed suicidal patients victimizes those depressed patients who do not respond quickly to treatment. Some years before I went to the Netherlands, I published the case of a woman who had a major depressive episode after her husband died of a heart attack while he greeted her on his return from work.[10] She had made several serious suicide attempts, and when I first saw her she had just come out of a barbiturate-induced coma. Since her husband's death she had been hospitalized several times, had received virtually every antidepressant medication then available, and had been given two courses of electroconvulsive therapy, all to no avail.

Her condition was incurable, she insisted, and suicide was the only solution. She would not consider treatment but came for a few sessions, and I remained in touch with her and her family to see how she was doing. Her children had reached a point where they half hoped she would die because they spent so much time thwarting her suicide attempts. Two more distressing years were followed by a nearly fatal suicide attempt from which she awoke after several days of coma to tell her daughter that she was finished with suicide. She agreed to see me, but could only tell me that she had a dream in which her husband came to her and said, "That's enough—you've put yourself and everyone else through enough suffering." She claimed she woke the following morning free of her depression. When I spoke to her a year later, and to her daughter a few years after that, they told me that she was living by herself, had made a new social life, and was no longer depressed or suicidal. Under a system that permitted legal assisted suicide for a chronically depressed patient, this patient, with the concurrence of her family and the assistance of her doctor, would have ended her life long before her recovery.

SUICIDE

Psychiatrists who have worked with many suicidal patients know that in their depression, their ambivalence about dying, and their need to test the affection of others, medically ill patients who request assisted suicide are not different from patients who become suicidal for other reasons. Physicians who assist in suicide often fail to hear that, despite the most severe medical problems, most patients are expressing a wish to live as much or more than they are expressing a wish to die. Most are looking for a response that indicates that their fears will be addressed, that their pain will be relieved, and that they will not be abandoned.

Suicidal patients commonly use the threat of their death to coerce and control others, including their doctors. The psychology of "if you do not help me kill myself I will do it in a more violent or disturbing way" is a variation on this theme. Patients who need to bring suicide into the relationship with their physician and use it coercively are often more severely depressed than their doctors recognize.

Studies of suicide clarify the nonrational elements of the wish to die in reaction to serious illness. Suicidal patients may have the unconscious wish to be put to death by their doctor. Psychiatrists treating suicidal patients may assume the patient sees them as a savior, when actually they are cast in the role of executioner,[11] with the patient sometimes fantasizing closeness or union with the doctor through death. Patients can feel that getting rid of a perceived bad part of themselves is necessary for such a union, and they may see death as a deserved punishment in this process.[12]

Similar dynamics can be seen in patients requesting assisted suicide and euthanasia. Often the illness is seen as part of the bad self that must be eliminated by death before the desired union can take place. Fantasies of achieving closeness through death are often shared by patient and doctor.[13] Timothy Quill and Diane, Boudewijn Chabot and Netty Boomsma, and Herbert Cohen and several of his patients shared such fantasies.

FAMILIES AND PHYSICIANS

Psychiatrists are more experienced than most physicians in recognizing the interactive nature of crucial decisions. Such understanding is helpful in dealing with requests for assisted suicide and euthanasia since the needs and character of family, friends, and physician play as big and often a bigger role than those of the patient in determining the outcome. Derek Humphry, his wife, Ann Wickett, and her parents; Timothy Quill and Diane; Reverend Mero and Louise; and several of the Kevorkian cases where the impetus for assisted suicide came from a spouse are examples. Sometimes the physician acts in concert with the family, and the patient's interests become secondary as in the case of Cees van Wendel, whose wife and doctor decided his fate with little regard for his needs.

Doctors who assist in such suicides seem not to recognize, or to be unwilling to acknowledge, their influence on the patient's decision in these matters. Psychiatrists are sometimes faced with a delicate situation of having to confront physician colleagues who have been caught up in the pressuring process.[14]

Physicians who perform euthanasia are often troubled by it even years afterward. Some speak of a need for absolution. One psychiatric advocate has even argued that the doctor being troubled afterward is a sign that the euthanasia is appropriate.[15] Another seems to maintain that providing absolution to medical colleagues is a legitimate function for psychiatrists in such cases.[16]

If euthanasia were a legitimate medical procedure, most doctors would not feel so disturbed after performing it. Although withdrawal of treatment that is only prolonging the dying process may be difficult for physicians, it seems to produce no such reaction afterward.

The average doctor's discomfort with ending a patient's life is not so surprising. Even when justified by the exigencies of war, most soldiers pay a price for participating in killing. Just as a minority of soldiers deal with the horror of war by embracing the power to end someone's life, a minority of doctors fervently embrace assisted suicide and euthanasia.[17] Several described the bonding with the patients they put to death as one of their closest and most meaningful experiences. For some, continuing to perform and advocate euthanasia appear to be a way of denying the guilt they feel over their initial involvement.

That a small number of doctors do a great number of the cases is one of the unexamined aspects of the Dutch euthanasia story; one admits to close to a hundred, while another is proud to have done many times that number.

COMPETENCE

In considerations of legalizing assisted suicide, psychiatrists are generally assigned the role of assessing whether patients are competent to make the request. Such an assessment is supposed to include an evaluation to determine the presence of depression and to distinguish it from the sadness that may accompany illness. Even patients with severe depression may pass tests of legal capacity to make medical decisions. This would all the more likely be true if physician-assisted suicide were to be legalized.[18] In the Netherlands, and in statutes being proposed to legalize assisted suicide in this country, depression per se is not accepted as indicating incompetence.

When the psychiatrist is in the role of gatekeeper, the patient tends to simply say or do what is necessary to persuade the psychiatrist to go along with the request to die. Netty Boomsma's behavior with Chabot is a prime example.

The Dutch acceptance of euthanasia for suicidal psychiatric patients seems the inevitable consequence of using such criteria as "competence" and "intolerable suffering" rather than sound clinical judgment. The idea that a patient who suffers from a chronic depression interspersed with major depressive episodes and psychotic behavior can—between such episodes —make a decision for suicide uninfluenced by his pathology only demonstrates the limitation of "competence" in evaluating those who are suicidal. On the Dutch model, the psychiatrist in such cases works to prevent suicide until the patient asks for his assistance in committing suicide; then the rules change, and the psychiatrist negotiates with the patient about which approach is best.

Evaluation of the prospective euthanasia patient by psychiatrists knowledgeable about suicide, depression, and terminal illness cannot provide us with a simple solution to a complex social problem. Nor should psychiatrists be reduced to the role of simply determining whether a patient is competent to make a decision regarding euthanasia. Since I was not the arbiter of his case, Tim, the patient with acute myelocytic leukemia, could talk freely with me about his fears of death, and he changed his mind about wanting an immediate end to his life.

Seriously suicidal patients want suicide. In a society that makes euthanasia accessible to them, they will be harder to treat. The Dutch experience illustrates how a culture transforms suicide into assisted suicide and uses euthanasia as almost a routine way of dealing with serious or terminal illness and even with grief. Unless one is prepared to agree that in euthanasia the Dutch have found an acceptable way to deal with depression and suicide, their experience should give the Dutch and everyone else reason to question where they are going.

Chapter 6

WHY THE
NETHERLANDS?
WHY THE
UNITED STATES?

Why is it that among the industrialized countries of the West, only the Netherlands has embraced assisted suicide and euthanasia? Why is there a strong impetus in the United States to follow in the footsteps of the Dutch? Although some Dutch euthanasia advocates like Pieter Admiraal believe that the pressure of an increasing elderly population will eventually move all of Europe to adopt assisted suicide and euthanasia, few European voices echo the American clamor for legalization. Indeed, the most savage criticism of Dutch policies has come from other European countries, from the same liberal democracies that were far ahead of us and the Dutch in providing medical care for all and giving women the freedom to choose abortion.

Those in the Netherlands who seek to explain Dutch policies on euthanasia begin by stressing the country's historical tradition of tolerance. In the sixteenth and seventeenth centuries, the Dutch fought to secure their religious freedom, and the Netherlands became a refuge for Jews, Catholics, and freethinkers like Spinoza and Descartes who fled from religious oppression. In the same period, the country became a major maritime power whose merchants had to learn to accept different cultures, traditions, and practices.[1]

In modern times, the Dutch point to the presence in their small country of fifty different religions—most due to schisms in the Protestant Church—and the presence of approximately twenty-five political parties. So much diversity in so small a country is seen as reflective of Dutch tolerance.[2]

Tolerance does not imply integration. Up until the 1960s, Dutch society was described as columnar in nature, resting on a secular pillar as well as strong Roman Catholic and Protestant columns. All three had a remarkable degree of autonomy, with their own schools, hospitals, and social organizations.[3]

Splitting up into so many smaller groups may also reflect an inability to tolerate the conflict that differences bring. Derek Phillips, professor of sociology at the University of Amsterdam, sees the Dutch dividing into so many parties and religious denominations as coming from their difficulty in accepting the ambiguity and tension that result when people of differing viewpoints are in the same group. In the academic world, for example, a Dutch professional journal does not reflect a diversity of viewpoints; more characteristically, the different opinions find expression in separate journals.[4]

Similarly, within the medical profession, the Dutch had no difficulty when religious physicians formed a separate medical group opposed to euthanasia. Dutch physicians are, in fact, comfortable believing that all opposition to euthanasia is religious in nature. They are intolerant of nonreligious physicians who do not wish to form a separate medical group but nonetheless oppose the secular consensus for euthanasia.

Most scholars see Dutch Calvinism as crucial to understanding Dutch attitudes toward euthanasia. Calvinism had a puritanical, self-righteous intensity in its dedication to work, its discouragement of pleasure, and its belief that the endurance of suffering was redemptive. These attitudes were associated with both the Dutch Reformed Church and the Catholic Church. When the Roman Catholic and Protestant churches lost influence in the 1960s, only the secular column remained to support the social structure.

A new and equally intense consensus formed. Perhaps in reaction to earlier values, it held that individual autonomy should prevail whenever possible in seeking pleasure and avoiding pain. It sought the greatest possible toleration for divergent behavior, transgression, or excess. Dutch toleration for drug abuse, exemplified by the crowds of young people who fill major public squares high on drugs; their acceptance of public displays of prostitution such that naked prostitutes sit in store windows in Amsterdam's red–light district; and the country's acceptance of euthanasia have been seen as a response to being freed of religious restriction. Certainly prior to the 1960s there does not seem to have been the interest in euthanasia in the Netherlands that had been present for some time in England and the United States and led to the formation of voluntary euthanasia societies in both countries in the 1930s—thirty-five years before such a society was organized in the Netherlands. The strength and intensity of the consensus that did develop in the Netherlands around euthanasia and other social changes were seen by Dutch observers as Calvinist in spirit, although organized largely in opposition to an earlier set of beliefs.[5]

It is somewhat misleading, however, to view Dutch toleration of drug abuse, pornography, prostitution, and euthanasia purely in a contemporary perspective and simply as a reaction against an earlier set of religious values. Calvinism became ascendant in the Netherlands during the miraculous Dutch achievement of the seventeenth century, when, for a period of at least fifty years, this small country—still establishing its freedom from Spain—became the preeminent commercial power in the world. In *Dutch Civilization in the Seventeenth Century,* Johan Huizinga reminds us that Calvinism in the Netherlands was never as puritanical as Calvinism in England or Scotland; while pastors still demanded that witches be burned alive, Dutch magistrates put a stop to the practice a century earlier than elsewhere.[6] Although Calvinism was granted a kind of public monopoly supported by the state, it never became a state or established religion in the way that Anglicanism did in England.[7] If the Dutch were swayed by Calvin's view of the utter depravity of human nature and man's inability to contribute to his own salvation, they never abandoned the Erasmian belief in the moral perfectibility of man through reason and rationality.[8] Huizinga's point is echoed by historian Simon Schama, who makes clear that Dutch capitalism, Dutch art, and Dutch social and sexual mores were in no way daunted by Calvinist sermons that condemned lust for money and sex as dirty equivalents.[9]

In Huizinga's view, and that of most Dutch social historians, Calvinist piety and faith were critical to the Dutch achievement, but urban society was the basis for seventeenth-century Dutch culture. He writes, "It was from a bourgeois dislike of interference with our affairs that our forefathers rose up against Spain."[10] It was middle-class merchant traders in the Dutch towns who organized trade between northern and southern Europe to create the Dutch commercial empire. Daniel Defoe's seventeenth-century description of the economic functions of the Dutch Republic has remained evocative:

The Dutch must be understood as they really are, the Middle Persons in Trade, the Factors and Brokers of Europe. . . . they buy to *sell* again, *take* in to *send* out, and the greatest part of their vast Commerce consists in being supply'd from all Parts of the World, that they may supply All the World Again.[11]

The middle class also impressed what Arnold Hauser has described as "an essentially bourgeois stamp on Dutch painting in the midst of a general European court culture."[12] He goes on to say that Dutch art owes its middle-class character—expressed in its interest in the possessions of the individual, the family, the community, and the nation—to the fact that it is free of ties to the church. The commissions for Rembrandt and his contemporaries came from the regents or governors of charitable institutions, the guilds, and most of all from individual affluent burghers.[13] Their distinctive group portraits celebrate both their success and good works together and imply that the moral as well as social values of the day were entrusted to them. In these matters they cherished the bourgeois self-image, seeing themselves as practical decision makers committed to moral relativism as a means of promoting mercantile success. Did this augur a future in which moral complexities would blur as issues of life or death were decided by the relativistic and pragmatic standards of professional groups increasingly committed to a utilitarian culture?

Dutch engineering suggests how great and how warranted was the faith of the Dutch in their own capacity for management and control. Any consideration of the origins of the modern Netherlands must include what Schama has described as the "diluvian" nature of the Dutch experience.[14] Political liberation, mercantile achievement, and the growth of Calvinism were matched by the simultaneous liberation from the sea by the Dutch of an enormous part of the land that forms the Netherlands today. Dutch mastery of the sea made possible the legendary resistance to the Spanish siege of Leiden in 1574.

The Dutch breached their dikes to flood the land, paralyzing Spanish troop movement and enabling the Dutch fleet to relieve the beleaguered city.

Dutch history and mythology are rooted in stories of individual and collective triumph over the sea. Dutch fiction is filled with stories of miraculous adventures in which courageous captains battle the sea, survive disasters, and through virtue and heroism emerge victorious. They contrast with the fiction, drama, and poetry of other maritime countries that view the sea fatalistically, as existentially immutable as life or death; efforts to vanquish its terrors are futile or insane.[15]

The Dutch saw their success as expressive of a covenant between God and, in Schama's words, "the children of the Netherlands." Schama explains that the "drowning of pharaoh's hosts in the Red Sea and the water that rid Leiden of its besiegers" furthered the Hebraic analogy of the Dutch as God's chosen people.[16]

Calvinism, mercantile success, and their triumph in claiming land from the sea shaped the Dutch as powerfully as the conquest of the Western frontier shaped the American experience. There was no way to hide the success of the Netherlands as a nation. The Dutch commercial empire, epitomized by the Dutch East India Company, aroused the envy of Europe. Although the Dutch viewed their military, political, economic, and engineering triumphs as preordained, as good Calvinists they also worried that their culture would perish if self-glorification and greed replaced godliness. They feared their own hubris, but at the same time saw themselves as a people capable of attempting and accomplishing the impossible.

If the seventeenth century was a defining experience in shaping Dutch character, so too was dealing with the decline that followed it. In the first half of the eighteenth century, England and France were able to use their military power to end the preeminent position of the Dutch as world traders.

Huizinga, however, sees the Dutch rise and fall as springing from the virtues and vices of the Dutch bourgeois character. In his remarkable essay "The Spirit of the Netherlands," he blames these vices for the decline of Dutch national life in the eighteenth century, although he worried over them in the context of the Dutch ability to resist fascism in Europe in the 1930s. He mourns the loss of heroism in the Dutch and finds his countrymen lacking in passion, insensitive to myth, self-satisfied, and obstinate. He believes or hopes, however, that the same qualities will lead them to avoid political extremism. He fears the Dutch like tranquillity to the point of passivity; he is tired of the Dutch obsession with cleanliness, complaining that the single Dutch word *schoon* expresses cleanliness and purity as well as beauty.[17]

The features of Dutch character noted by Huizinga are described by most Dutch social historians. Qualities like sobriety, domesticity, commercial spirit, honesty, thriftiness, cleanliness, and maintaining a show of respectability are consistently observed and praised, while the Dutch are pictured less admirably as unromantic, unemotional, unimaginative, stiff, and stubborn.[18]

Writing decades before the issue of euthanasia became a Dutch preoccupation, Huizinga was concerned that the emergence of technical power coincided with a weakening of judgment and morality. It was not crime, prostitution, or drunkenness that worried him as much as a "betrayal of the spirit."[19] While praising Dutch tolerance, he notes that "tolerance is a virtue that can become a vice. Respect for the rights and opinions of others too often leads to respect for their wrongs."[20] In a sentence that could be an epigram for euthanasia in the Netherlands, he states, "The belief that what is evil becomes good if only enough people want it is one of the most terrifying aberrations of the age."[21]

Derek Phillips shares Huizinga's concerns about Dutch social and moral attitudes. He sees the Dutch as relatively uninterested in moral philosophy, which has been the focus of attention in other Western countries, as unwilling to accept any moral absolutes, and as lacking in moral passion. The Dutch, he points out, tend to equate morality with religion, seeing themselves as nonreligious. He considers the single most important social fact regarding morality in the Netherlands to be that indifference often masquerades as tolerance.

Phillips, who was born in the United States but who has lived for twenty-five years in the Netherlands, was impressed by the paradox between the love of freedom felt by the Dutch and their extreme conformity. He found them to be "uncomfortable with anything that distinguishes one individual from another."[22] In the words of Duke de Baena, a Spanish observer, "the Dutch are passionately fond of their freedom and meekly subservient to the tyranny of petty social convention. . . . the Dutchman is as free as he can be according to laws of his kingdom, but he is terrified of his own personal liberty."[23] A common Dutch aphorism is "Be just like everybody else and that will be foolish enough." Phillips found that the standard for conformity was usually narrow: people of one's own age, religion, class, occupation, etc. As a corollary of what he sees as a lack of individualism, the Dutch are unwilling to hold an individual responsible for his or her actions. They are prone to seek external explanations for misconduct.[24]

In contrasting the Dutch with his own culture, Phillips has also been struck by the Dutch discomfort with the notion that the capacity for guilt is critical to moral behavior; he sees the Dutch as having a culture more characterized by "shame" than by "guilt."[25] Since shame is less internalized than guilt and more dependent on the reaction of others, a greater role for shame is consistent with the social pressure for conformity that exists in the Netherlands. Shame can also serve as a way of denying guilt and avoiding moral conflict. It makes external what is really internal. I was impressed with efforts to deny guilt on the part of Dutch euthanasia practitioners, rather than its absence. The tone of moral superiority adopted by many Dutch euthanasia practitioners also suggests the need to deny guilt.

Carlos Gomez, the American philosopher Daniel Callahan, and I were each troubled by what we regarded as Dutch indifference to both their systems' failure to protect patients and their physicians' failure to follow their own euthanasia guidelines.[26] I found that euthanasia advocates, while willing to admit abuses in general, and even to agree that in a particular case euthanasia should not have been performed, or to concede a wrongful death, did not express anger or indignation that a life had been taken unnecessarily. The common attitude was that the doctor may have been mistaken but that he was entitled to his judgment of the matter. This casualness, or what appears to a foreign observer as callousness, is consistent with Phillips's description of the Dutch lack of moral passion and unwillingness to assign individual responsibility.

The need for conformity is related to an aspect of Dutch Calvinism and Dutch character that seems particularly significant, that is, an ambivalent attitude toward authority. Although Calvinism was born in opposition to papal authority, magistrates were seen as "ministers of Divine Justice, vice-regents of God."[27] In modern times the impulse seems to be to resist open authoritarianism—the Catholic Church itself in the Netherlands is uniquely resistant to papal authority[28]—and to replace it with authority that is less direct and obvious; doctors and judges fall into this category.

Other residues of Calvinism still permeate Dutch life. Gomez quotes William Roose of the NVVE (Dutch Volun-

tary Euthanasia Society): "Everybody in Holland is a Calvinist. The Protestants are Calvinists, but so are the Catholics.
Even atheists like me are Calvinists. And the Communists here
are the worst Calvinists of all. What does this mean? We like
many rules, but we don't like to be told what the rules
mean."[29]

Phillips writes that it is the sheer number of rules that is striking to foreign observers. In his own field of education, there
are rules about how many pages per hour students can be asked
to read and how many hours per week teachers can be expected to work. These kind of rules are strictly adhered to. He
goes on:

> But there is also the belief that one can formulate rules as
> to how many citations constitute an adequate review of the
> literature, how many pages for an adequate hypothesis. . . .
> And there are even rules as to how much time one gets off
> for a funeral: a whole day for a spouse or close family mem-
> ber, a half for . . . etc., as well as how much one is expected
> to pay for flowers for the death of a colleague, a neigh-
> bor. . . . There are rules for everything![30]

Certainly the belief that with specific guidelines one can
regulate the private interactions between doctors and patients
regarding euthanasia suggests a faith in rules that transcends the
possible. The flexible way in which physicians interpret these
rules to suit themselves is consistent with Roose's insight.
Calvinist fatalism may also be reflected in the untroubled acceptance of mistakes resulting in death.

Other aspects of Dutch character described by social scien-
tists seem related to how the Dutch have dealt with assisted
suicide and euthanasia. What is described as unimaginative-
ness or insensitivity to myth reflects a concreteness illustrated
by the way in which doctors did not hear the ambivalence ex-

pressed in patients' requests for euthanasia. Johanna Groen-Prakken was right to fear that Dutch doctors in the nursing home would not understand her mother's remarks with regard to her violets that "one should not throw out living things."

Forging Consensus on Euthanasia

When a political or legislative consensus on euthanasia seemed impossible to achieve in the Netherlands, the judicial system became the catalyst for developing one through a series of decisions made in euthanasia cases. The special position of Dutch judges made this possible;[31] judges are appointed for life, cannot be removed by the electorate, and do not have to deal with juries but only with each other, because trials are adjudicated by panels of three judges.

Dutch doctors and the medical profession have also been invested with a remarkable degree of authority. The patient's unquestioning acceptance of that authority makes it likely that if the patient is ambivalent about euthanasia and the doctor favors it, euthanasia will be performed. Herbert Cohen and Robert Dillman agreed that the idea of patient protection in dealing with the medical establishment would be foreign to the Dutch. Public and judicial deference to organized medicine—that is, to the Royal Dutch Medical Society (KNMG)—enabled the KNMG to play a key role in the development of Dutch policy on euthanasia. Developed alongside if not actually together with the courts, KNMG euthanasia guidelines have virtually been adopted by the courts as a national standard. If, as we have seen, these guidelines do not seem to work, the difficulty that Dutch doctors and the medical establishment have in admitting it may partly reflect the obstinacy described by social historians.

The medical profession has become both participant and

regulator in the practice of euthanasia: only the doctor knows what took place with the patient, doctors do not report all their euthanasia cases to the authorities, and the courts defer to medical judgments of professional conduct. The Dutch exhibit a remarkable degree of trust in the medical profession, a trust particularly striking when the profession seems to show more inclination to support doctors than to protect patients where euthanasia is concerned.

Trust in doctors also stems from the unique role of the "house doctor" *(huisarts),* or family physician, in the Netherlands.[32] The doctors live and practice in the neighborhood, make frequent house calls, and usually maintain an office in their homes.

Fifty percent of Dutch patients die at home (compared with about 20 percent in America), usually after the patient has left a hospital because treatment can no longer be helpful.[33] Like Herbert Cohen, who visited his first euthanasia patient for a hundred consecutive days, the doctor often makes daily house calls to dying patients. The house doctor has to a degree replaced the parish priest as a moral arbiter. Cohen acknowledged this in discussing Dutch acceptance of doctors' making decisions without consulting patients by saying, "There is a certain paternalism built into our system."

While the Dutch parliament has resisted the KNMG demand to remove from euthanasia the threat of legal sanction and punishment and to place it under medical control, in actuality this has occurred de facto. Euthanasia, initiated in the service of greater patient autonomy, may provide it to some patients, but overall seems to have increased physicians' power at patients' expense.

Ernst Hirsch-Ballin, the former Christian Democratic minister of justice long concerned with the increasing acceptance of euthanasia in the Netherlands, gave an interesting class analysis of its development.[34] Euthanasia was advocated initially by liberal intellectuals who were concerned with "self-realization" and the avoidance of suffering. They saw no danger to themselves in legalization. They felt equal to the task of dealing with doctors, and they did not fear being pressured by doctors or anyone else. Most working people, though, are less assertive with doctors, more accepting of medical authority, and more in danger of accepting the doctor's prescription of euthanasia.

Over time the Dutch people grew horrified by news stories and TV coverage showing medical technology prolonging painful death. Driven by this mass media sensationalism, euthanasia became appealing to the people who had most to fear from its routinization.

By the 1980s, some movement toward acceptance of euthanasia became inevitable. Better reporting of deaths from euthanasia, combined with the avoidance of formal legalization, seemed to offer the best protection against its abuse, and this is what Hirsch-Ballin and the Christian Democrats have fought to maintain.

Hirsch-Ballin did not believe that the Netherlands had de facto legalized euthanasia; as long as it was not formally legalized, it might be possible to reverse the course of its increasing normalization. In addition, he thought it important to insist that doctors be obliged to justify why *force majeure* applied in each particular case.

He did not believe that the new Dutch government necessarily would legalize euthanasia. Instead, he saw more danger that officials in the government might be lax in insisting on proper reporting and review. Recent events (discussed in Chapter 4) seem to justify his fears.

Unlike René Diekstra, who hoped that foreign criticism might force some modification of Dutch euthanasia policies,

Hirsch-Ballin is counting on change prompted from within. External criticism so far seems only to make the Dutch defend their position more adamantly. One of Huizinga's main criticisms of his countrymen was that they are self-infatuated with regard to how they do things and obstinate in their rejection of criticism.[35] Herbert Cohen reflected the moral superiority of Dutch euthanasia advocates who see foreign criticism as evidence that the United States and the rest of the world are not as enlightened as the Dutch. For example, he maintained that death in the Netherlands is seen as peaceful whereas in the United States it is seen in violent terms. He cited the U.S. acceptance of capital punishment and the high U.S. homicide, abortion, and suicide rates as indicative of this. He was surprised to learn that the Dutch suicide rate has historically been about the same as that of the United States.

Cohen's views would not explain the fact that among developed countries, the United States has experienced the most pressure for euthanasia. Furthermore, there is little such pressure in countries like Sweden, Norway, and Denmark that have no capital punishment and low homicide rates. Moreover, fantasies of peaceful death often mark violent lives; some patients feel that only dying can end a violence that threatens them with a loss of control more fearful than death itself.

Any discussion of the cultural factors that may influence the Dutch acceptance and practice of assisted suicide and euthanasia must recognize that the Dutch embraced euthanasia as a way of dealing with terminal illness before the developments in palliative care in the past decade. Given their experience and the discontent of Dutch doctors with legal regulation, it is far from sure that they would do something similar if they were starting right now. It will probably not be possible, however, for the Dutch to back away completely from legally sanctioned euthanasia. Euthanasia, once sanctioned, creates its own irrational demand that some are all too willing to meet. A medical system that develops around the easy option of euthanasia is hard to reverse.

The Dutch have come to accept euthanasia for reasons that seem quite different from those that draw Americans to its legalization. The Dutch have buried the moral complexities of euthanasia and assisted suicide, as well as the emotional ambivalence of dying, under a modern ethos that prizes management, usefulness, and control. The doctor, the judge, and the patient may share a common culture, which takes a utilitarian view of the diminished meaning of living with illness. In both the Netherlands and the United States, however, an "anything goes" attitude toward individual choices regarding death may have in common the fact that in each country there has been a marked breakdown in previously held values.

The United States

In the United States a more gradual waning of the influence of religion contributed to the questioning of traditional prohibitions against self-induced death.[36] Physicians, however, were not significantly involved in this questioning until the discovery in the nineteenth century of analgesics and anesthetics that could relieve suffering in dying patients, as well as easily and painlessly end life.[37]

Interest in medical euthanasia coincided with birth a century ago of the modern hospital as an institution that could provide curative medical and surgical treatment. As medicine learned to control acute infectious disease, and as life expectancy began its gradual increase from a norm of 40 in 1850 to double that figure today, degenerative and late-onset diseases, of which cancer was the epitome, made the discussion of end-of-life care more urgent and the role of the physician in palliation more important.[38] By the beginning of the twentieth century the principle of the double effect was introduced into medicine; that is, in the interests of relieving suffering it was appropriate to give treatments that risked death.

The first articles in the United States advocating euthanasia in the context of modern medicine appeared in the 1870s. The first proposal for the legalization of euthanasia was made and defeated in Ohio in 1905. Following a similar defeat in Iowa, no further proposals were made for three decades. Interest in euthanasia revived in the United States in the 1930s, when the first euthanasia society was formed. Accounts of suffering patients who desired euthanasia began to appear, as well as accounts by physicians who had surreptitiously performed it. In 1937 the Nebraska legislature defeated a bill to legalize euthanasia.[39]

The postwar revulsion at the use of euthanasia by Nazi Germany to eliminate handicapped and retarded children, the mentally ill, Jew, Gypsies, and others in the name of racial and genetic improvement discredited the movement.[40] The cooperation of German doctors and the use of medically run camps for this extermination made people wary of the involvement of physicians in euthanasia.

Modern medical technology that permits us to maintain a pointless semblance of life and that creates fear of painful and undignified deaths was blamed for the revival of interest in euthanasia in the 1970s and 1980s. At the same time, medicine appeared to some degree to be replacing religion as the institution people turn to for relief from their fears of death and to fulfill their desires for immortality. Physicians have some power to prolong our lives and can also provide us with some illusion of control over death through determining how and when it occurs.

If fear of suffering through prolongation of the dying process were the entire explanation, we would educate the public about the right to refuse unwarranted and unwanted treatment. Doctors would learn about the care of terminally ill people, and more hospices would be established. We should, in any case, be doing all of these things.

Something more, however, seems to lie behind the current U.S. interest in euthanasia. Something that leads people to become members of the Hemlock Society in their forties and fifties and to want to end their lives at the earliest signs of serious illness. Something that led almost half the voters of Washington and California, and more than half in Oregon, to support bills legalizing assisted suicide and euthanasia. I believe that this something is an increased anxiety in our culture about death itself.

How to manage the anxiety associated with death has been a problem for all cultures throughout history. Most people never fully accept death, but how they do depends on its cultural context. In a culture in which life has no continuity, in which life lacks significance beyond itself, death becomes more threatening and intolerable. Robert Lifton cites a World War II study of English children during the air raids on Britain to illustrate this point. The children's fear of death and dying during the bombing raids depended not so much on the intensity of the raids but on the mood and attitude of their mothers and other significant adults.[41] The child's death anxiety, assuaged by the mother, matures into the dying adult's finding comfort and meaning in connection to family, religion, country, and work.

Connectedness somewhat relieves our anxiety about death; it helps fulfill our need for immortality or at least for what Lifton has called symbolic immortality.[42] Religion comes first to mind, although not necessarily in the sense of an afterlife.

Some believers may not accept a literal afterlife, but they may achieve a sense of symbolic immortality by sharing the enduring values and purpose of life prescribed in church teachings. Symbolic immortality is obviously achieved biologically, by living on through one's sons and daughters and, in an extended way, through the continuity of the family with larger social units such as the culture and the nation. Creative immortality is achieved through work, not simply from doing something that achieves recognition, but from the feeling of influencing the lives of others, and in that sense of connecting in a human experience that transcends oneself—whether through teaching, writing, preaching, building, or business. The Protestant concept of works as opposed to work reflects a recognition of the importance of such experience. In a period when family integration is threatened, when government is not trusted, when religion is less influential, when few find significant meaning in their work, a greater anxiety about death is not surprising.

American attitudes toward older people intensify these problems. Arnold Toynbee, the English historian, once said that death is un-American.[43] He explained that death has no place in a culture that emphasizes progress, strength, and the vitality and beauty of youth and so devalues the wisdom and dignity of age. In such a society, dying can be a terribly lonely and desperate experience.

How differently older people can be treated in other cultures was made clear to me some years ago when I was working on a study of suicide in the Scandinavian countries. On a Sunday in Oslo you could see elderly couples walking arm in arm on the streets with pride and confidence, with a certain sense that this was their city, that they had lived in it, that they had helped to build it. One seldom sees such couples in American cities. Older patients whom I saw in Norwegian hospitals had a bearing about them that implied that they expected to be treated (as they were) with a deference due their age and experience. It was a striking contrast to what I see in municipal hospitals in the United States, where older people are often treated as an inconvenient nuisance.

A hundred years ago, there were no old-age homes; people died at home, surrounded by loved ones. Here the dying person and the family were conscious of the connection and continuity of their lives and had a sense of death as a part of life.[44] Pain, suffering, and death itself were easier to bear in this context.

Not surprisingly, given their social isolation, patients with AIDS have also become a significant group attempting and committing suicide and requesting assisted suicide and euthanasia.[45] Research has shown that the absence of social support—including good medical care—is as significant as actual symptoms or the stage of the disease in determining the desire of AIDS patients to end their lives or to request help in doing so.[46] The alienation from family, frequent in AIDS patients, the absence of children, and isolation from the larger community all contribute to increased anxiety about death.

Social historians have described us as a culture of narcissism.[47] Psychiatrists increasingly see what they describe as narcissistic pathology. Whatever else these terms imply, they refer to an egocentric quality that is derived from a lack of connectedness. Heinz Kohut sees the shift in pathology as the product of families in which children are more isolated and less involved with parents in contrast to the less severe pathology associated with the overinvolvement between parents and children that was more common forty years ago.[48] The diminished connectedness that develops in such an environment of isolation leaves the individual vulnerable to anxieties of disintegration. Age and approaching death threaten everyone's sense of self, but are particularly intolerable for narcissistic individuals. In a culture that fosters narcissism, aging and death are harder to bear.

A consequence of the fragmentation evident in the culture is the increasing absence of a shared set of values, leading many to believe that anything goes if it is chosen freely, regardless of social consequences. Understood in this context, the concern for autonomy used to justify euthanasia is a euphemism for "narcissism" and less a new value than a reflection of the loss of social cohesion.

Anxieties about death and disintegration aggravated by cultural fragmentation seem to have led to an increasing need for individuals to feel some control over death by determining how and when it occurs.

Alexis de Tocqueville observed that Americans rush to law to solve all problems.[49] In America's eagerness to legalize assisted suicide and euthanasia, he surely would recognize our wish to legislate a quick fix for those who are terminally ill. Although we have referred to assisted suicide and euthanasia as a "cure" for suicide, they are intended to offer the even loftier goal of providing us with an illusory control over our fears of death.

Chapter 7

THEORY AND PRACTICE

Long before the current concern with euthanasia, writers and philosophers from Seneca to John Donne and David Hume defended the right to suicide. In more modern times, Nietzsche succinctly expressed this position when he wrote, "There is a certain right by which we may deprive a man of life, but none by which we may deprive him of death."[1] From that standpoint, attempts to prevent suicide can be seen as an interference with that right. Removed from its social and psychological context, suicide then becomes an issue of personal freedom.

Decriminalization of both suicide and attempted suicide and the abolition of such punishment as confinement in prison and ignominious burial did not come about because society approved of suicide or considered it a human right. The changes reflected the view that punishment was unfair to the relatives of the suicide and, more important, that those who attempted or committed suicide were usually suffering from mental illness.[2]

As a consequence we now try to help rather than punish those who are suicidal. Although the right to kill oneself can be exercised without assistance by most of those who are sufficiently determined, those who involve others—someone on the window ledge of a tall building who is threatening to jump or someone who is found unconscious after swallowing sleeping pills—force society to pay attention, whether or not that person is hoping to be saved or helped. Surely some intervention in the hope of providing help is indicated. When behavior is psychosocial—when the community has a stake in it—personal rights are not unlimited.[3]

Thomas Szasz, professor of psychiatry at the State University of New York at Syracuse and an articulate spokesman for the right to suicide, believes that successful suicides intend to die and unsuccessful ones do not.[4] He does not accept the ambivalent quality of most suicides. Yet the clinical evidence contradicts him. Three-fourths of all suicides communicate their intentions, often with the hope that something will be done to make their suicide unnecessary. Studies of those who survived serious suicide attempts frequently reveal a fantasy of being rescued.

What misleads clinicians is that many who attempt suicide are not really ambivalent about suicide—they clearly want to live. A large number of those who kill themselves, however, act irrevocably while in a state of uncertainty. People have speculated about whether someone who has jumped from a tall building might wish to change his mind in midair. Over the past forty years I have seen four people who survived six-story jumps. Two wished to survive as soon as they jumped; two did not, but one of the latter who professed to be furious at surviving made no subsequent suicide attempts.

Ambivalence often extends to those who are close to the would-be suicide. Sometimes they wait for hours before getting help for an unconscious suicide attempter. Sometimes they call for help but argue that the patient should not be resuscitated. It may be hard to say how much their wish that the patient should be out of the way contributed to the suicide attempt, but psychosocial intervention with such patients and their families has been shown to change the atmosphere so that the patient is no longer suicidal.[5]

It is not so surprising that the attitudes of those close to a patient often determine the outcome in euthanasia cases. Requests for assisted suicide usually reflect the same ambivalence that is seen in other suicides. The outcome in such cases is often determined by whether family or physicians choose to hear the wish to continue living or only to support the wish to die.

A doctor who suggests assisted suicide as an option to a patient, or relatives who respond too readily to a patient's mention of euthanasia, send a powerful message that they believe the patient should not continue to live. In such cases we are not dealing with autonomy or the patient's right to die but with the will of the doctor and the relatives and their right to influence the ending of a life that has become a burden, or that they think is not worth living.

The "right to die" is a good slogan designed to sell euthanasia. Historically, however, it is life that has been considered an inalienable right; death is a biological fact. One could with equal or more justification speak of legalization as establishing the doctor's right to kill. The notion of a right to die has a preposterous quality, conjuring up images of the state denying us that right and granting us immortality.

Neither Szasz nor Nietzsche claims that society should help, support, or encourage the suicide in his efforts to kill himself. Szasz explicitly tells us that it would be sufficient if society recognized that it had no right to interfere. But supporters of euthanasia go further with the right to die. They believe in the utility of suicidal death and want support, encouragement, and even help in carrying out suicide.

Autonomy and Social Policy

In making the case that personal autonomy dictates a right to choose the time and place of one's death, Ronald Dworkin, professor of law at New York University and university professor of jurisprudence at Oxford, maintains that respect for the consistency and integrity of the way individuals live their lives and the issues they deem most important, including the way they wish to die, requires that we grant their requests for euthanasia.[6] Just what does it mean in this context to respect the integrity of how an individual has lived his or her life?

For those individuals who respond to every life crisis with depression, panic, and the desire to die, does the fact that the crisis is now serious or the illness terminal demand that we heed their request to die because it is consistent with their character? For others the panic that accompanies serious or terminal illness is not in keeping with their prior life or character. When that panic is addressed, it usually subsides and the request for death disappears. If the panic is not addressed, it may be perceived as the "autonomous" desire of an individual.

In making the argument for the wrongfulness of assisted suicide and euthanasia, the philosopher Daniel Callahan reasons that since euthanasia and assisted suicide entail assistance by another person, they are no longer private acts but are a form of communal action, even though the community in question may be only two people. We have never allowed killing as a form of contractual relationship between two consenting adults, just as we do not permit people to sell themselves into slavery. The killing of another is now publicly justified only in cases of self-defense, capital punishment, and a just war. In none of these cases is the killing for the benefit of the person killed, but only to protect the lives or welfare of others.

Callahan goes on to say that taking a life can only be justified by a strong public interest. We have considered the power to kill too great a power to be given to individuals to serve their private ends, even good ends like compassion and relief of suffering. Finally, if a case can be made that an individual has the right of self-determination unto death, it does not follow that the right can be transformed into the right of someone else to kill that person. The individual has, in fact, no right to authorize another individual to kill him. Callahan concludes, "No human being, whatever the motives, should have that kind of ultimate power over the fate of another. It is wrong for a community to sanction private killing among its members in pursuit of their individual goals."[7]

Callahan makes a good case. If a strong public interest must be involved in taking a life, however, many euthanasia advocates will argue that relieving the suffering of those who are terminally ill is such an interest. Society can change its view of when it will sanction killing; this has happened with capital punishment.

Yet, few well-functioning societies are apt to legalize and encourage self-destructive behavior on the part of their members, singly or with assistance. If society modifies this attitude it should be because the problem addressed is overwhelming and no other solution can be found. A better solution than legalizing euthanasia *can* be found for the social problem we face in helping those who are seriously or terminally ill, just as a better solution can be found for most individuals who are contemplating euthanasia.

Ethical Questions

We have reached a consensus that permits us to withhold or withdraw futile treatment when patients are terminally ill, but some insist euthanasia and withdrawing futile medical treatment

are no different. The ethicist Dan Brock rejects the argument
that the disease and not the doctor kills the patient when futile
treatment is withdrawn. Brock observes that if for personal, self-
ish reasons a son disconnects the respirator of his mother dying
with amyotrophic lateral sclerosis, we would not accept his
contention that the disease killed her, while we do accept this
rationale from the doctor. Brock wants us to regard both actions as killing; the moral difference is that some killings are justified and some are not.[8]

Callahan points out, however, that when we maintain that
the physician in Brock's example caused the death, we confuse causality (directly physically causing death) and culpability (our attribution of moral responsibility):

> The physician's omission can only bring about death on the
> condition that the patient's disease will kill him in the ab-
> sence of treatment. We may hold the physician morally
> responsible for the death, if we have morally judged such
> actions wrongful omissions. But it confuses reality and moral
> judgment to see an omitted action as having the same causal
> status as one that directly kills. A lethal injection will kill
> both a healthy person and a sick person. A physician's omit-
> ted treatment will have no effect on a healthy person. . . .
> It will only, in contrast, bring the life of a sick person to an
> end because of an underlying fatal disease. . . . the doctor
> who, at the patient's request, omits or terminates unwanted
> treatment does not kill at all. Her underlying disease, not
> his action, is the physical cause of the death; and we have
> agreed to consider actions of that kind to be morally licit.
> He thus can truly be said to have "allowed" her to die.[9]

Callahan has the better of the argument. Of more importance perhaps, most people understand and accept the distinction between killing and allowing to die in such cases.

Most people also are able to value the distinction between giving pain medication in doses necessary to provide relief, even at the risk of causing death, and giving pain medication with the intention of causing death. Some euthanasia advocates do not. Dr. Thomas Preston of the University of Washington Medical School, who is active in Compassion in Dying, maintains that physicians routinely end patients' lives behind the screen of giving pain relief in the form of a high morphine dose. He argues that if we are to avoid such deception we must legalize assisted suicide.[10] Certainly there are some physicians in this country who use painkilling medication to end the life of patients whose lives they feel should be ended.

The relationship between doctor and patient and the attitude of each in facing serious or terminal illness are at the heart of the matter. Former U.S. Surgeon General C. Everett Koop captured the essence of this relationship in discussing "the intent of the heart" in treating a hypothetical older woman with a powerful painkiller. "The intent behind the gradual administration of drugs is to be her ally in her remaining hours or days of her life and to keep her comfortable as she slips away. The intent behind . . . the drug overdose, is to get her 'out of her misery' and 'off our hands' as quickly as possible."[11] Koop's attitude toward persons who are terminally ill seems to reflect a finer and more humane quality of medical care than simply calling for the legalization of euthanasia.

In the words of Dr. Kenneth Praeger, chair of the ethics committee of the Columbia Presbyterian Medical Center, one of the goals of euthanasia advocates is to "desensitize society to euthanasia by blurring the distinction between mercy killing and the merciful use of drugs that may unintentionally hasten death."[12] Richard Doerflinger, an executive with the National Conference of Catholic Bishops, makes the point even more strongly: "If some doctors are so anxious to hasten death that they evade crystal-clear laws against homicide, it would be madness to place such a recipe for discretionary killing in their hands."[13]

It will not always be possible to know the "intent of the heart" or to uncover the ambivalence that terminal illness and imminent death engender in both doctors and patients. There are now and will continue to be abuses in the care of people who are terminally ill. But as long as deliberately producing death is illegal, as long as physicians know that in case of a complaint they will be called to justify their actions to their peers and to the legal system, the extent of such abuse will be limited. If a doctor chooses to break the law, he should do so with full knowledge of the seriousness of his action. Protecting the honorable physician does not warrant legalizing physician-assisted suicide or euthanasia in a society where the public is uninformed of present abuses and does not recognize the potential for much greater ones.

The Nature of Medicine

Euthanasia proponents maintain that the advances of modern-day medicine have made euthanasia necessary by painfully prolonging dying. Freeing death from the technological control of doctors was the worthy goal of many patients and their families who fought the battles for the right of patients or their surrogates to refuse unwanted treatment. As health attorney Giles Scofield points out:

A central concern has been to enable patients to die without the encumbrances of tubes, ventilators, cardiopulmonary cerebral resuscitation, dialysis, surgery, transfusions, and drugs . . . preserving the right to die the way we used to die before advances in medicine and medical technology enabled physicians to attenuate the dying process; it has been about insuring that patients, not doctors, determine when such a death is to occur.[14]

Scofield points out, however, that advocacy of physician-assisted suicide paradoxically encourages the view that medical technology can solve the problems of dying. As D. J. Bakker, a Dutch surgeon, points out, "Euthanasia is then chosen as the wrong solution for a wrong development in medicine. A medical science that is in need of euthanasia has to be changed as soon as possible to a medicine that cares beyond cure."[15]

Viewing euthanasia as a corrective misunderstands the nature of the relationship between patients and doctors. In regard to the role of autonomy in that relationship, Leon Kass reminds us that "physicians serve the needs of patients not because patients exercise self-determination but because patients are sick. A patient may not insist, for example, on a treatment the physician feels is not consistent with sound medical practice."[16]

The case that the essential moral structure of medicine requires that "doctors must not kill" has been argued vigorously by many physicians who note that for centuries physicians have not participated in capital punishment because to do so would compromise their role as healers. Edmund Pellegrino, physician and ethicist at Georgetown University, points out that the healing relationship requires the doctor to restore health when possible, and to enable the patient to cope with death and disability when cure is not possible and death is inevitable.[17] He sees medicine as ineradicably grounded in trust, with the patient "dependent on the physician's good will and character. The physician to be faithful to the trust must seek to heal and not to remove the need for healing by killing the patient."[18] Pellegrino asks, "Whose agent is the doctor when treatment becomes marginal and costs escalate?"[19]

Advocates of euthanasia do not share Pellegrino's perception that euthanasia intrinsically opposes healing. They insist that euthanasia can be considered a proper part of medical caring, justified when it prevents pain, incompetence, or undignified dying, justified because the prevention of suffering is a proper part of a doctor's activities. Dr. Els Borst-Eilers states directly: "There are situations when the best way to heal the patient is to help him die peacefully. The doctor who, in such a situation, grants the patient's request acts as the healer par excellence."[20]

Yet justifying euthanasia by "healing" and "helping," the ethicist and legal scholar Alexander Capron believes,

"opens the door to people who have never made their wishes known, but whom one would 'objectively' say must be suffering a good deal. Since in those cases autonomy is not the benchmark, pain and suffering become all-important as they are in euthanizing pets."[21]

But there is no objective way of determining what is unbearable pain and suffering, leaving the decision to the doctor's subjective assessment.

Although today euthanasia advocacy is centered more on compassion for people who are terminally or incurably ill, the specter of using euthanasia to deal with the social problem of those who are sick and elderly is always in the background. Until the last decade, eugenic considerations were an intrinsic part of the argument for euthanasia. The increasing number of old people, the inadequate care provided by nursing homes, and the economic cost to both families and society were used to support the view that euthanasia was to be accepted and encouraged. As Eliot Slater, a prominent English euthanasia advocate, put it, "If a chronically ill man dies, he ceases to be a burden on himself, his family, on the health services and the community."[22] As we noted in the last chapter, Pieter Admiraal, one of the foremost Dutch practitioners of euthanasia, thinks it likely that in twenty-five years Europe may resort to euthanasia to deal with the problem of a large population of older people. Admiraal said he was glad he would not be there to see it; this from a man who was one of the pioneers of euthanasia in the Netherlands and remains one of its strongest advocates.

The Legal Argument

While efforts to justify euthanasia and assisted suicide have sought support in philosophy and medicine, advocates have been active on the legal front. In Michigan, New York, and the state of Washington there have been constitutional challenges to state laws prohibiting assisted suicide. The opinions expressed by the courts in these cases have been contradictory.

The arguments rejecting a constitutional right to suicide were well expressed in an opinion written by Judge John T. Noonan for a three-judge panel of the U.S. Court of Appeals for the Ninth Circuit. In declaring unconstitutional the state of Washington's statute prohibiting assisting in a suicide, a federal district court in Seattle had cited the U.S. Supreme Court's limited acknowledgment in the Nancy Beth Cruzan case of a patient's right to refuse treatment as tantamount to an acceptance of assisted suicide. The Ninth Circuit Court's opinion pointed out that the district court had ignored the more relevant part of the *Cruzan* opinion affirming the state's interest in protecting and preserving life, and noted that most states have laws forbidding assisted suicide. In distinguishing the right to refuse treatment from the acceptance of a right to assisted suicide, Judge Noonan concluded, "Whatever difficulty the district court experienced in distinguishing one situation from the other, it was not experienced by the majority in *Cruzan*."[23]

The district court had also cited *Planned Parenthood v. Casey* to maintain that assisted suicide was a personal decision like abortion, and thus a right protected by the Fourteenth Amendment. In rebuttal, the appellate panel referred to an article by Yale Kamisar[24] which pointed out that such a right or liberty interest could not be limited to persons who are terminally ill; i.e., it would have to apply to everyone. The appellate opinion concluded,

> If at the heart of a liberty protected by the Fourteenth Amendment is this uncurtailable ability to believe and to act on one's deepest beliefs about life, the right to suicide and the right to assistance in suicide are the prerogative of at least every sane adult. The attempt to restrict such rights to the terminally ill is illusory. If such liberty exists in this context, . . . every man and woman must enjoy it. . . . The conclusion is a "reductio ad absurdum."[25]

In March 1996, however, in an 8 to 3 decision, a larger panel of the Ninth Circuit Court of Appeals overturned this ruling, declaring (in line with the district court) that the Washington State ban on assisted suicide was unconstitutional.[26] In writing for the majority of the court, Judge Stephen Reinhardt saw "compelling similarities between right-to-die cases and abortion cases."[27] He found both to involve intimate and personal choices central to personal dignity and autonomy. He went on to declare that although preservation of life is a legitimate function of the state, "when patients are no longer able to pursue liberty or happiness and do not wish to pursue life, the state's interest in forcing them to remain alive is less clearly compelling."[28] The Ninth Circuit's decision further maintained that the Supreme Court ruling in *Cruzan* allowing patients to terminate unwanted treatment did indeed signal recognition of "a constitutionally recognized 'right to die.' "[29] The opinion aroused strong reaction and the state of Washington appealed the decision to the U.S. Supreme Court.

In April 1996 a three-judge panel of the U.S. Court of Appeals for the Second Circuit also overturned a lower court's opinion and declared invalid New York's ban on assisted suicide. The rationale given by the Second and Ninth Circuit Courts for their decisions differed markedly. The Ninth Circuit had drawn on the liberty protections afforded by the due process clause of the Fourteenth Amendment to the Constitution. The Second Circuit judges, however, said that New York law prohibiting assisted suicide violates the equal protection clause of the Fourteenth Amendment since it permits one class of patients to end their lives by withdrawing treatment, but requires another class to stay alive by denying them suicide.[30] New York state also appealed the decision.

To further complicate the issue, the Michigan Supreme Court had earlier declared not only that a statute barring assisted suicide is constitutional under the U.S. Constitution but that even in the absence of such a statute, assisting in a suicide could be prosecuted as a felony under Michaigan common law. Although the U.S. Supreme Court declined to review the Michigan case, given the legal chaos of these conflicting decisions one or both of the New York or Washington cases seemed likely to be accepted by the Court.

Kamisar doubted that the Supreme Court would sustain the Ninth or Second Circuit Courts' opinions. As far as the parallel to abortion goes, he pointed out that the Supreme Court in *Roe v Wade* cleared the way for its ultimate decision by rejecting the argument that a fetus is a "person" under the meaning of the Constitution; a terminally ill person, however, clearly is.[31]

Kamisar also read the Supreme Court's 1990 decision in the

Cruzan case differently from Judge Reinhardt. Kamisar pointed out that in ruling that a state could require clear and convincing evidence of a patient's past wishes in order to terminate life-sustaining treatment even of someone in a vegetative state, like Nancy Cruzan, Chief Justice Rehnquist carefully distinguished between ending use of artificial life-support systems and assisting in a suicide. The opinion characterized the right of even a competent person to refuse life-sustaining nutrition and hydration as deriving from a Fourteenth Amendment potential "liberty interest" rather than from a constitutionally protected right of privacy. The use of "liberty interest" language rather than "constitutionally protected right" may give the state greater freedom of action in such cases.

Kamisar saw the *Cruzan* decision as a signal of the Court's reluctance to constitutionalize an area marked by social and legal debate, and an inclination to defer to the states' judgment. He concluded by saying' "A Court that refused to 'constitutionalize' a 'right to die' broad enough to uphold the claims of the Cruzan family is hardly likely to 'constitutionalize' a right to assisted suicide."[32] The *Cruzan* decision also specifically ruled that a state may express an "unqualified" interest in protecting life regardless of the diminished quality of life that may be caused by illness. The circuit court decisions insisting that states selectively allow assisted suicide for certain conditions seemed to be in conflict with this aspect of *Cruzan*.

In the fall of 1996, the U.S. Supreme Court accepted the New York and Washington cases. In a decision released on June 26, 1997, the Court unanimously upheld the New York and Washington prohibitions on assisting suicide.[33]

In the New York case, the Court rejected the Second Circuit's contention that the right to refuse life-sustaining medical treatment "is nothing more or less than assisted suicide." The Court held that the state's ban on assisted suicide involved no violation of the equal protection clause of the Constitution, which declares that no state shall "deny to any person within its jurisdiction the equal protection of the laws." The opinion written by Chief Justice Rehnquist pointed out that the clause created no substantive rights but simply embodied the general rule that states must treat like cases alike, yet may treat unlike cases accordingly.

The Court based its analysis on intent and causation, two legal principles used to distinguish acts that may have the same result. Under a causation analysis, the Court reasoned that a patient refusing life-sustaining medical treatment dies from an underlying disease, while a patient ingesting lethal medication prescribed by a physician is killed by the medication. The physician's intent is also different in the two situations: A doctor withdrawing or not administering treatment does not necessarily intend the patient's death. The doctor may simply be complying with patient wishes to desist from futile or excessively burdensome treatment. By contrast, a doctor assisting in a patient's suicide can have no intention other than to help see to it that a patient dies. The patient who commits suicide with the help of a doctor has the specific intention of ending his or her life; the patient refusing or discontinuing treatment might not.

Since refusal of life-sustaining treatment is not identical with assisted suicide and since *everyone,* regardless of physical condition is entitled if competent to refuse life-sustaining medical treatment while *no one* is allowed to assist a suicide, the Court found that the New York law applies evenhandedly to all and protects all equally.

Finally, the Court found that New York had valid and important public interests for its law—"prohibiting intentional killing and preserving life; preventing suicide; maintaining physicians' role as their patients' healers; protecting vulnerable people from indifference, prejudice, and psychological and financial pressure to end their lives; and avoiding a possible slide toward euthanasia."[34]

In upholding Washington's law against causing or aiding suicide, the Supreme Court rejected the Ninth Circuit's contention that a liberty interest protected by the due process clause of the Fourteenth Amendment was violated by the statute. The Court pointed out that the clause particularly protects fundamental rights and liberties rooted in our nation's history. The Court then traced a history of prohibition against assisted suicide in the country, noting that such prohibitions have been long-standing and that they were reexamined and reaffirmed in many states.

The Court also rejected the Ninth Circuit's view that the patient's interest involved "a right to die." The Court felt the more precise issue was whether the due process clause included the right to commit suicide, which included a right to assistance in doing so. Here the Court refused to reverse "centuries of legal doctrine and practice" to overrule the policy choices of almost every state.

The Court furthermore rejected the Ninth Circuit's reliance on past Supreme Court precedents on abortion *(Planned Parenthood v. Casey)* or withdrawal from treatment *(Cruzan)* to argue for a right to assisted suicide. It emphasized that its opinion in *Cruzan* was rooted in common law protection against forced medical treatment (a form of battery) rather than in any broad-ranging concept of a constitutional right to die. The Court explained that the Ninth Circuit incorrectly interpreted *Casey* to apply to matters other than family intimacy or reproductive capacity.

The majority of the Justices were more concerned with a patient's right not to suffer than they were with creating a right to assisted suicide. The fact that patients involved in the two cases could obtain relief from suffering short of death was a crucial factor in the Court's decision. The Justices made clear their willingness to revisit the issue if such relief were not provided.

The Supreme Court, while challenging the states to experiment in ways to improve the care of dying patients, and not precluding their right to consider assisted suicide in doing so, gave powerful reasons in their opinion (see Preface) for considering that there were better alternatives.

In 1994, Oregon had become the only state to pass a law permitting physician–assisted suicide. That act, known as Measure 16, was still being contested in court and, at the time of the Supreme Court decision in the New York and Washington cases, was going to be reconsidered in a state referendum; the Court made a specific point of not prejudging the Oregon law.

Measure 16 permits Oregon's physician's to prescribe lethal drugs to competent, terminally ill, adult patients who request them. Two physicians must determine that the patient has a disease that is likely to kill him or her within six months. Only if one of the physicians believes the patient is depressed or suffering from a mental disorder should a referral be made "for counseling" by a licensed psychiatrist or psychologist. The physician who prescribes the lethal drug may or may not be present when the patient takes the medication. If he follows certain guidelines and acts in "good faith," the physician is immune from civil or criminal liability or professional disciplinary action.[35]

The law was challenged by patients who were terminally ill, doctors, and administrators of health care facilities as violating the constitutional rights of people who were terminally ill who would not be given the equal protection of Oregon statutes prohibiting assisted suicide.[36] In an opinion for the U.S. District Court of Oregon (August 3, 1995), Judge Michael

Hogan declared the law unconstitutional. His opinion in the case is worth examining since many states are considering laws similar to or modeled after the Oregon law.

Judge Hogan pointed out that the Oregon laws against assisted suicide were designed to protect vulnerable people who might otherwise seek suicide in response to treatable depression, mental illness, or coercion.[37] He considered that "a crucial inquiry under an equal protection analysis is whether the safeguards provided in Measure 16 are sufficient to justify treating terminally ill patients differently than others."[38]

Judge Hogan found that the procedures in Measure 16 designed to differentiate between competent and incompetent patients were not sufficient. The measure required physicians, who need not be psychiatrists or psychologists, to make an initial evaluation as to whether a condition was causing impaired judgment, or if the patient was depressed or suffering from a mental disorder.[39] But there is no requirement for a psychiatric or psychological referral in every case; and there is no mechanism in Measure 16 at all for evaluation at the time the lethal drug is actually to be taken. Judge Hogan considered that "the problem of inadequate mental evaluation is compounded by imprecision in defining 'terminal disease'. . . . only in hindsight is it known with certainty when someone is going to die."[40]

Under the statute, the treating physician would have been exclusively responsible for presenting the patient with feasible alternatives, including comfort care, hospice care, and pain control. There was no requirement that a patient consult a certified social worker or other specialist to explore social services that might enable the person to live in greater comfort. There is no requirement that the patient consult with a specialist in pain relief. The same treating physician would be deciding when a person's request was voluntary and not subject to undue influence. There was no provision for an independently chosen physician to confirm that a person is capable and acting voluntarily.

In his opinion, Judge Hogan noted there was no independent oversight for the decision and implementation of assisted suicide by medical professionals, such as review by a probate court, as there is with civil commitment: "With death at issue under Measure 16, the court is unable to conceive of a set of facts under which it would be rational to not require mental and social evaluations by appropriately trained professionals."[41]

Remarkably, Measure 16 exempted physicians from the ordinary standards of care, skill, and diligence required by Oregon of other physicians in other circumstances, standards applying, for example, to a physician's conduct in withdrawing life-support. Instead, under Measure 16 a physician is immunized from liability for actions taken in "good faith" irrespective of medical community standards in other matters. As Judge Hogan put it,

> The plain inference from Measure 16 is that it is irrelevant whether physicians objectively act reasonably, or instead act negligently. . . . this defect goes to the very heart of the state's reliance on a person's consent to die. . . . the physician is allowed to negligently misdiagnose a person's condition and competency and negligently prescribe a drug overdose, so long as those actions are in "good faith."[42]

Since there is no requirement that a person be under the supervision of a physician at the time of taking the lethal overdose, Judge Hogan was also concerned that Measure 16 "does nothing to ensure that the decision to commit suicide is rationally and voluntarily made at the time of death."[43] He indicated that under the statute "a person decides when, where, and most important, whether to take the prescribed drug without any legal protection."[44]

For all of the above reasons, Judge Hogan concluded that Measure 16 singles out terminally ill persons who want to commit suicide and excludes them from equal protection under Oregon laws that apply to all others. Since Judge Hogan restricted his opinion to equal protection issues, he did not address a number of other questions raised by the law.

Commenting on the case prior to the decision, ethicist and health attorney George Annas reminds us that physicians are already able to supply terminally ill patients with potentially lethal medications that have a legitimate medical use if the physicians believe the medication will help the patients to live better. Under the Oregon law, and comparable laws being considered in other states, the patient's request must not be for the purpose of living better but only "for the purpose of ending his or her life." In other words, "the physician must agree with an explicit plan of suicide by his patient and must participate in the suicide directly and unambiguously."[45]

The Oregon law was also vague as to whether the six-month estimate of life expectancy necessary to qualify a patient for assisted suicide is based on accepting or refusing treatment. If the estimate is without treatment—most likely, since treatment cannot be mandated—the law would make assisted suicide available to many thousands of people whose illness or life-threatening condition is controllable through medication or surgery, but who would die within six months without treatment. This very large class of patients will not inevitably die, but, if suffering from undiagnosed clinical depression, may consider their lives not worth living and choose assisted suicide.

Since under the law there were no mandatory requirements for reporting assisted suicide on the death certificate, Judge Hogan believed effective monitoring was not possible. The only ones protected by the law were physicians, since their "good faith" virtually immunizes them against all prosecution.[46]

Much of Judge Hogan's opinion was specific to the situation in Oregon and to the particular safeguards or lack of them in Measure 16. One could imagine revising the statute so as to meet at least some of his concerns. Of course, Oregon might create a different situation by repealing all laws it has prohibiting assisted suicide. No such equal protection problem would then exist. But who would suggest that assisted suicide should be legal for everyone in every circumstance?

Many legal scholars, including those who consider state laws allowing assisted suicide to be unwise, believe on purely constitutional grounds that the states are entitled to make their own decisions and mistakes in these matters and should correct them if and when they see fit.[47] If they are right and a state law permitting assisted suicide is passed that does reach the Supreme Court, the Court, which is inclined to defer to states in these matters, may be reluctant to strike it down.

Judge Hogan's opinion, however, has the merit of dealing with the real world and with the actual difficulties encountered in implementing statutes regarding assisted suicide and euthanasia based on theoretical abstractions. His analysis should be contrasted with the cavalier dismissal by Judge Stephen Reinhardt of the dangers of abuse were assisted suicide to be legalized. Recall that in his opinion for the Ninth Circuit in the Washington case, Judge Reinhardt wrote, "Should an error actually occur it is likely to benefit the individual by permitting a victim of unmanageable pain and suffering to end his life peacefully and with dignity. . . ."[48] The implication seems to be that since the patient is going to die anyway, what's the difference? The presumption that even a mistaken death would be a benefit to any terminally ill person is painfully removed from the needs of terminally ill patients, most of whom want to live as long and as comfortably as they can.

Judge Hogan's ruling had stopped the Oregon law from taking effect. In February 1997, however, the Ninth Circuit

Court of Appeals vacated this ruling on technical grounds, finding that since the law had not been in effect no one had suffered under it, so the plaintiffs had no standing to bring suit. The plaintiffs filed briefs urging the Supreme Court to review this decision, but the Court declined to do so, accepting the argument that the plaintiffs had no standing and leaving the decision in the hands of the Oregon voters.

In a referendum in November 1997, Oregon voters reaffirmed their support for Measure 16. Oregon's actions will encourage advocates of assisted suicide to pursue similar initiatives in other states. Although such initiatives are not likely to pass in most states, the struggle over them becomes an enormous distraction from efforts to improve the quality of end-of-life care.

Crafting a Law

A model proposal put forward in the *Harvard Journal of Legislation* by Charles Baron and eight colleagues from the fields of law, medicine, philosophy, and economics attempted to meet some of Judge Hogan's objections to the Oregon statute. The proposal provides for a review of patient competency by a licensed psychiatrist, clinical psychologist, or psychiatric social worker. It *"allows* patients the opportunity of consulting with a social worker about alternatives to suicide" (emphasis added). It holds physicians legally responsible for following defined guidelines, but protects them if they subjectively have "an honest belief" that they have done so.[49]

The group was divided about permitting euthanasia, but decided not to do so because public perception of the greater voluntariness of assisted suicide would secure greater acceptance of their proposal for assisted suicide. Other than this limitation and the requirement of a consultation regarding competency, the procedures and safeguards of the model proposal are similar to those of the Dutch: the decision must be voluntary, the request must be repeated over time (two weeks in this statute), there must be "unbearable suffering"—although anyone with an incurable condition, not necessarily a terminal illness, who feels that "the accompanying suffering is worse than death," is eligible—alternative treatments that might improve the patient's condition must be discussed, another physician must confirm the diagnosis and prognosis, and the death must be reported as assisted suicide to the authorities.

Clinical depression per se is not a barrier if the patient is deemed to be making a "reasoned decision consistent with his or her long-term values." Although the model's authors recognize that ideally a physician with a close professional relationship with the patient should be involved, if that physician has "ethical constraints" about assisting in the suicide, then another physician should be sought.

The model's authors view the patient as one might a person applying for a license who must meet certain formal requirements and the requirements are not intended to protect the patient so much as the person granting the license, in this case the doctor. In fact, requests for assisted suicide are made out of desperation. It makes a world of difference whether a doctor explores the sources of that desperation, which can usually be relieved, or says, "We can go ahead in two weeks provided you meet these requirements."

The physician most apt to hear more than just a request to die is the patient's regular physician. But in this proposal, if that physician does not think assisted suicide is appropriate, then he or she is said to have "ethical constraints" and the patient is diverted to another physician. The same need to circumvent the family physician who knew the patient best led to the "angels of death" in the Netherlands.

Under the model, if the depressed patient makes a decision for death consistent with his or her values, then this is deemed sufficient to proceed. But such a patient's values may well have included responding to other crises in life with a wish to die. Why should he or she be treated differently because the crisis is physical illness?

Another model proposal for "regulating physician-assisted death," put forth in the *New England Journal of Medicine* by Franklin Miller, Timothy Quill, Howard Brody, John Fletcher, Lawrence Gostin, and Diane Meier, is more forthright in that it calls for legalization of euthanasia as well as assisted suicide. Like the Baron et al. proposal, it recommends the procedures for "competent patients suffering not only from terminal illness" but also for those with "incurable, debilitating disease who voluntarily request to end their lives."[50] The plan of Miller and his colleagues seeks to avoid certain risks of other proposals by mandating that a physician have the patient seen by a palliative care consultant; cases are reviewed after death by an interdisciplinary palliative care committee.

Including euthanasia as well as assisted suicide is seen to eliminate the legal and ethical unfairness of denying the ability to end their lives to those who want to but are physically or psychologically unable to do so without assistance. By refusing to limit assisted suicide and euthanasia to those who are terminally ill, the proposal seeks to avoid the impossible task of determining what exactly is "terminal illness" or the even more impossible task of determining when patients have six months to live. Extending euthanasia beyond patients who are terminally ill to those who are chronically ill avoids the ethical and legal unfairness of denying those who are chronically ill and have longer to suffer whatever "benefits" are made available to those who are terminally ill.

Of course, "incurable debilitating disease" would include conditions like diabetes and arthritis. And the provision that patients do not have to be in the last months of their lives will, as in the Netherlands, encourage requests from patients who are not in great pain but who are fearful of death. As in the cases we have described, their requests for death are likely to be granted with no recognition of their emotional state.

The interdisciplinary palliative care committee, with which the Dutch experimented for ten years and to which cases could be referred for consultation for assisted suicide or euthanasia (see Chapter 3), did stop assisted suicide and euthanasia from being performed in a number of cases. But the committee reviewed cases before death—a procedure Miller and his coauthors find too obtrusive—not after death became a *fait accompli*. In time the Dutch also found the procedure too burdensome and it was dropped.

Miller and his colleagues wish us to feel reassured by the use of a palliative care consultant, saying they had gone beyond the Dutch, who merely require consultation with another physician. The Dutch have and use many such palliative care consultants. Herbert Cohen, who directs a palliative care unit, is a frequent consultant in such cases. My experience suggests that when such consultants are euthanasia advocates they are far more of a danger than the average physician, who is more likely to see assisted suicide or euthanasia as a last resort.

Many Dutch physicians perform euthanasia only a few times in a career, each time with a good deal of anguish. To state that the average Dutch physician performs euthanasia once every two years—a figure that Herbert Cohen likes to cite—is misleading. Such an estimate lumps together the one-half of Dutch physicians who have never performed euthanasia, and those who have done it a few times with euthanasia consultants like Herbert Cohen, who have performed euthanasia between 50 and 100 times, or those like Pieter Admiraal, who are proud to have done it many times that number.[51]

Such consultants seem to believe that controlled death can accomplish wonders and see it as a fairly routine way of dealing with serious illness. Given their outlook, euthanasia practitioners are less apt than other physicians to present their patients with feasible alternatives. In the Dutch euthanasia cases presented to Carlos Gomez, a recurrent theme was the failure to explore such alternatives.[52]

These consultants are seldom qualified to explore the terror of death that many patients feel they can alleviate only by determining the when and how of their death. They often share the belief that if you cannot be fully in control of your life, or if life does not meet your conditions, then you are better off dead. As a result, they may not see how their attitudes predetermine their patients' fate. Moreover, in the proposal of Miller and his colleagues, psychiatric evaluation takes place only if called for by the treating physician or the palliative care consultant.

If assisted suicide and euthanasia were legalized in this country in the manner proposed by the proposal's authors, some cases that meet their criteria would go through the system with the already inadequate "safeguard" of palliative care consultant. Consultants, who are generally also euthanasia advocates, would, as in the Netherlands, be cooperative colleagues, not providers of an independent second opinion. The evidence from both this country and the Netherlands suggests that if psychiatrists are consulted, those interested in doing such consultations would be euthanasia proponents who would limit their evaluations to a determination of competency; enabling the euthanasia to proceed without any deeper psychological inquiry.

Palliative care committees reviewing cases after the fact are apt to behave like the medical tribunals in the Netherlands. After the euthanasia is performed, more emphasis is put on protecting the doctor than on revealing any mistake in judgment.

The proposal uses as its title the misleading and euphemistic "regulating physician-assisted death." "Regulating physician-assisted death" could include many things—adequate pain management, hospice care, withdrawal of futile treatment— that do not involve legislating permission to end the patient's life. "Legalizing euthanasia" would be a more accurate description.

Remarkably, in 1992, only two years before this current proposal, one of Miller's coauthors, Timothy Quill, wrote that while assisted suicide should be legalized, euthanasia should not, because "access to medical care in the United States is too inequitable and doctor-patient relationships too impersonal to tolerate the risks of condoning active voluntary euthanasia."[53] Has access to medical care and the quality of doctor-patient relationships so changed in the past two years?

Although no doctor in this country has yet been convicted of assisting in a suicide, the fear of prosecution is, of course, a central concern of euthanasia advocates. In their proposal, Miller, et al. subscribe to the view that since some physicians perform euthanasia anyhow, legalizing the practice would make them law-abiding and free us of this hypocrisy.

Coauthor Diane Meier now rejects this argument and considers that legalization would create more problems than it would resolve. Her subsequent work, which indicates that a small but significant percentage of physicians are giving medication to end patients lives, sometimes without the consent of patients or families, leads her to believe that if they are willing to break the law as it now stands, they surely will not be constrained by any guidelines. Meier and Miller, who also no longer favors legalization, have coauthored a paper discussing how patient refusal of artificial nutrition and hydration combined with palliative care offers a better way of relieving suffering in intractable cases without the dangers of physicianassisted suicide or euthanasia.[54] Meier's work with dying patients and her observation of the work of other physicians has persuaded her that assisted suicide and euthanasia are not capable of regulation.[55]

Meier's conclusion is borne out by the Dutch experience. Despite their best efforts, the Dutch have been able to get doctors to report only 41 percent of their euthanasia cases (and there is reason from the government-sanctioned studies to question whether all of them are reporting truthfully). Since following the legal guidelines would free from the risk of prosecution Dutch doctors who admit to not reporting most of their cases and the 20 percent of doctors who say that under no circumstances will they do so, it is a reasonable assumption that these doctors are not following the guidelines. The Dutch government-sanctioned research as well as the cases presented to me and to Carlos Gomez bear this out.[56]

Moreover, the cases that come to trial are often the cases that doctors report because they want the courts to sanction actions that would widen the guidelines. They are invariably successful, as Chabot was in getting the Dutch courts to agree that mental suffering was grounds for euthanasia. Legal sanction creates a permissive atmosphere that seems to foster not taking the guidelines too seriously. The notion that those American doctors—who are admittedly breaking some serious laws prohibiting assisting in a suicide—would follow guidelines if assisted suicide were legalized is contradicted by the Dutch experience. Nor is it likely given the failure of American practitioners of assisted suicide to follow elementary safeguards in cases they have published.

Daniel Callahan and attorney-ethicist Margot White reviewed bills introduced in twelve states that would permit assisted suicide; in six states the bills were modeled after the Oregon law. They found that with regard to safeguards concerning informed consent, mental competence, voluntariness, and restriction of eligibility to the terminally ill, all twelve bills had the same failings as the Oregon law or were even worse.

Why is it that there is so little attention given to safeguards designed to protect patients? Callahan and White concluded that the bills appeared to be primarily written for the protection of doctors, not patients.[57]

A law that would at least protect some patients would require an ombudsman to look at the overall situation, including the family, the patient, the doctor, and, above all, the interaction among them prior to the performance of assisted suicide or euthanasia. This would involve an intrusion into the relationship between patient and doctor that most patients would not want and most doctors would not accept.

Without such intrusion before the fact, there is no law or set of guidelines that can protect patients. After euthanasia has been performed, since only the patient and the doctor may know the actual facts of the case, and since only the doctor is alive to relate them, any medical, legal, or interdisciplinary review committee will, as in the Netherlands, only know what the doctor chooses to tell them.

Who Is Most Vulnerable?

The United States is alone among the industrialized democracies in not guaranteeing medical care to large numbers of its population. Without such care, euthanasia would become a forced choice for large numbers of the poor, minority groups, and older people; many of them would be vulnerable to pressure for assisted suicide and euthanasia by family, physicians, hospitals, and nursing homes. In the words of the 1994 report on physician-assisted suicide and euthanasia by the New York State Task Force on Life and the Law:

> The risk of harm is greatest for the many individuals in our society whose autonomy and well-being are already compromised by poverty, lack of access to good medical care,

advanced age, or membership in a stigmatized social group. The risks of legalizing assisted suicide and euthanasia for these individuals, in a health care system and society that cannot effectively protect against the impact of inadequate resources and ingrained social disadvantages, would be extraordinary.[58]

Some awareness of these possibilities may be responsible for the fact that in contrast to younger groups that support euthanasia—56 percent of those in the fifteen to thirty-four age group favor it—it is opposed by 55 percent of those over sixty-five, the presumed beneficiaries of the practice. While a slight majority of whites favor the practice, African-Americans oppose it by more than 2 to 1.[59]

No group is more justifiably concerned about legalization than people with disabilities. When people with disabilities become depressed and suicidal, their condition is mistakenly viewed as the inevitable and untreatable result of their disability. The court battle over legalization has also revealed how many physicians and jurists consider that death is preferable to needing help in eating, bathing, and going to the toilet. Yet large numbers of those who are disabled lead satisfying and productive lives despite needing such help. Given such prejudice, if assisted suicide and euthanasia are given legal sanction, disabled persons are, in disproportionate numbers, likely to be seen as appropriate candidates.

Even the Dutch question where we are going. Virtually all Dutch advocates of euthanasia familiar with the United States, including strong advocates like Herbert Cohen and René Diekstra, see our legalizing euthanasia as unwise for a variety of reasons. From a Dutch perspective, the legal and medical systems of the United States do not foster social harmony but instead pit one profession against the other. They believe that the litigious tendency of American patients would make euthanasia a nightmare for physicians. The Dutch believe their hospitals are not subject to the economic pressure to get rid of terminally ill patients that would be present in this country. In the United States, the relative absence of the family doctor, the core of medical practice in the Netherlands, eliminates what the Dutch perceive as a major source of patient protection. Further contaminating the process in the United States would be the difficulty of preventing the profit motive from making euthanasia and assisted suicide a lucrative business.

The Dutch concern for our welfare has a patronizing quality, implying they are advanced enough as a society to be able to reap the benefits of euthanasia, but we are not. Yet one senses as well that they would be delighted for the United States to legalize euthanasia, since then they would not be so isolated in their position.

As we have seen, having a less adversarial legal system and a more equitable medical system has not protected the Dutch. Depressed patients regardless of economic status are vulnerable there and would be endangered here as well. Those who are terrified of serious illness are also most vulnerable to suicide, assisted suicide, and euthanasia.

The burden of caring for people who are chronically and terminally ill leads to pressure for euthanasia from family and doctors that is not necessarily economic. Margaret Battin, a euthanasia advocate, admits that social acceptance would undoubtedly lead to situations in which families might pressure older members to end their lives, "for the good of all concerned." Although Battin believes the right to suicide must be accepted on philosophical grounds, she is conscious of the "moral quicksand into which this notion threatens to lead us."[60]

If legalization is generally adopted, the pressure for euthanasia is also likely to become internalized so that social acceptance may become a form of coercion. Yale Kamisar asks:

> In a suicide-permissive society, in a climate in which sui-
> cide is the "rational" thing *to* do, or at least a "reasonable"
> option, will it become the unreasonable thing *not* to do?
> The noble thing *to* do? In a society unsympathetic to jus-
> tifying an impaired or dependent existence, a psychologi-
> cal burden may be placed on those who do not think their
> illness or infirmity is reason for dying. The presence of a
> socially approved option becomes a subtle pressure to re-
> quest it.[61]

Ultimately all people who are seriously or terminally ill are
vulnerable. As D. J. Bakker points out, "A very ill or terminally ill patient is completely dependent on others who
through their attitude, gesture, tone of voice, and so on and
so on, can suggest that the patient, even unconsciously, should
ask for euthanasia."[62] Pellegrino sees much of the suffering of
dying patients coming from "being subtly treated as nonper-
sons. The decision to seek euthanasia is often an indictment
against those who treat or care for the patient."[63]

The physician's influence is particularly troublesome. As we
have seen, Dutch doctors who favor euthanasia routinely ask
themselves, "Would I want to live if I were in that situation?"
For those who are not euthanasia advocates, the question
would only be relevant if it were the doctor who was terminally ill. Their attitude, however, is consistent with the admission by Dutch euthanasia advocates that legal acceptance
has encouraged physicians to feel they are best able to make
the decision as to who should live and who should die. Although in theory patient autonomy is the justification for euthanasia, on the evidence of the Dutch experience, practice
belies theory.

Chapter 8

WHO SHOULD DECIDE? COMA AND DEMENTIA

The fear of being kept alive indefinitely in a comatose state has understandably colored our attitudes toward the end of life. Although relatively few people experience this fate, the image of patients dying slowly in an irreversibly comatose condition, referred to as a persistent vegetative state (PVS), and of families suffering the ordeal of watching seems to symbolize our helplessness in the face of foolishly applied medical technology.

Over the past two decades we have developed a medical, ethical, and legal consensus that families or other proxies may authorize the discontinuation of life-sustaining treatment for such patients. Now the opposite situation has emerged as a problem. Some families are insisting that relatives in a persistent vegetative state be kept alive as long as possible. Doctors and hospitals are being asked to provide indefinite care in hopeless cases.

Who should decide whether to use medical treatment to prolong the life of people who are irreversibly comatose or in a state of advanced dementia? Although the Dutch are inclined to give the doctor sole decision-making authority in such cases, that may not be a policy acceptable to most people in the United States.

A case that epitomizes the problems involved was recently argued in a Massachusetts court where a jury acquitted Massachusetts General Hospital and two of its doctors of failure to provide treatment that a patient wanted. The suit was brought by Joan Gilgunn, the daughter of a seventy-two-year-old woman who was comatose and brain-damaged; she was being kept alive by life-support systems at the insistence of her daughter, who was following her mother's wishes. Mrs. Gilgunn was in generally poor health when she entered the hospital for diabetes-related problems and a fractured hip. A few days after admission she began having seizures that could not be immediately controlled with anticonvulsant medication, leaving her brain-damaged and in a coma. Physicians initially followed the family's request that everything possible be done. After several weeks, however, the doctors felt that continuing treatment was futile and, in consultation with the hospital's ethics committee but not the family, weaned the woman from the ventilator; she died soon afterward.

In commenting on the case, Kenneth Praeger points out that prior to the court decision there was no limit to what patients and their families could request of doctors even though the medical outlook was hopeless. He is concerned that scarce critical-care beds are often occupied by patients for whom there is no chance of recovery, that the cost of such care is prohibitive, and that it is unethical to subject "moribund patients to treatments that are painful and disfiguring. In these cases doctors play not God, but Satan."[1]

Praeger is aware of the dangers of inappropriate termination of treatment for patients in a cost-conscious medical system. He wishes to limit the dangers by restricting the definition of futility to treatments for those unconscious patients who have no chance of leaving the hospital alive. He sees those who support the rights of patients to assisted suicide and those who advocate unlimited rights to medical care even when it is futile as having in common the notion that patients should have the right to whatever they want of the medical profession.

There is another side to this question, reflected in the view of Giles Scofield, who is concerned with the exclusive power over dying that physicians seem to be claiming in such cases. As Scofield, who shares with Praeger an opposition to assisted suicide, puts it,

> it is no coincidence that some in the medical profession are seeking immunity for denying patients medically futile treatment at the same time they are seeking immunity for physician-assisted suicide. Although each purports to protect the interests of patients, each is simply about protecting the power and authority of the medical profession by seeing to it that death is completely medicalized.[2]

Alexander Capron is concerned that doctors and the public may be misled by the *Gilgunn* case into thinking that the law has placed the decision about which treatments to use with critically ill patients solely in physicians' hands.[3] He cautions us that, in the absence of review by an appellate tribunal, a jury verdict has limited legal significance. Confounding the issue was the disagreement among the Gilgunn family members about both the use of the respirator and possible cardiopulmonary resuscitation (CPR).

Since the part of the case that went to the jury dealt with Joan Gilgunn's claim of emotional suffering, it did not address the hospital's failure to provide procedures to resolve the dispute between the family and the physicians. Nor did it deal with the hospital's decision to stop treatment before the dispute was resolved in court, which runs counter to the recommendations of the presidential commission that addressed the issue of withdrawal of treatment. Finally, the judge's instruction to the jury that treatment was futile if it did not provide cure made the jury decision a virtual certainty.

Capron sees the abrogation of power by the physicians in the case as exacerbated by an abandonment of the patient, accompanied by an absence of protective legal guidelines that could have the potential for much future harm. He is concerned with a broader spectrum of cases than comatose patients like Mrs. Gilgunn. In the area of coma many physicians might agree with the conclusions of the doctors in the *Gilgunn* case, but could hardly agree with the arbitrary treatment of the Gilgunn family by the doctors and the hospital.

A presidential commission and court decisions beginning with the Karen Quinlan case and extending through that of Nancy Beth Cruzan have helped develop the consensus that it is acceptable to withdraw treatment from patients in a persistent vegetative state. Reliable criteria for the determination of PVS and clarification of the conditions with which it can be confused—established by the Multi-Society Task Force on PVS—have helped.[4]

We need now to reach a consensus as to how to proceed when families and doctors disagree on the decision to withdraw treatment from comatose patients. Unless the public is involved in developing this consensus, fear of the medical profession's control of these deaths will increase. Families like the Gilgunns will be on their own; the care patients receive will be subject to arbitrary, varying, and inconsistent hospital policies.

A consensus on withdrawing futile treatment in PVS patients has been compared with the consensus that was reached when the cessation of brain function rather than the cessation of heart and lung function became the criterion of death. It will take longer to achieve if only because in a persistent vegetative state patients may look alive. In brain death not just the upper brain but the brain stem and hypothalamus have ceased to function, so the heart will soon stop. In a persistent vegetative state all the higher brain functions are lost but the brain stem and hypothalamus function, so the heart and lungs can continue working and the patient may survive for many years with artificial feeding. The person is gone, but it takes time for the family to realize it. Even the concept of brain death, which we now take for granted, shocked the public before it learned its meaning. When it did, there were virtually no disagreements between doctors and the families of patients.

To the judge in the *Gilgunn* case, futility meant inability to cure; Kenneth Praeger sees it as applying if treatment will not enable a comatose patient to leave the hospital. Others see it applying when treatment cannot end dependence on intensive medical care. The defense in the *Gilgunn* case introduced a paper by the American Thoracic Society that recognizes futility when intervention is unlikely to result in "meaningful survival of the patient"; survival in a permanent state of unconsciousness is considered not to be meaningful.

Calling treatment "futile" when it will not lead to hospital discharge or the end of medical dependency implies that short-term survival is not a goal worth pursuing. Patients, families, and physicians may not agree with placing this value judgment on the remaining days, weeks, or months of life.[5] In these situations, physicians and other caregivers are consistently poor judges of patients' wishes concerning intensive care.[6]

The concept of futility, as physician-ethicists Robert Truog, Allan Brett, and Joel Frader point out, permits physicians to limit therapy without acknowledging that value judgments, the need to allocate scarce resources, and unspecified questions of statistical probability concerning the effectiveness of treatment underlie the decision to withdraw treatment.[7] All these questions need to be considered, as do others ranging from what constitutes the best interests of the patient to whether physicians should be asked to continue what they may see as inappropriate or unethical treatment. Truog, Brett, and Frader conclude that "the problem with futility is that its promise of objectivity can rarely be fulfilled. The rapid advance of the language of futility into the jargon of bioethics should be followed by an equally rapid retreat."[8]

We are, of course, not close to a consensus when doctors want to withdraw futile treatment, families do not, and the patient is not in a persistent vegetative state. The complexity and ambiguity of such end-of-life decisions is illustrated by the story a colleague related about his father's death. Dying of lung cancer, his father gave strict instructions to his son and daughter—both doctors—and to his wife that he wished never to be put on a respirator. While undergoing chemotherapy in the hospital he developed pneumonia, from which his doctor thought he could recover with the help of a respirator. The family went along with the recommendation, and the father was intubated.

The father recovered from the pneumonia, no longer needed the respirator, and lived for some additional months. During this period my colleague asked his father if he regretted that the respirator had been used and was told no, and when he asked whether his father would want it used again in a similar situation, the answer was an unequivocal yes.

By some definitions the father's treatment could be considered futile, since it would not end his dependence on intensive medical care, nor would it restore him to a "meaningful" life. Suppose a different doctor regarding the treatment as futile did not want to employ it and the family did. Do we want to give the doctor the exclusive authority to make such a decision?

While PVS is a rare fate, dementia, most frequently from Alzheimer's disease but also from cerebral vascular failure, is common. Over 11 percent of those over sixty-five develop Alzheimer's disease.[9] If one lives long enough and escapes cancer and cardiac disease, the probability of developing dementia increases dramatically.

Those who have witnessed the last stages of Alzheimer's in relatives—who are unaware of themselves and their surroundings, bedridden, incontinent, and unable to eat or even swallow—never forget the experience. The desire to avoid this condition is one of the principal fears of many with regard to the end of their own lives.

Alzheimer's disease usually progresses slowly, so that the individual may have many years of gradually decreasing functional capacity after the diagnosis is made. Some individuals shorten the final stages of Alzheimer's by advance directives indicating that they wish nothing but palliative care for the various medical problems that afflict terminally ill Alzheimer's patients. They may refuse to be tube-fed if they stop eating.

Although many people feel that they would not want to live if they became demented, even the Dutch have been reluctant to sanction an advance request for euthanasia to be implemented when dementia occurred. Ronald Dworkin claims that respect for the integrity and autonomy of the person before that person became demented requires us to honor such requests even if the now demented individual seems happy and wants to live. He reasons that the demented person no longer has an integrated self, nor is that person capable of genuine autonomy. So while it may seem cruel to end the life of a person who seems to want to live and to be enjoying the limited pleasures of a restricted existence, respect for the earlier autonomous person demands it.[10]

People change throughout life; competence is not so clearly

defined a condition as Dworkin presumes. What if the person writing such an advance directive changed his mind in one month? Or six? It would need more than a King Solomon to know when such an advance directive should go into effect. Although virtually no one who has seen partly demented people enjoying their lives is going to put them to death against their will, Dworkin's attempt to circumvent the fact that the two persons he describes occupy the same body highlights some of the dilemmas we face in dealing with Alzheimer's disease and other dementias.

The strange mixture of lucidity and confusion that characterizes Alzheimer's disease was brought home to me by a recent patient. A successful attorney, Robert had retired at the age of seventy-four partly at the urging of his family and perhaps because he sensed that he was no longer able to function as well as he once had. When his wife asked me to see him a year later, she was concerned about his being depressed, which she felt might be contributing to the memory difficulties he was having.

Robert could discuss intelligently and empathically a variety of subjects and spoke with love and affection about his wife and daughters, but was at the same time more mentally confused and more severely depressed than his family realized. He could come to my office by himself but would have difficulty finding his way out of the office. He could discuss the problems of his immediate family while referring to himself as eighty-seven years old and his parents (long dead) as alive and in their nineties.

Although Robert had a number of interests such as music, literature, and walking, he was unable to enjoy pursuing them because of his mood. Depressed by the loss of his faculties, he was preoccupied with suicide. He planned to exsanguinate himself by sticking a large needle into one of his veins and letting the blood run out. It was clear, however, that he felt that life had already been drained from him. He was put on antidepressant medication, and I saw him weekly for psychotherapy.

He had a recurrent dream in which he was traveling in some foreign land but did not recognize himself. He was then working, but not as an attorney, and was trying to help a new employee who did not know what was expected of him. The dream seems to reflect the divided image of himself as observer of his strange situation and hard-to-recognize self. He was able with minimal help to comprehend the dream and derived great relief from talking about his difficulties in knowing who he now was or what he could or should expect of himself.

He felt that since his illness his wife treated him overprotectively and somewhat condescendingly. She had never been a good listener, but he had regarded that as a foible in a woman he loved and who loved him. Now he tended to take her not listening as a sign of lack of respect for his opinions because of his mental decline. She also had a tendency to test and correct his memory in a way that made him tense. Meetings I had with her alone and with the two of them together seemed to improve the situation. He was gradually able to set new goals for himself with regard to his interests and to take pleasure in sharing music and speed-walking with his wife. His depression lifted and his preoccupation with suicide disappeared. He enjoyed our sessions, and the fact that he sensed that I did too was important to him. There was an admirable nobility to the way in which he dealt with his situation. Of course, his ultimate prognosis is poor; yet he and his wife were now deriving enjoyment from their lives together while having time to come to terms with the future.

I can best illustrate the medical and social problems involved in the care of Alzheimer's patients as the disease progresses with the recent death of my own mother. I grew up at a time when you did not discuss with your mother her wishes for terminal medical care. In the absence of any instruction to the contrary, I felt my responsibility was to see to it that she received the best medical care possible. At eighty-four, although in good physical health, she was beginning to lose her mental faculties and could no longer be cared for at home.

In a nursing home during the next nine years, she deteriorated slowly. At one period she was depressed, seemingly at the realization that she was losing her faculties. Later she did not recognize me and I had to introduce myself anew at each visit, but she still showed some responsiveness and grew more cheerful during a visit and, according to the nurses, remained so afterward. My family and I have a poignant memory of her during this period. After my younger son played a song for her on the guitar, she smiled, could not find the words to praise him, and said in an affectionate tone, "That was terrible." As her faculties failed further and she became more and more oblivious to her surroundings, she seemed less depressed. In her ninety-second year, however, she stopped talking, ate little, slept most of the day, and was nonresponsive when awake.

One Sunday, we were called to the nursing home because she had developed pneumonia, with high fever and difficulty breathing. Although a doctor at the home had administered antibiotics, and I preferred that she continue to be treated in the nursing home, he felt he could not treat her there, adding that on a Sunday no pulmonary consultant was available to see her. She was transferred to a hospital and was given intravenous fluids in the emergency room. I spoke by phone with the attending physician who had seen her and left; he sounded annoyed at receiving such a case on a Sunday night. He told me that she would probably not survive the night, would certainly not do so without a respirator, and probably should be allowed to die. I had one minute to decide whether to permit her to be intubated and put on a respirator, which I did. She was transferred to an intensive care unit, and subsequently a naso-gastric tube was inserted to feed her.

She seemed to be in great distress during this period. Her pneumonia subsided, but without the respirator she could not breathe strongly enough to get rid of carbon dioxide. After a week her doctor suggested a tracheostomy and then a gastrostomy to make her more comfortable and reduce the danger of complications. They were done, and she did indeed seem more comfortable. She gained weight, and seemed to be sleeping constantly but peacefully, although she would respond to the pain of an injection by opening her eyes slightly. She looked better than she had in the past two years.

Her condition seemed to have stabilized, so she was transferred off the intensive care unit, but could not be returned to the nursing home while on a respirator. Her improvement was illusory and short-lived. After a relatively calm week her respiratory difficulties worsened. She required 100 percent oxygen to breathe; her X-rays showed a recurrence of the pneumonia. She developed a paralytic ileus and could not absorb food. She could have been fed intravenously, but at the doctor's suggestion and with my concurrence this was not done. It was decided to simply see to it that she had enough fluid. She died within a few days.

Many questions could be raised about her treatment. Should she have been given antibiotics? Should she have been transferred to the hospital? Should she have been intubated? Should the nasogastric tube have been inserted? Should the respirator have been disconnected when she recovered from the pneumonia? Should the tracheostomy and the gastrostomy have been performed? Should intravenous feeding have been introduced when she could no longer absorb food through her abdomen?

I learned how subjective are the decisions made when confronted with death. Had the nursing home doctor not seemed so anxious to be free of responsibility for my mother I might have resisted transferring her to the hospital. If the attending doctor who saw her in the emergency room had not conveyed an anxious sense of wanting to end the problem by letting her die, without knowing much about her or her underlying condition, or had he been willing to talk with me in person instead of by phone, I would have trusted him more. Instead both he and the nursing home doctor aroused in me an impulse to protect my mother that may or may not have been in her best interest. It was only after she had been on the ward and I felt compassion on the doctor's part, reflected in his recommendation that since we had decided to treat her the tracheostomy and gastrostomy would make her more comfortable, that I felt able to agree not to feed her intravenously.

Initially I told myself that all of my decisions were determined by not having a health care proxy, but I realized that was not true. If I had felt strongly that it was not humane to keep her alive, I would not have consented to her transfer to the hospital, or had she been transferred before I was contacted, I would not have authorized the use of the respirator in the emergency room. The doctors in the emergency room had left that decision up to me, although they were not entitled to do so since New York law requires evidence of a patient's wishes before a surrogate is allowed to decide whether to not initiate or to withdraw medical treatment. In the structured atmosphere of the intensive care unit, her doctor explained to me later, we could not have disconnected the respirator even if we wished to, since that violation of law would have been noticed and challenged.

On some level I suspect that my mother would have wished

to die sooner than we allowed. I know that transferring her to the hospital was partly motivated by my not being ready to accept her death. Despite her obliviousness, the time I spent saying goodbye to her in the hospital meant a great deal to me. I also know that had she known I needed that time she would have told me to take it. I had not realized that at her age she was likely to remain permanently on the respirator or that her illness and treatment would hasten her mental deterioration so that she could not be roused during her thirty days in the hospital.

I do not claim that my decisions were right or wise. When I asked the attending physician after my mother's death what he would have done had it been his mother, he replied that he probably would not have intubated her. On the other hand, I do not find that I regret my decisions or think that I would have done things differently. I do regret that most of my decisions were made in a state of urgency. I wished in retrospect that I had had a calm conversation with the physician in which the likely consequences of the treatment we were undertaking were spelled out. I wished that long before the pneumonia crisis I had discussed with the doctor the possibilities that awaited my mother. Such a conversation would have led me to seek a health care proxy from her while she was still competent and to ascertain her wishes regarding medical treatment. Such conversations should probably be mandatory nursing home policy.

As the population ages, we will be forced to address the social and economic considerations that play a part in determining the medical care we provide demented patients. Society will not be willing or able to afford indefinite life-support for large numbers of patients who are oblivious to their surroundings, but neither should we be willing to let helpless people die without palliative care.

At what point in advanced dementia would one restrict the

medical care provided? I suspect that my mother's doctors went as far with her as any group of physicians would agree to go. We will need a medical consensus to crystallize a social consensus as to what is acceptable in such situations.

Social consensus makes it easier for the individual to know what to expect. It makes it easier for families to forgo futile treatment that they otherwise might feel obliged to provide. Although this would not stop those who are able and willing to pay any cost for treatment deemed futile, they too might feel less pressure to do so. Oregon can be criticized for hastily adopting an ill-conceived law embracing assisted suicide; in dealing with the allocation of Medicaid funds, however, the state utilized public hearings that permitted extensive community participation in deciding what treatments would be covered. The success of the Oregon plan owes much to its widespread acceptance by the residents of the state, which resulted from their sense of participation in achieving a social consensus.

No consensus, of course, can substitute for the need for doctors to discuss with families the alternatives in an individual case; families need the assurance they are doing the right thing. The guidelines provided by such consensus, however, will encourage this communication and make it far more useful.

Social consensus achieved through public discussion is a powerful and necessary but underutilized tool. Withdrawal of treatment for comatose or demented patients involves ethical, legal, and medical considerations that must reflect community values; it will take more than doctors and hospitals acting alone to make social policy regarding such decisions.

Chapter 9

CARING BEYOND CURE

Not long ago I received a letter from a California woman in her eighties who was not terminally ill but was concerned about how she might be treated when she was. She believed that in ten or fifteen years we could establish a level of care for terminally ill people that would make euthanasia unnecessary, but, she asked, "What about me, what should I and others like me do now to protect ourselves?" This woman's concern—I'll call her Mrs. L—is certainly warranted.

In fact, under current law she can protect herself, though it is not easy. The necessary first steps she must take to manage the final phase of life are not widely known or readily available. What should Mrs. L do now?

A practical first step would be to prepare advance directives—a living will and a health care proxy—stipulating what she would want done should she become incapable of making decisions. She can bring the same foresight to planning for the end of life that she brought to her earlier life. Mrs. L can acquire standard forms for California from her doctor, from her county medical society, or from Choice in Dying, a New York–based organization that pioneered the adoption of advance directives and keeps on file the forms and explanatory instructions for every state. Although hospitals are obliged to inquire if a patient has prepared an advance directive and to make forms available on request, by the time hospitalization is required, a patient may be too ill to consider the matter carefully. Advance directives are simple to prepare, and do not require the services of a lawyer or a notary.

The "California Declaration"—the state's version of the living will—is a one-page document. The basic substance is contained in one long sentence:

> If I should have an incurable and irreversible condition that has been diagnosed by two physicians and that will result in my death in a relatively short time without the administration of life-sustaining treatment or has produced an irreversible coma or persistent vegetative state, and I am no longer able to make decisions regarding my medical treatment, I direct my attending physician, pursuant to the Natural Death Act of California, to withhold or withdraw treatment, including artificially administered nutrition and hydration, that only prolongs the process of dying or the irreversible coma or persistent vegetative state and is not necessary for my comfort or to alleviate pain.[1]

On the form, Mrs. L can list specific treatments she may not want, such as cardiac resuscitation, mechanical respiration, or antibiotics. Or she may write other instructions such as "I do not want to be placed in a nursing home," or "I want to die at home," or "I want maximum pain relief even if it may hasten my death," or, conversely, "I want all life-prolonging treatments that might be effective."

She must sign the document in the presence of two witnesses, at least one of whom must not be a beneficiary of her estate and neither of whom can be health care providers. If Mrs. L is a resident of a nursing home, one of the witnesses must be a state-designated patient advocate or ombudsman. She should give copies of the document to her doctor and to anyone else who might become involved in her health care, such as relatives, close friends, or a health care proxy. She should have photocopies available for the records of any nursing home or hospital she may enter.

Why should Mrs. L have a health care proxy in addition to a living will? No living will can anticipate all the possible complications of illness that may require on-the-spot decisions by someone who can adapt Mrs. L's wishes to the current situation. Deciding when the time has come to implement advance directives is such a major decision. Her proxy, like her doctor, must be a person whom she trusts, with whom she can talk, and who is prepared to act in accord with her wishes.

In California, Mrs. L can designate a health care agent or proxy by signing a document known as a "Durable Power of Attorney for Health Care." The proxy can be a family member or close friend, but cannot be her attending physician or someone connected with a health care facility. On the proxy form Mrs. L can also make specific requests or place limitations on what the proxy should decide. She can appoint a substitute proxy to fill in if the person she appoints is unavailable at the appropriate time. She can have the document witnessed by a notary, or she can sign in the presence of two adult witnesses, neither of whom can be her proxy, her doctor or other health care provider, or an operator of a health care facility. At least one of the witnesses must not be a relative or a beneficiary of her estate. If she is a resident of a nursing home, just as with the living will, one of the witnesses must also be a patient advocate or ombudsman.[2]

Mrs. L can revoke the health care proxy at any time by notifying her proxy either orally or in writing. Although California law states that she can revoke the living will at any time and in any manner, if she decides to do so, it is advisable for her to put her revocation in writing.

The laws governing living wills and health care proxies differ slightly from state to state. In New York, for example, the living will is authorized by law created by the New York courts, not by statute, so there are no specific requirements for its use. Most people follow the legal requirement that exists in New York for the health care proxy, that is, that the will be witnessed by two adults (a notary cannot substitute). Although New York law does not prohibit relatives or estate beneficiaries from being witnesses, it is not advisable to use them for this purpose. It is wise to add a statement to the New York health care proxy stating, "My proxy knows my wishes concerning artificial nutrition and hydration." The statement is necessary because of the specific provision in New York law that requires your proxy to be able to state that he or she knows your wishes on this matter.

To improve the effectiveness of advance directives the American Medical Association and the Medic Alert Foundation, a nonprofit emergency medical information service, have created a national repository for advance directives. A standardized medical directive form is being mailed to every practicing physician in the country. Once patients have discussed their end-of-life care preferences with their physician and named a health-care proxy, the information will become part of their medical records and will be filed in a central repository filed with Medic Alert. Participating patients will wear a bracelet indicating that there is an advance directive on file. Should patients be in a situation where they are unable to speak for themselves, the directive can be read, faxed, or E-mailed to any location.

Living wills and health care proxies are only a beginning. If Mrs. L wants to make sure that good palliative care is available—care for relief of symptoms when cure is no longer possible, practicable, or desired—she should inquire about hospice programs in her area. The modern hospice movement, initiated in the 1960s in England, is gradually humanizing death by addressing the dying patient's emotional, social, and spiritual as well as physical needs. In a sensitive account of their experiences, home hospice care nurses Maggie Callanan and Patricia Kelley demonstrate how the hospice approach combines compassionate care with sophisticated palliative medicine. One of their stories illustrates how enabling patients to express their fears about dying and to communicate them to their families can provide relief that makes palliative care and a peaceful death possible:

Laura, who was dying of a colon cancer that had spread to her liver, was being cared for by her husband, Joe. One morning the hospice nurse found her restless and preoccupied, while Joe was agitated at her uncharacteristic behavior. Laura told the nurse, "It's time to get in line." Exploration revealed that Susan—her daughter of a previous marriage who had died many years earlier—was in line but that Joe could not go in line with her. Laura felt she was getting ready to die soon; while comforted by the thought of being reunited with Susan, she was concerned that Joe, who was dependent on her, was not prepared for her death and would have trouble managing without her. Only when the nurse was able to encourage Joe to discuss with Laura how he planned to manage after she was gone did Laura's restlessness and Joe's agitation cease; Laura died peacefully a few days later.[3]

Good palliative care is now being implemented in many medical settings. It is strongly associated, however, with hospice programs, sometimes in a residential facility dedicated to caring for those who are dying, more often in a formal pro-gram designed to provide palliative care in the patient's own home.[4] The patient's primary physician and a primary hospice nurse will most often coordinate the patient's care; the re-sources of a team that includes social workers, nurses, volun-teers, clergy, and physician consultants can be called upon when needed. Unlike a residential hospice, home hospice does not provide round-the-clock supervision; a large portion of the responsibility for the patient's care is placed on friends and relatives. If Mrs. L wants to die at home, as most people do, she should discuss with friends or relatives, well in advance, whether they will be available to help with her care.

Even if Mrs. L is among the small fraction of patients whose suffering cannot be relieved, sedation—with barbiturates if necessary—is now a medical, ethical, and legal option. She should make sure that her doctor would provide this option. If a patient knows that a doctor is committed to relieving suf-fering by sedation, the knowledge itself may provide the re-lief that makes the use of sedation unnecessary.[5]

Perhaps most important for Mrs. L is to find a doctor who can assure her that he will be with her to the end and see to it that she does not suffer unduly. Her physician must respect her wishes, whether for aggressive treatment or for palliative care; he must tell her everything necessary to enable her to make an informed choice between the two approaches.

Mrs. L needs a physician who will treat her as a person, not as a disease; a physician who understands pain but realizes that suffering is a complex social and psychological phenomenon that can include physical pain but is not limited to it.[6] Suffer-ing originates in severe distress that threatens the intactness of the person; pain is just one such threat. Pain is more apt to cause suffering if it is out of control, if it is overwhelming, if its source is unknown, or if its meaning is frightening. A typ-ical example reported by Dr. Eric Cassell of Cornell University Medical College, who helped educate physicians about the nature of pain and suffering, is that of a woman who could control the pain in her leg with small amounts of codeine when she believed it was sciatica but needed much more medicine when she learned her pain was caused by malignant disease.

Cassell described terminally ill cancer patients whose suffering could be relieved by demonstrating that their pain really could be controlled; they would then tolerate the pain without medication, preferring to avoid the side effects of the analgesics.[7] We now know that giving analgesic medicine to patients at regular intervals rather than waiting for their pain to intensify provides better relief for chronic pain. Even our recent discovery that antidepressant medication can be effective in relieving otherwise intractable pain suggests the complexity of the perception of pain.

Cassell saw doctors as often unable to relieve suffering because they were trained to deal only with the physical aspects of personhood. To paraphrase Cassell, before he can relieve suffering, a physician must understand that a person has personality and character, a past, ties to others, a cultural background, regular patterns of behavior, a private life, a perceived future, and a transcendent dimension, i.e., a life of the spirit as well as a body. With this in mind, Cassell says, we can "realize how someone devoid of pain, even devoid of physical symptoms, may suffer. People suffer from what they have lost of themselves in relation to the world of objects, events, and relationships."[8]

Therefore, Mrs. L needs a physician able to understand the personal meaning of illness to her, with whom she can discuss her concerns before she is terminally ill. She should not be afraid to ask her physician how he will feel about caring for her when she is dying. What she requires demands much from a doctor and tests the ability to extend the humanistic traditions of medicine into the final phase of life. How does this work in practice?

Dr. Carlos Gomez, of the University of Virginia School of Medicine, reports the case of a forty-two-year-old white male, HIV-positive for six years, who was seen in an AIDS clinic one month after he had been hospitalized for staph pneumonia.[9] He subsequently required a respirator in breathing and, during the course of his intensive care unit (ICU) stay, was found to have a widespread bacterial infection associated with AIDS, a low platelet count, and a cystic lung infection that was also AIDS-related. His ICU course was complicated by two episodes of blood infections with a drop in blood pressure lasting about ninety minutes to two hours. He recovered from both of those episodes and was successfully removed from the respirator, but developed painful inflammatory deterioration of the nerves in his arms and legs.

When first seen in the clinic this young man was lethargic, emaciated, and wheelchair-bound. The physician was able to lift him from the wheelchair to the examination table. The patient complained bitterly of pain in his hands, shins, and feet. He also complained of difficulty sleeping, although several times during the examination he fell asleep. His sister, who was present during the examination, expressed concern that the patient was overmedicated. He apparently took pain medications and tranquilizers at will in seeking relief.

Two of the pain medications given to the patient on discharge from the hospital were discontinued, and a lower dose of gradual-release morphine sulphate was prescribed. He was also given morphine elixir for breakthrough pain. The tranquilizer he had been given was gradually eliminated, and he was given medication to help him sleep. Arrangements were made for his sister to count the pills he took.

Two weeks after the initial assessment, the patient appeared more alert, but still complained of severe pain and was unable to get around without the wheelchair. At this point, he raised the issue of suicide, saying he did not want to live this way. An intensive discussion with the patient and his sister ensued. The patient expressed his terror of dying alone, specifically during the work day when his sister was away from home. He also felt trapped in the wheelchair and was afraid he would be in pain with no access to transportation. Each of these issues was addressed: the physician gave the patient his pager number and his home phone number, and told him to call anytime that he felt in crisis; the morphine was increased; and the patient was started on a corticosteroid in the hope it would help relieve his peripheral nerve inflammation while elevating his mood. He was also started on antidepressant medication.

The patient called about three times in the intervening period, basically to ascertain if the physician would respond promptly. Each time the physician was able to return the call within five minutes of the patient's page. During the next clinic visit, the patient looked markedly improved. He had gained about five pounds, "because I eat like a horse all the time." He was sleeping better at night and was more alert during the day, and with the exception of some mild gastrointestinal upset after he took the corticosteroid, he tolerated his medicines well.

About two weeks later, the patient came in on an emergency basis with a complaint of shortness of breath. He had fluid in his lungs and swollen arms, legs, and face, probably secondary to the corticosteroids. Rather than tapering the corticosteroids, he was given a diuretic and told to adjust the dose, with his sister's help, to the symptoms. He went home, and over the course of the next three days he discharged the fluid and became essentially asymptomatic, remaining on a daily dose of the diuretic.

About six months later, the patient came into the clinic and said, "I've got something to show you." He got up from his wheelchair, walked into the examining room, and hopped up on the table. He said he had been working on a physical therapy program at home, which consisted of hydrotherapy and exercise in his sister's pool. He had gained weight, and his fluid problem remained under control. He said that he "wanted to simplify" his life, stopped his AIDS medication, and was only going to use those medicines that he felt would improve the quality of his life. When informed that the long-term use of corticosteroid could mask other symptoms, especially fever and abdominal pain, the patient said the corticosteroid had given him a new lease on life and was worth the risk.

Approximately ten months after starting the corticosteroid, the patient came to the hospital emergency room complaining of "black, tarry stools" and saying that he felt "like I'm going to die." His blood pressure was low and his abdomen was distended. An emergency endoscopy showed a small perforation along the posterior aspect of the stomach. On hearing this the patient smiled and said, "I guess that's it." He was admitted to a subacute ward of the hospital, started on a morphine drip, and given his corticosteroids intravenously. He was in no pain and died quietly twelve hours after coming to the emergency room.

This man's emotional and physical needs had been heard and met by a doctor and a sister who cared for and valued him. His acceptance of his death was undoubtedly influenced by the meaningful ten months that had been added to his life by a physician who understood that he needed and wanted more than a literal response to his request for assisted suicide.

Psychosocial interventions of this kind are needed not just for the patient but to help relieve the burden on the patient's family. An improvement in the family atmosphere can make a crucial difference in determining whether a patient cares about living.

———

Work at Memorial Sloan-Kettering Cancer Center with the families of terminally ill patients demonstrates how much the families themselves are suffering: from grief, from concern over inadequate resources to carry out home care, or from unrealistic expectations that members of the family have for what they should be able to do to relieve the patient. All of these contribute to what palliative care specialists have come to know as the "profoundly fatigued family."[10] Meetings with a patient's relatives are critical in helping family members come to terms with what they should expect of themselves, each other, or health care providers.

How profoundly burdened families can be was demonstrated by Danuta Wasserman, professor of psychiatry at the Karolinska Institute in Stockholm, who studied the response of relatives to the suicide attempts of elderly patients with somatic illnesses. Family members, overwhelmed by what they felt were the relentless needs of the patient, were likely to delay calling the doctor, to urge nonresuscitation of the patient, and to have expressed death wishes to the patient. Once help from social welfare agencies was arranged, family attitudes changed and the patients wanted to live.[11]

Gomez created an atmosphere that encouraged his patient to play an active role in the decisions regarding his treatment. Several decades ago in two books recounting his recovery from a potentially lethal connective tissue disease and later a heart attack, writer and editor Norman Cousins helped make the public and the medical profession aware of how critical a patient's participation was in his or her treatment. Elevation of mood, the will to live, and the outcome of treatment are all affected.[12]

Gomez also enabled his patient with AIDS to express his fears about death; he listened to them carefully and responded effectively. Patients do not readily express such fears. In studies of assisted suicide and euthanasia, most of which have been done in the Netherlands, physicians reported that patients' reasons for requesting euthanasia were loss of dignity, pain, not wishing to die in an "unworthy way," being dependent on others, and being tired of living. The fear of death itself is not mentioned; Pieter Admiraal was the exception among Dutch doctors in recognizing that such fear underlies other concerns in euthanasia patients. The reticence of patients to speak of their fear of death is heightened by their perception of doctors as unwilling or unable to deal with such fear.

Patients' silence and attempts to deny their fear only increase their desperate feeling that their lives are out of their control. Their fear and their desperation are too often reinforced by doctors' anxieties over being powerless in the face of terminal illness. Choosing death and determining its time and place seem to both to offer a solution.

Male patients with AIDS have a particularly high risk for suicide,[13] but cancer sufferers, because of their sheer numbers and the frequent chronicity of their illness, are the patients who make most requests for euthanasia.[14] Although most cancer patients do not express a wish to die, a significant minority express a transitory wish for death.[15] The small number with a persistent wish to die are invariably suffering from a clinical depression.[16] Our greater experience in treating patients with cancer and the generally better care provided these patients have enabled us to document how frequently those cancer patients requesting euthanasia change their minds when provided with good palliative care, including treatment for their depression.[17] The following case reported by Dr. Kathleen Foley, chief of the pain service in the department of neurology at the Memorial Sloan-Kettering Cancer Center, illustrates this point.[18]

A sixty-four-year-old woman with advanced lung cancer and severe chest-wall pain requested that she be aided in death.

She was tearful, felt hopeless, and stated that there was no purpose or meaning to her life; she also viewed herself as a burden to her husband. She could not go on and threatened that she would seek assistance from a friend, who had aided her own mother to die, if she was not helped immediately. Her husband viewed the request as a sign of profound depression and requested help to keep her alive. He argued that he could not aid her in death, but felt that he was letting her down by not assisting her. He felt guilty that he could not be more supportive of her and expressed frustration and anger when she kept him awake at night.

After an emergency admission to the hospital, it was determined that the tumor was invading the woman's chest wall. She was treated with a combination of analgesics (morphine and acetaminophen) on a regular basis, initially by the intravenous route, and she underwent a nerve block to interrupt the nerves to her chest wall and reduce her pain. Her pain diminished to the point that she had only mild pain infrequently during the day. She was also started on antidepressants in low doses and agreed to talk with a psychiatrist. Her mood improved rapidly, there was dramatic reduction in her pain, and she began to view her life more positively. She spoke openly about dying but wanted to be alive as long as her pain could be controlled. When asked whether the doctors should have "killed" her when she requested it, she responded with a definite no, recognizing that pain had so depressed her that she could only wish for death.

The woman was discharged from the hospital and lived for another four months with good pain control and renewed energy. She was able to come to closure with her children over some difficult family issues, and died in her own home with her husband caring for her.

Patients who request euthanasia are usually asking in the

strongest way they know for mental and physical relief from suffering. When that request is made to a caring, sensitive, and knowledgeable physician who can assure them that he or she will remain with them to the end and relieve their suffering, most patients no longer want to die. Nothing is more heartening than to see what these physicians are accomplishing with terminally ill patients.

The Exceptional Case

What if a patient is one of that small group whose suffering cannot be relieved by any palliative care measure now available to us? It is now accepted practice—supported by the American Medical Association, the courts, and most churches—that when patients cannot be helped in any other way, they can refuse food and fluids and request sedation. Gomez's AIDS patient eventually required sedation. People must be made aware that this alternative is available, doctors must learn when it is appropriate, and hospitals must ensure that patients will be given such sedation when it is requested and needed.

Euthanasia advocates maintain there is no difference between withholding food and hydration for semiconscious, dying patients and deliberately ending their lives. At a conference on coma patients, a Swedish professor told me the story of his mother's death. He was called to her hospital bedside after she suffered a massive, terminal stroke. He knew that she would not want to exist in a vegetative state. Her doctor placed a bed for him in his mother's room; he kept her lips moist over the period of a day during which she received no nutrition or hydration and was allowed to die. I asked him how he would respond to euthanasia advocates who asked why she should not have been given an injection to speed up the process. He replied, "It would have made no difference to her but it would have made an enormous difference to me and to her doctor."

What about a patient who is terminally ill but not in the last days of life, and requests euthanasia, saying he or she does not want to live with the physical and psychological distress of illness? Palliative care specialists see such patients frequently; so do psychiatrists doing consultation-liaison work in general hospitals. If physicians respond to them empathetically, making it possible for them to discuss their fears of death while addressing their physical suffering, most of these patients regain the desire to live.

What of those who, like Netty Boomsma, say, "I don't want treatment even if you think it will help me; I just want to die"? Or those who can no longer be helped and simply want to end their suffering quickly? Should respect for their wishes require society to legalize assisted suicide and euthanasia?

Given the overwhelming numbers who, if responded to sensitively by a caring and capable physician, will accept relief and will want to live, and given that those who cannot be helped can be sedated and allowed to die, we must recognize that other options are available. To say, however, that people should make out advance directives, designate a health-care proxy, arrange for hospice care, and find a doctor who is willing to see that they do not suffer unduly while dying requires us to admit how difficult this currently is to achieve. Advance directives are sometimes ignored, a suitable health-care proxy may be hard to find, hospice care is often not available, and perhaps only a minority of physicians know how to provide the palliative care needed by dying patients.[19] Moreover, the supportive care and social services needed by families to care for dying patients who do not warrant hospitalization are often unavailable under our present health care system. Patients need foresight, intelligence, assertiveness, and even a little luck to get the kind of care that is required.

The difficulties involved lead many to believe that euthanasia is the answer. On the surface, euthanasia would seem to increase patient autonomy. Since suffering is ultimately subjective, only the patient can judge if it is unbearable. Respect for autonomy becomes the criterion for the right to suicide, and when it does it becomes, as Judge John T. Noonan expressed it in his opinion in the Washington case, "the prerogative of at least every sane adult"—from Netty Boomsma, who was physically healthy, to the Dutch man who was HIV-positive but might have been years away from any symptoms.

Whatever the court's concerns about a slippery slope, patient autonomy would seem to be enhanced. In fact it is not. In practice it is still the doctor who decides whether to perform euthanasia. He can suggest it, not give patients obvious alternatives, ignore patients' ambivalence, and even put to death patients who have not requested it. Euthanasia enhances the power and control of doctors, not patients.

If the Dutch experience teaches us anything, it is that euthanasia brings out the worst rather than the best in medicine. In the name of an illusory and self-righteous compassion for the patient, the decisive role of the physician's needs and values in the decision for euthanasia remains concealed. Instead of expanding patients' choices, euthanasia becomes a seemingly simple solution for a myriad of problems; palliative care languishes as a consequence

Given the inequities in our health-care system and the inadequacies of our care of people who are terminally ill, palliative care would be an even more likely casualty of euthanasia in this country. Euthanasia will become a way for all of us to ignore the genuine needs of terminally ill people. In the words of Dr. Joanne Lynn, director of George Washington University's Center to Improve Care of the Dying, "If society continues not to make caring alternatives available, but allows the option of being killed, then we must not wear blinders to what is really at stake—that is, whether this society prefers to leave dying people so bereft of hope that being killed is to be preferred to living."[20]

The question is often asked whether these requests to die are rational. Although it may be true that no one suffering while confronted with death can be fully rational, that does not mean too much. The question is not whether individual decisions are fully rational but whether it is rational for society to sanction them. One could maintain, as George Bernard Shaw facetiously did about marriage, that "when two people are under the influence of the most violent, most insane, most delusive, and most transient of passions," to require them "to swear that they will remain in that excited, abnormal, and exhausting condition continuously until death do them part" is not rational;[21] it has been in society's interest, however, to sanction marriage.

Wise social policy dictates that a personal choice for euthanasia cannot outweigh all other considerations, including the palliative care now available and the needs of the vast numbers of other patients who, if legalization occurs, will die inappropriately, just as in the Netherlands. To legalize euthanasia would truly be what Daniel Callahan has called "self-determination run amok."[22]

Social Policy

We seem to be the last country to accept that dying is an inevitable part of the aging process, not simply the product of a disease that can be prevented or cured. If patients live long enough and escape heart disease, stroke, cancer, and

Alzheimer's disease, they die without identifiable cause. Physicians are beginning to attribute such death to the aging process rather than to a specific disease.[23] Such a shift in attitude may help us to undo partially what social historian Philippe Ariès has referred to as the "medicalization" of death.[24] It will induce us to put the same effort into helpful palliative care that we expend on the unwise utilization of medical technology.

We need to educate physicians to recognize depression, understand its relation to suicide, and realize that most requests for assisted suicide among those who are terminally ill are motivated by the same impulses that generally lead people to seek suicide. We know that about half of all patients who commit suicide see a doctor in the month prior to the suicide, often requesting treatment for the physical symptoms that frequently accompany depression, such as insomnia, loss of appetite, and loss of energy. Yet the depression that underlies such symptoms too often goes unrecognized.

Physicians need to learn to ask about the psychological symptoms of depression, such as feelings of worthlessness and guilt. Even with patients known to be depressed, it is the rare physician who asks about preoccupation with death and thoughts of suicide. Training physicians to recognize depression and to respond to depressed patients is as important as any other aspect of palliative care.

Physicians also need to learn to distinguish treatable depression from the sadness that is likely to accompany any serious physical illness. Like most suicidal patients, those who are responding to serious or terminal illness are ambivalent about their desire to die. This is particularly true for patients who are not in their last days or weeks. Whether they continue to feel they want to die is very much influenced by the response of those to whom they communicate their despair.

Our knowledge of how to minister to the needs of terminally ill people is one of medicine's finest achievements in the past decade, but dissemination of that knowledge to the average physician has only begun. There is a great deal of evidence that in the United States, as in the Netherlands, doctors are not sufficiently trained in the relief of pain and discomfort in terminally ill patients.[25] Routine palliative care cannot be reserved for palliative care specialists; it must be the province of every physician.

In cancer, which has been most studied, it is clear that most pain can be relieved. Nevertheless, there are obstacles to patients' receiving the relief they require. Kathleen Foley points out that physicians undertreat even the most severe states of pain based on inappropriate fears of heavy sedation.[26] Foley is concerned that knowledge alone does not mean that patients will receive appropriate treatment. Although close to 90 percent of physicians agree that it is sometimes appropriate to give pain medication to relieve suffering even if it may hasten a patient's death, fear of hastening death is a major reason physicians give inadequate doses of pain medication.[27] The conflict between what physicians know and what they do will be erased only when providing palliative care becomes an intrinsic requirement for every physician.

Medical school is the place to confront future physicians with the painful truth that they must develop skill to comfort and help those patients they cannot cure. Medical students can no longer be kept away from dying patients on the grounds that there is nothing they can learn from them; on the contrary, they must be encouraged to learn that communicating with and caring for those who are dying is necessary to truly be a physician.

We need to involve patients more in the decisions relevant to their illnesses. All those who care for terminally ill patients must remind them of their right to refuse or withdraw futile or unwanted treatment. Physicians must be encouraged to discuss with seriously ill patients and their families their wishes regarding terminal illness before the final phase of the illness. In nursing homes such discussion should be mandatory.

Although most people indicate their intention of preparing a living will or designating a health care proxy, fewer than 20 percent say they have actually done so.[28] Some members of the Dutch Voluntary Euthanasia Society sheepishly admitted to me that they had not prepared advance directives. Nor is this so surprising. Many people avoid any kind of will until the birth of children or some serious illness forces them to face to some degree their own mortality.

We need public education courses in how to manage the last phase of life—courses that cover every aspect from aging and terminal illness to living wills and the right to sedation if pain is intractable. Such an educational process will need the involvement of public officials as well as lawyers, ethicists, and doctors.

We need to remove administrative and legal barriers that in many states prevent proper care of terminally ill patients—for example, difficult regulations intended to control narcotic distribution make it impossible for hospitals to acquire narcotics in adequate amounts to provide pain relief for terminally ill patients.

Unless we make address all of these issues, large numbers of terminally ill patients will consider suicide to be their only choice. They may not be able to choose their doctor. If they can, the doctors may not know how to relieve their suffering. If the doctors are knowledgeable, state regulations may make needed medications hard to obtain. If the medications are obtainable, their cost may be prohibitive and managed-care companies may not be willing to pay for them.

The Supreme Court decision encouraged the states to address these issues, ideally through the formation of state commissions that will be devoted to improving the quality of care provided to those who are terminally ill. New York's Attorney General Dennis Vacco, who argued the New York case before the Supreme Court, has made a major contribution to this effort by organizing a Commission on Quality Care at the End of Life, which is addressing virtually every aspect of this care, from changing regulations that constrain the ways in which physicians can treat pain and training physicians in palliative care, to educating the public about their rights and fostering proper reimbursement for end-of-life care.

One of the issues the New York commission is addressing is the enactment of pending legislation[29]—initiated by the New York State Task Force on Life and the Law—permitting relatives and other surrogates to make decisions concerning life-sustaining treatment for patients not competent to do so themselves. New York is one of the only states not to have such a surrogacy law, and the suffering that results as a consequence is considerable. Passage of such a law is a crucial first step toward the commission's larger goals.

Such state commissions could be aided by the creation of a presidential task force that would identify barriers to providing palliative care and would propose ways to overcome them. The state commissions would profit from such guidance in working to develop a consensus on specific guidelines for the care of terminally ill patients as well as on how best to allocate medical resources for palliative care. The absence of such consensus creates confusion for patients, their families, and their physicians.

Another significant factor that will influence the development of high-quality palliative care is the transformation of the American health care system under managed care. In the last few years, the birth pangs of the managed care industry have separated many patients from the doctors who grew to know them and to respect their wishes and values. As the managed care industry matures, their places will be taken by new relationships with primary care physicians. These primary care physicians are the gatekeepers at the core of managed care, and it is they who will have to provide the palliative care to their terminally ill patients.

Will they know what to do? Can managed care plans be persuaded to approve quality palliative care for their patients? They will if the accrediting agencies that set the standards for such plans insist that they do. They will if insurance companies are persuaded that it is in their interest to include palliative care—far less expensive than medicine dominated by life-support systems and ICUs—in their managed care programs. They will if managed care plans catering to the elderly and guaranteeing palliative care are successfully organized.

None of this is likely to happen if managed care plans are presented with the easier and cheaper option of assisted suicide and euthanasia. Whatever danger there is in the power given to physicians under legalization will be multiplied many times if the decisions are made by administrators in managed care companies. Avoiding legalization is but a necessary first step. Ensuring that good palliative care is available to all will require a banding together of physicians, lawyers, ethicists, religious leaders, and senior citizens determined that enlightened care for people who are terminally ill become a priority not just for medicine but for society.

The more people know about the care of those who are terminally ill the less they support legalization.[30] Yet the public is still grossly misinformed. A recent poll indicates that only 61 percent of people are aware that under current law, patients may refuse any and all unwanted treatments. Ten percent of the population believe that the law requires a patient to accept *whatever* treatment a doctor wants to provide.[31] Among physicians, support for euthanasia is strongest among those who are least knowledgeable about palliative care.[32]

Recently I saw a vivid example of how knowledge and experience affect decisions for euthanasia, decisions that are rationalized as growing out of a respect for patient autonomy. At a small international workshop that addressed problems in the care of the terminally ill, two American cases were presented—both discussed earlier in this chapter—in which terminally ill patients requested assisted suicide.

One was Dr. Carlos Gomez's patient who had been confined to a wheelchair with advanced symptoms of AIDS that included cystic lung infection, severe pain due to inflammation of the nerves in his limbs, and marked weight loss. By the appropriate use of steroids, antidepressants, and psychological sensitivity in dealing with his fears of abandonment, he was enabled to gain weight, be free of his pain and his wheelchair, and live an additional ten months, for which he was grateful.

The other was Dr. Kathleen Foley's patient, a woman in great pain due to lung cancer that was invading her chest wall, and who also wished assisted suicide. A nerve block relieved her pain, and she was happy to be able to leave the hospital and live her remaining months at home.

A Dutch ethicist at the meeting asked if raising alternatives to assisted suicide was not paternalistic and did not compromise the patient's autonomy. I later presented these cases to several euthanasia advocates in the Netherlands and in this country. They agreed that the patient had a right to have euthanasia performed in the first case but were not so sure after they heard the actual outcome. In the second case, aware that a nerve block could provide relief, most would not perform euthanasia. They felt free to ignore patient autonomy when they knew how to help the patient.

Patient autonomy was in essence the rationale for assisted suicide when doctors felt helpless and did not know what else to do. This seems a powerful argument for educating doctors, not for legalizing assisted suicide,

There are some who try to assure themselves that what happened in the Netherlands would not happen here in the United States. The laws proposed by euthanasia advocates in various states in this country, however, do not protect patients any more than the Dutch laws and guidelines; the cases presented by Drs. Kevorkian and Quill and organizations like Compassion in Dying demonstrate the same abuses seen in Dutch cases. And Dutch doctors are not so different from our own. Since most doctors, even if they support euthanasia, refuse to become involved themselves, large numbers of cases will go to specialists who are believers in the virtues of euthanasia and are less inclined or able to find better alternatives.

Nor is it possible to regulate what those doctors do with patients. Carlos Gomez and I went to the Netherlands at different times and with totally different perspectives, since he is a palliative care specialist and I am a psychiatrist. Yet after hearing detailed cases of euthanasia presented by Dutch physicians, we independently came to the same conclusion: it is not possible to sanction and regulate euthanasia within any prescribed guidelines.[33]

To normalize euthanasia and assisted suicide as social policy is to offer an illusory solution that will only usher in new and worse difficulties. Institutionalizing controlled death in effect enshrines the need for control as a greater value than humanity in dying. Some years ago, after seeing so many people respond to the knowledge of serious or terminal illness with a desire for immediate death, I speculated that if life were so structured that people knew that they would die on their eighty-fifth birthday but would live in good health up to that time, many would probably kill themselves months or years early to avoid anxiety over the inevitability of their fate and their lack of control over it.

Subsequently, I had occasion to read *The Fixed Period,* Anthony Trollope's nineteenth-century satire on euthanasia. Trollope describes a fictional society in which all people are to be put to death on their sixty-eighth birthday to spare society the cost of maintaining the elderly and to spare the elderly and their families the problems attendant on old age. For the year prior to their sixty-eighth birthday, people give up their worldly responsibilities and live in a retreat where they are treated with respect and have time to prepare for a dignified death. The first person scheduled to enter the retreat reveals his feelings on the subject to his friend, Mr. Neverbend, the president of the country, who, as his name suggests, is a great advocate for such control:

> I should have gone mad. . . . I should have committed suicide. . . . The fixed day, coming at a certain known hour; the feeling that it must come, though it came at the same time so slowly and yet so fast; every day growing shorter day by day. . . . A man should have been an angel to endure it,—or so much less than a man. . . . Life under such a weight became impossible to me.[34]

Trollope's sense of the social and psychological aberration that would be created by legalized euthanasia is still germane. Uniformity of control as the proposed solution to anxiety becomes the main source of anxiety; assisted suicide is the cure that causes another form of disease. In the name of controlling death, it even manages to dominate the living, the survivors who are involved in implementing it. It is a kind of contagious disease in its own right.

In a 1995 *New Yorker* article, Andrew Solomon tells the

haunting story of how he, his brother, and his father assisted in the suicide of his mother, who had decided on suicide as soon as she learned that she had ovarian cancer.[35] She orchestrated the event, wanting her sons and husband to participate. "Don't think you are paying me some kind of tribute if you let my death become the great event of your life," she told Solomon.[36] But it seems clear that is exactly what she needed to have happen. Like many suicides, hers was an instrument for affecting those who would survive her.

Solomon describes how he and his father and brothers are united by the "weird legacy" of their sorrow and by their participation in their mother's death.[37] He considers that he, his brother, and his father are "signatories to a sealed pact of the conscious soul,"[38] that they will end their lives when terminally ill as their mother ended hers. He considers their plan a way of being reattached to his mother.

Solomon's article is also filled with people who consider assisting in a suicide the most meaningful experience of their lives. One nurse who assisted her mother's death told him, "I know some people will have trouble with my saying this but it was the most intimate time I've ever had with anyone. It was the most intimate thing I've ever done."[39] The feeling that participating in death permits an intimacy that they are otherwise unable to achieve permeates euthanasia stories and draws patients and doctors to euthanasia.

Solomon is struck by the fact that two of the founders of the Hemlock Society killed themselves when they were not terminally ill. He wonders if involvement with euthanasia may have depressed them. Here he has the sequence wrong. It is often depressed people with inordinate needs for control who are drawn to euthanasia long before they are ill.

Both the impulse to control and to connect in a complete way find perverse expression in assisted suicide. Those affected and disturbed by it discuss it as if it were a contagious disease. "Euthanasia breeds euthanasia," Solomon tells us.[40] He considers that "euthanasia is a toxic subject: if you think about it too much, it will begin to quietly poison you."[41]

People who participate in assisted suicide or euthanasia are frequently drawn into encouraging others if only to alleviate their own sense of uneasiness or guilt. Unlike most relatives or doctors who have shared his experience, Solomon does recognize that "the act of writing or speaking about your involvement is, inevitably, a plea for absolution."[42] The quest for absolution for a deed they suspect is wrong, or that violates some deeper instinct, also creates a need in many euthanasia advocates to justify, to advocate, to recruit, or even to emulate.

If the advocates of legalization prevail, we will lose more lives to suicide (although we will call the deaths by a different name) than can be saved by the efforts of the American Foundation for Suicide Prevention and all the other institutions working to prevent suicide in this country. The tragedy that will befall depressed suicidal patients will be matched by what will happen to terminally ill people, particularly older poor people. Assisted suicide and euthanasia will become routine ways of dealing with serious and terminal illness just as they have in the Netherlands; those without means will be under particular pressure to accept the euthanasia option. In the process, palliative care will be undercut for everyone.

Our success in providing palliative care for those who are terminally ill will do much to preserve our social humanity. If we do not provide such care, legalization of assisted suicide and euthanasia will become the simplistic answer to the problem of dying.

Euthanasia advocates appeal to the fearful in the name of ideals of compassion and autonomy even as they promote policies which, despite their best intentions, can only result in coercion and cruelty. If successful, advocates will have the effect of dehumanizing older people as much as or more than any indiscriminate use of medical technology. Euthanasia advocates have more in common with those who insist on futile medical technology than they realize: both are unable to accept death as a fact of life not totally subject to our control.

Euthanasia advocates have been seduced by death. They have come to see suicide as a cure for disease and a way of appropriating death's power over the human capacity for control. They have detoured what could be a constructive effort to manage the final phase of life in more varied and individualistic ways onto a dangerous route to nowhere. These are not the attitudes on which to base a nation's compassionate social policy. That policy must be based on a larger and more positive concern for people who are terminally ill. It must reflect an expansive determination to relieve their physical pain, to discover the nature of their fears, and to diminish suffering by providing meaningful reassurance of the life that has been lived and is still going on.

AFTERWORD:
THE CULTURE OF
EUTHANASIA

When I began studying assisted suicide and euthanasia, my apprehensions were rooted in experience with people who became suicidal in response to serious illness. I feared they would become willing victims if assisted suicide and euthanasia were given legal sanction. What I learned in the Netherlands indicated that such fears were justified.

I had assumed, however, that euthanasia in the Netherlands, where there is comprehensive health insurance for everyone, was surely set in a framework of providing better care for patients who were terminally ill than we were providing in this country. I learned that not only was that not true but that the development of such care was being stunted in the Netherlands by Dutch acceptance of euthanasia as an alternative. Euthanasia, which had been proposed as an unfortunate but necessary solution in rare cases, had become an almost routine way of dealing with anxiety, depression, and pain in seriously or terminally ill patients. What I have seen subsequently in this country as well as the Netherlands has persuaded me that legalization should be prevented because it would markedly worsen the care we provide to terminally ill patients.

As surprising as this discovery was, it was matched by my realization that legal sanction for assisted suicide and euthanasia, contrary to the expectations of its proponents, increased the power of doctors, not patients. I have tried to convey that this happens because the doctor can suggest euthanasia, which has a powerful influence on patients' decisions, can ignore patients' ambivalence, cannot propose suitable alternatives, and can put to death patients who have not requested it.

Of equal importance to me was the realization derived from studying the research sanctioned by the Dutch government, from talking to the principal investigators that did it, and from cases presented to me that it was not possible to regulate the practice of euthanasia within any established guidelines. That legal sanction creates a cultural climate which encourages the violation of guidelines is only most dramatically demonstrated by the 25 percent of doctors who admit to giving drugs to end the lives of patients who have not given their consent. Consultation is pro forma. Alternatives are not presented. The fact that the majority of cases are not reported makes regulation impossible.

In the hope of ensuring that we go in the direction of improved care for the dying rather than legal sanction for assisted suicide, I have tried to share what I have learned. In the process I have found that even consideration of legalization in the United States has affected the ways in which doctors, families, and patients view serious illness without necessarily illuminating that condition. The culture of euthanasia often seems a culture that obscures rather than assists in solving problems.

At the simplest level is the surprising amount of misinformation on end-of-life issues that exists even among doctors. Proponents of euthanasia have so muddied the waters that several doctors who told me they had performed euthanasia turned out to mean that they had consented to requests to withdraw treatment from dying patients.

In addition, few doctors realize that it is possible to relieve all pain by adequate palliative care if it includes sedation for those who require it. When they understand this, most doctors would prefer such an approach since it is possible to establish medical guidelines for sedation that avoid the nonmedical regulation doctors find so onerous and which legalization would bring.

More fixed in their opinions are those people, including doctors, who are influenced by their traumatic experience with the painful death of a parent or other loved one; they have become persuaded that legal sanction of assisted suicide is the only way to prevent the suffering they witnessed.

Dr. Marcia Angell, a euthanasia proponent and editor of the *New England Journal of Medicine,* which published the story of the death of her father as an argument for the legalization of physician-assisted suicide, provides an excellent example. Her father, who committed suicide by shooting himself when ill with metastatic prostate cancer, had a life expectancy of longer than six months, was not in extreme pain, but was suffering from nausea, weakness, and incontinence. Angell tells us that her father was depressed and felt hopeless but would not have considered psychiatric treatment. She says he was protective of his family and would have preferred sparing his mother the shock of finding his body. He did not tell Angell's mother what he planned to do because he knew that she would stop him. Angell believes that her father would have chosen physician-assisted suicide if it had been available and would have waited longer before ending his life.[1]

One hesitates to comment on so personal a case. But in publishing it and using it as an argument for legalization, which would affect the lives and deaths of so many, Angell obliges one to overcome such inhibition.

White men over fifty are the group most vulnerable to suicide; for most of them physical illness is an important part of their motivation for suicide. Angell is maintaining that they should be able to choose physician-assisted suicide as the treatment for their suicidal depression.

Whether or not there had been legalization, to avoid dying angry and alone her father needed someone he could talk to about what he was feeling. That someone could have been a psychiatrist, his wife, his physician-daughter, or a hospice worker. If the need to be protective of his family prevented him from talking to them, he was undoubtedly angry with them for this. In shooting himself at home where his wife would find his body he is expressing that anger while obliging her to clean up the mess. The method and setting of a suicide usually express what the suicide wants to convey.

Families are apt to feel troubled and guilty after such an event. Blaming society for not permitting assisted suicide is one way of dealing with such emotion.

The social change that would help future sufferers like Angell's father would be one that makes it easier for families and doctors to talk more openly with those who are dying. Remarkably, when this happens, patients no longer are in a rush to die, are grateful for their remaining time, and do not feel they are dying alone and abandoned.

Even more fixed in their opinion are those proponents who have actually assisted in the suicide of a friend, relative, or patient. Many have a need to justify what they did by proclaiming not only that it was right but that society should acknowledge this by making assisted suicide public policy. Timothy Quill, George Delury, and Andrew Solomon are but a few examples.

Most people, however, are educable. When they say they favor assisted suicide, they mean that they want a doctor to be able to do whatever is necessary to relieve their suffering. When they understand that there are other options than suffering or a quick death, they change their minds. When they understand what happens when assisted suicide and euthanasia are actually practiced, they are even more persuaded.

People are being exposed, however, to a great deal of misinformation by euthanasia proponents. Not the least of this is the attempt to promote assisted suicide as a solution that will make euthanasia, which is more distasteful to the public, unnecessary. But both euthanasia proponents and opponents know that it is not possible legally, medically, or morally to permit patients who want lethal medication and can swallow to be given it while the large number of patients who are terminally ill and cannot swallow are not.

The medical and legal problems facing doctors and patients in Oregon, which now has a law permitting physician-assisted suicide, are enormous. Doctors have no clue about what medication to prescribe, how effective it will be, or what the side effects will be. The lethal dose of barbiturates—which, based on the Dutch experience, is recommended by the Hemlock Society—does not produce death in 3–4 hours in 25 percent of the cases.[2] Those of us who work with suicide see patients who have taken several times the lethal dose of barbiturates go into coma that lasts for several days. Some die and some live with the outcome virtually unpredictable.

In the Netherlands, when extended coma follows an assisted suicide, the doctor then gives a lethal injection. In this country, families and friends cannot stand the watchful uncertainty of an extended coma and end up feeling obliged to suffocate the patient with a plastic bag. That is what happened to Jane, the only patient described in Timothy Quill's second book to whom he gave a lethal prescription of drugs.[3] Jane's friends told Quill some months later that they had to use a plastic bag to end her life. That is also what happened to George Delury, who admitted that he had had to use a plastic bag because his wife had not died from the lethal dose of medication that he had prepared for her. Of course, if a physician is present or called, he would probably intervene with a lethal injection; either way one is dealing with euthanasia.

Each assisted suicide patient in Oregon will essentially be a guinea pig in an experiment performed by a doctor. Since the physician may not know if the prescribed drug was used, and to what effect, and is not required to report the information in any case, we will learn nothing from the experiment. Oregon has gone hastily and unwisely down a path with consequences that are only beginning to be realized.

Physician-assisted suicide is felt to have the safeguard that the patient has more control over the process. We have seen from the experience of Louise (Chapter 2) that it offers little protection against coercion. Physician-assisted suicide also has some inherent dangers. More than euthanasia, it is used with people who are not close to death. They are also more likely to be patients who are depressed in response to medical illness and who, if treated properly, would want to live.

Euthanasia proponents have exaggerated the numbers of doctors practicing assisted suicide and euthanasia and then argued that legalization will create guidelines to regulate the practice. The argument is hardly persuasive that if some physicians are breaking current law, we should change the law to accommodate them or believe that they will then follow guidelines. The Dutch experience suggests that guidelines create a sanction that encourages their violation. In any case, no law is going to permit doctors to end patients' lives without their consent; doctors doing so now are apt to feel even freer to do so in a climate that sanctions euthanasia.

Part of the misinformation put out by euthanasia proponents is that opposition to the practice comes essentially from the Catholic Church or the religious right. Oregon voters were asked: Are you going to let the Catholic Church dictate how you die?

Proponents ignore the fact that the American Medical Association (AMA) is probably the most significant organization opposing legalization. It was the AMA's brief in opposition to legalization—a brief that was joined by the American Nurses Association, the American Psychiatric Association, and numerous other health care organizations—that was most cited by the Supreme Court in its recent decision on physician-assisted suicide and euthanasia. In addition to the AMA, the American Geriatrics Society, the American Hospital Association, the American Foundation for Suicide Prevention, Choice in Dying, 49 Bioethics Professors, the National Hospice Association, the National Legal Center for the Medically Dependent and Disabled, the National Spinal Cord Injury Association, Not Dead Yet and Americans Disabled for Attendant Programs Today (ADAPT), the Open Society Institute's Project on Death in America, and the U.S. government were among those filing *amicus curiae* briefs with the U.S. Supreme Court opposing legalization of assisted suicide.

Within organized medicine, the groups of physicians most opposed to legalization are palliative care specialists, physicians caring for elderly patients, and psychiatrists with extensive experience with suicide. Thus physicians with the most knowledge and experience in caring for patients who request assisted suicide are the ones most generally opposed to legalization: they know that legalization is an uninformed response to the challenge of helping these patients.

Proponents claim that they, too, are in favor of palliative care. But they seem much more in favor of assisted suicide and euthanasia. Their claim, echoed in their Supreme Court brief, that withdrawal of treatment was the same as assisted suicide served only to confuse physicians and families, making it harder for them to respect and follow patient requests for treatment withdrawal. Proponents' equally misleading contention that sedation sometimes required at the end of life amounted to torture was just as pernicious. Fortunately, the Supreme Court decisively rejected both arguments. The leadership in palliative care in this country and abroad is coming from physicians who are strongly opposed to euthanasia. They know that ultimately physician-assisted suicide and euthanasia are bad medicine—bad for doctors, bad for patients, and bad for society.

Dancing with Mister D

The Dutch provide ongoing evidence of the corrosive effects societal acceptance of euthanasia has on physicians, their practice of medicine, and their attitudes toward terminally ill patients. There is no more vivid picture of what happens to terminaly ill patients when palliative care is subordinated to hastening death than *Dancing with Mister D,* a best-selling memoir by Dr. Bert Keizer, a physician in a Dutch nursing home for patients who are terminally ill.[4] The Dutch public praised the book's frankness, scope, and literary quality, and, sharing Keizer's vision of what dying is all about, sees euthanasia as the better option.

In his performing euthanasia without trying to understand his patients, in his indifference to palliative care, and in his attitude toward medicine, Keizer is surely more jaundiced than the average Dutch euthanasia practitioner. His detached, "what's the use," fatalistic attitude toward his patients, however, appears to be shared by his colleagues in the nursing home facility.

Keizer tells us early and forcefully that his encounters with dying patients are a constant source of revulsion to him. Of one such encounter, he writes:

I was about to take out my stethoscope when suddenly she sat up straight in the bed, her eyes wildly staring and on her face an expression of intense disgust while with great effort she tried to keep something down by swallowing repeatedly. Instinctively I took a step backward. It would not have surprised me if an enormous turd had come slithering out of her mouth. But she managed to keep it down and finally to swallow it entirely. Then she fell back on the pillow and was dead.

Keizer seems to see his work as requiring him to do the same sort of swallowing.

His irritation with his patients is pervasive. To a woman who wants him to decide whether she should stay in bed for the day he replies:

Mrs. van Eyk. I cannot stand the way you are clinging to me. Don't try to pass your life on to me all the time, burdening me with it, letting me worry about your problems. You are 78 years old now, and if not wise, are at least old enough to decide for yourself how you are going to spend your day: in bed, beside your bed, or, for all I care, underneath your bed.

His irritation with his patients extends to their relatives. When the brother of a patient dying of prostate cancer arranges to have the patient brought to the nursing home because their aging father is also there, he sees only malice in his motivations. The brother's over-solicitousness, which Keizer describes as "detestable" and "self-serving," is likely to reflect anxiety, guilt, and affection as well as the hostility attributed to it by Keizer.

Keizer feels obliged to force patients to face death free of illusions, whether religious, medical, or about their past. He says critically of a patient who just died that "he was so naive in the beginning about his disease, treating it as though it were a wicked fairy tale." At times Keizer seems almost comical, as when he needs to insist to a dying woman, who wants him to confirm that those who mistreated her in the past will surely go to hell, that there is no hell. He is most intolerant of patients and colleagues who find consolation in religion. The most positive emotion Keizer expresses is a grudging admiration for those patients who can face death without illusion—which he feels he can—and without fear, which he feels he cannot.

Although a proponent of euthanasia, Keizer has his own criteria for performing it. The patient should not be too eager, or too flip, or have made a suicide attempt. He says his "First Commandment" is not to terminate a life merely because it is hard on the spectators to watch the suffering. It is a commandment he easily violates under pressure from a staff member or relative who approaches him in the right way. He fears the consequences of ending the life of someone who has not requested it but indicates that quietly giving an excessive dose of morphine can at times be useful in such situations.

He agrees to perform euthanasia on a patient with a presumed lung cancer even though tuberculosis has not been completely ruled out. He has no desire to question why the patient and his granddaughter are eager for him to go ahead although the patient is in no great physical distress. Nor is he receptive to the suggestion of a colleague that cortisone might make the patient feel better. Once he has decided on euthanasia, he wants it over with as soon as possible; he knows he will be angry if the patient wants a postponement. He writes, "If anyone so much as whispers 'cortisone' or 'uncertain diagnosis' I'll hit him."

When another patient who had expressed a desire for assisted suicide hesitates after a letter from his brother urging him not to, he writes, "I don't know what to do with such a wavering death wish. It's getting on my nerves. Does he want to die or doesn't he? I do hope we don't have to start the whole business again, right from the very start."

Nevertheless, euthanasia is traumatic for him. It is usually accompanied by migraine headaches and nightmares; in the worst of the nightmares he is in danger of catching his patients' dreaded diseases. One suspects he must fear punishment and retaliation for the anger and cruelty that seem to pervade his attitude toward them. During his waking hours, his emotional distance protects him. Of a patient who is himself distant and isolated Keizer writes, "it would have been worse if I had succeeded in cutting a breach in his defense, through which all the inspissated pus of the years would have come gushing out in a hideous wave."

Occasionally the patients, but more often the relatives, are critical of his insensitivity. A son accuses him of taking his mother's wish for death too literally and of not understanding that her request came from her fear of dying, not from the symptoms of her disease. Misunderstanding the son as well, Keizer sees him simply as wishing to deny the reality of his mother's approaching death.

Keizer is disillusioned with medicine, explaining that "in all probability, not whoring, but doctoring is the oldest profession." Medicine seems spoiled for him by its helplessness in the face of death. He makes no distinction between painfully futile treatment, which only prolongs the process of dying, and palliative care, which relieves suffering. Since death will come in the end, distinctions are not important. If medicine has failed him, it is not by its inability to cure more patients, but by its inability to teach him to want to care for people whom he cannot cure.

Patients in this nursing home surely suffer more in their last months by the revulsion they encounter. The attitudes of the doctors treating them encourage their seeking a quick death. The staff of the nursing home seems little more than impatient custodians in a warehouse for dying patients.

Dying patients are themselves often revolted by their condition. It is remarkable how their perceptions change when they encounter caregivers who accept their humanity and do not perceive them this way. Such caregivers are harder to find in a cultural climate that encourages the easier option of euthanasia. Within a culture that provides no vision for making the last phase of life more meaningful, an attitude of revulsion becomes part of a cultural narrative moving both doctors and patients toward euthanasia. That attitude in turn reflects what happens when medicine is used to hasten death rather than to relieve suffering.

REFERENCES

Preface

1. The names used to describe the New York and state of Washington cases changed as the cases passed through the courts depend-
ing on who was listed as the plaintiff and who as the respondent.
When the New York case reached the Supreme Court, it was described as *Vacco v. Quill.* New York's Attorney General Vacco was
listed first since, on behalf of the state of New York, he was then
the plaintiff appealing to the Supreme Court to reverse a lower
court opinion in favor of Quill. For comparable reasons, the
Court's opinion in the Washington case is referred to as *Washington v. Glucksberg.* Some names that appeared on the lower court
briefs were dropped when the case reached the Supreme Court.
To avoid confusion, throughout this book the cases will simply be
referred to as the New York and Washington cases.

1: Suicide, Assisted Suicide, and Medical Illness

1. H. Hendin, *Suicide in America* (New York: Norton, 1995).
2. R. Twycross, "A View from the Hospice," in *Euthanasia Examined,* ed. J. Keown (Cambridge: Cambridge University Press,
1995).
3. T. B. MacKenzie and M. K. Popkin, "Medical Illness and Suicide,"

in *Suicide over the Life Cycle,* ed. S. J. Blumenthal and D. J. Kupfer (Washington, D.C.: American Psychiatric Press, 1990), 205–232.

4. E. J. Emanuel, D. L. Fairclough, E. R. Daniels, and B. R. Clarridge, "Euthanasia and Physician-Assisted Suicide: Attitudes and Experiences of Oncology Patients, Oncologists, and the Public, *Lancet,* 1996, 347:1,805–1,810.

5. H. Hendin and G. L. Klerman, "Physician-Assisted Suicide: The Dangers of Legalization," *American Journal of Psychiatry,* 1993, 150:143–145.

6. E. Robins, G. E. Murphy, R. H. Wilkinson Jr., S. Gassner, and J. Kayes, "Some Clinical Considerations in the Prevention of Suicide Based on a Study of 134 Successful Suicides," *American Journal of Public Health,* 1959, 49:888–889; P. Sainsbury, *Suicide in London: An Ecological Study* (New York: Basic Books, 1956); C. P. Seager and R. S. Flood, "Suicide in Bristol," *British Journal of Psychiatry,* 1965, 111:919–932.

7. H. Hendin, "Suicide and the Request for Assisted Suicide: Meaning and Motivation," *Duquesne Law Review,* 1996, 35:285–310.

8. Y. Conwell, E. D. Caine, and K. Olsen, "Suicide and Cancer in Late Life," *Hospital & Community Psychiatry,* 1990, 41:1334–1339; T. L. Dorpat, W. F. Anderson, and H. S. Ripley, "The Relationship of Physical Illness to Suicide," in *Suicidal Behaviors: Diagnosis and Management,* ed. H. L. P. Resnick (Boston: Little Brown, 1968).

9. S. Perry, "Suicidal Ideation and HIV Testing," *JAMA,* 1990, 263:679–682.

10. T. L. Dorpat and H. S. Ripley, "A Study of Suicide in the Seattle Area," *Comprehensive Psychiatry,* 1960, 1:349–359; B. Barraclough, J. Bunch, B. Nelson, and P. Sainsbury, "A Hundred Cases of Suicide: Clinical Aspects," *British Journal of Psychiatry,* 1974, 25:355–373; D. C. Rich, D. Young, and R. C. Fowler, "San Diego Study I: Young vs. Old Subjects," *Archives of General Psychiatry,* 1986, 43:577–582; Robins et al., "Some Clinical Considerations."

11. J. H. Brown, P. Henteleff, S. Barakat, and C. J. Rowe, "Is It Normal for Terminally Ill Patients to Desire Death?" *American Journal of Psychiatry,* 1986, 143:208–211; H. M. Chochinov, K. G. Wilson, M. Enns, N. Mowcun, S. Lander, M. Levitt, and J. J. Clinch,

"Desire for Death in the Terminally Ill," *American Journal of Psychiatry,* 1995, 152:1185–1191.

12. E. J. Emanuel et al., "Euthanasia and Physician-Assisted Suicide."

13. J. Fawcett, W. A. Scheftner, L. Fogg, D. C. Clark, M. A. Young, D. Hedeker, and R. Gibbons, "Time-Related Predictors of Suicide in Major Affective Disorder," *American Journal of Psychiatry,* 1990, 147:1,189–1,194.

14. H. Hendin, "The Psychodynamics of Suicide with Particular Reference to the Young," *American Journal of Psychiatry,* 1991, 148:1,150–1,158.

15. M. B. Keller, G. L. Klerman, P. W. Lavori, J. Fawcett, W. Coryell, and J. Endicott, "Treatment Received by Depressed Patients," *JAMA,* 1982, 248:1,848–1,855.

16. G. E. Murphy, "The Physician's Responsibility for Suicide (1) An Error of Commission and (2) Errors of Omission," *Annals of Internal Medicine,* 1975, 82:301–309.

17. Hendin and Klerman, "Physician-Assisted Suicide."

18. Hendin, "Suicide and the Request for Assisted Suicide."

19. A. Hoche, "Vom Sterben," in *Aus der Werkstatt* (Munich: Jehmann,) 210–232.

20. L. Thomas, "Dying as Failure?" *American Journal of Political Science,* 1984, 444:1–4.

21. D. Hendin, *Death as a Fact of Life* (New York: Norton, 1973), citing Herman Feifel, "Physicians Consider Death," unpublished manuscript presented at 1967 meeting of the American Psychological Association.

2: Selling Suicide

1. T. E. Quill, "Death and Dignity—A Case of Individualized Decision Making," *New England Journal of Medicine,* 1991, 324:691–694.

2. T. E. Quill, *Death and Dignity: Making Choices and Taking Charge* (New York: Norton, 1993).

3. Quill, "Death and Dignity," 692.

4. P. Wesley, "Dying Safely," *Issues in Law and Medicine,* 1993, 8:467–485.

5. Quill, "Death and Dignity," 692.

6. Ibid.

7. Ibid., 693.

8. Wesley, "Dying Safely," 480.

9. Ibid.

10. Ibid.

11. Quill, "Death and Dignity," 693.

12. Ibid., 694.

13. L. Belkin, "Doctor Tells of First Death Using His Suicide Device," *New York Times,* June 6, 1990, A1.

14. Hon. A. L. Gilbert, *People ex rel. State of Michigan v. Kevorkian,* No. 90-390963-AZ, Michigan Circuit Court, Oakland County, February 5, 1991.

15. J. Finkelstein and K. Lewis, "Suicide Doctor Questioned in 2 Deaths: Kevorkian Leads Cops to Bodies, Machine Use Probed," *Detroit Free Press,* October 24, 1991, A1.

16. J. Kevorkian, *Prescription: Medicide: The Goodness of Planned Death* (Buffalo, N.Y.: Prometheus Books, 1991), 318.

17. M. Betzold, "The Selling of Doctor Death," *The New Republic,* May 26, 1997, 22–28.

18. G. R. Redding, "The Challenge of Patholysis to Forensics and Psychiatry," *American Journal of Forensic Psychiatry,* 1998, in press.

19. Ibid., in press.

20. Betzold, "Selling of Doctor Death," 27.

21. J. Kevorkian, "A Fail Safe Model for Justifiable Medically Assisted Suicide," *American Journal of Forensic Psychiatry,* 1992, 13:7–81.

22. J. Kevorkian, "The Fundus Oculi and the Determination of Death," *American Journal of Pathology,* 1956, 32:253–269.

23. J. Kevorkian, *Current Biography* (New York: Wilson Press, 1994), 55:32–35.

24. G. Borger, "The Odd Odyssey of 'Dr. Death'," *U.S. News and World Report,* August 27, 1990, 27–28.

25. Associated Press, "Michigan Board Suspends License of Doctor Who Aided in Suicides," *New York Times,* November 21, 1991, A14.

26. T. Lewin, "Judge Clears Doctor of Murdering Woman with a Suicide Machine," *New York Times,* December 14, 1990, A1.

References

27. R. Fornoff and A. Arellano, "Kevorkian Challenges Law: In Detroit, Suicide Doctor Is Present as Ill Man Dies," *Detroit Free Press,* May 17, 1993, A1.

28. D. Humphry, *Jean's Way* (New York: Quartet Books, 1978).

29. *Assisted Suicide: The Compassionate Crime* (Los Angeles: Hemlock Society, 1982), 32.

30. D. Humphry, *Final Exit* (Secaucus, N.J.: Carol Publishing, 1991).

31. P. M. Marzuk et al., "Increase in Suicide by Asphyxiation in New York City after the Publication of *Final Exit,*" *New England Journal of Medicine,* 1993, 329:1508–1511; B. Angelo, "Assigning the Blame for a Young Man's Suicide," interview in *Time,* November 18, 1991, 12.

32. A. Wickett, *Double Exit* (Eugene, Ore.: Hemlock Society, 1989).

33. T. Gabriel, "A Fight to the Death," *New York Times Magazine,* December 8, 1991, 46.

34. Gabriel, "A Fight to the Death"; A. Fadiman, "Death News: Requiem for the *Hemlock Quarterly,*" *Harper's,* April 1994, 74–82.

35. "The Hemlock Solution," *Prime Time Live,* March 20, 1992.

36. Y. Kamisar, Physician-Assisted Suicide: The Last Bridge to Active Voluntary Euthanasia," in *Examining Euthanasia,* ed. by J. Keown (London: Cambridge University Press, 1995); Y. Kamisar, "Are Laws Against Assisted Suicide Unconstitutional?" *Hastings Center Report,* 1992, 23:33–41.

37. M. P. Battin, "Assisted Suicide: Can We Learn from Germany?" *Hastings Center Report,* 1992, 22, 2:44–51.

38. L. Belkin, "There's No Simple Suicide," *New York Times Magazine,* November 14, 1993, 50–55, 63, 74–75.

39. W. Shakespeare, *Macbeth,* act I, scene VII, lines 1–2 (New York: Folger Library Press, 1958).

40. H. Hendin, "Selling Death and Dignity," *Hastings Center Report,* 1995, 25, 3:19–23.

41. G. Pierre-Pierre, "Man Sentenced to Six Months in Wife's Suicide," *New York Times,* May 18, 1996, B22.

42. G. Delury, "Countdown: A Daily Log of Myrna's Mental State and View Toward Death" (diary released to the New York prosecuter's office), 7.

43. *Dateline NBC,* aired September 27, 1996.

44. G. Delury, *But What If She Wants to Die?* (Secaucus, N.J.: Birch Lane Press, 1997).
45. E. R. DuBose and M. Walters, personal narratives in *Choosing Death: Active Euthanasia, Religion and the Public Debate,* ed. by R. Hammell (Philadelphia: Trinity Press International, 1991).
46. Genesis 18.

3: Seduced by Death

1. "Psychiater Vrijuit Na Hulp bij Zelfdoding" [Psychiatrist goes free after help with suicide], *Algemeen Dagblad* (Rotterdam), April 22, 1993, 1; "Psychiater Niet Gestraft voor Hulp bij Zelfdoding" [Psychiatrist not punished for help with suicide], *Volkskrant* (Amsterdam), April 22, 1993, 1; W. Drozdiak, "Dutch Seek Freer Mercy Killing," *Washington Post,* October 29, 1993, A29.
2. H. Hendin, "Seduced by Death: Doctors, Patients and the Dutch Cure," *Issues in Law and Medicine,* 1994, 20:123–68.
3. C. Gomez, *Regulating Death: Euthanasia and the Case of the Netherlands* (New York: Free Press, 1991), provides a comprehensive description of Dutch euthanasia practices.
4. J. K. M. Gevers, "What the Law Allows: Legal Aspects of Active Euthanasia on Request in the Netherlands," in *Euthanasia: The Good of the Patient, the Good of Society,* ed. R. I. Misbin (Frederick, Md.: University Publishing Group, 1992).
5. C. Gomez, *Regulating Death,* 37–38.
6. Ibid., 38.
7. "KNMG, Standpunt Inzake Euthanasie" [KNMG's standpoint on euthanasia], *Medisch Contact* (1984), published in abridged form in KNMG, "Guidelines for Euthanasia," trans. W. Lagerwey, *Issues in Law and Medicine,* 1988, 3:429.
8. The Hague Editor, "The Netherlands Is the Only Country with a Statutory Regulation: Euthanasia Law Barely Passed by Senate," *Brabants Dagblad* (Den Bosch), December 1, 1993, 1.
9. C. Gomez, *Regulating Death,* 48–55.
10. R. Fenigsen, "A Case Against Dutch Euthanasia," *Hastings Center Report,* Special Supplement, 1989, 19, 1:22–30; C. I. Dessaur and C. J. C. Rutenfrans, "The Present Day Practice of Euthanasia,"

Issues in Law and Medicine, 1988, 3:399–405, reprinted from C. I. Dessaur and C. J. C. Rutenfrans, *Mag de dokter doden?* [May the doctor kill?] (Amsterdam: E. M. Querido, 1986).

11. The formal name of the group was the Commission of Inquiry into the Medical Practice Concerning Euthanasia. It became known by the name of its chairman, Jan Remmelink, as the Remmelink Commission; the report of the investigative team is referred to as the Remmelink study.

12. P. J. van der Maas, J. J. M. van Delden, and L. Pijnenborg, *Euthanasia and Other Medical Decisions Concerning the End of Life* (New York: Elsevier, 1992).

13. Ibid., 49, table 5.14.

14. *An Appointment with Death* (K.A. Productions in conjunction with TV Ontario, Canada, 1993).

15. R. Diekstra and N. Speijer, *Hulp Bij Zelfdoding: Een Onderzoek Naar Problemen Rondom Hulpverlening Bij De Zelfgekozen Dood* [Help with suicide: research into problems with assisted suicide] (Alphen aan de Rijn: Samson, 1980).

16. R. Diekstra, "Assisted Suicide and Euthanasia: Experience from the Netherlands," *Annals of Medicine,* 1993, 25:5.

17. R. Diekstra, "Suicide and Euthanasia," *Italian Journal of Suicidology,* 1992, 2:71; Diekstra and Speijer, *Hulp Bij Zelfdoding.*

18. Diekstra and Speijer, *Hulp Bij Zelfdoding.*

19. Few cases have been brought to trial. The recommended guidelines are not fixed conditions, so even when they were not followed, judges have generally exonerated physicians on the grounds of *force majeure.* Only one doctor, the physician in the infamous De Terp nursing home case, who confessed to putting to death without their consent patients under his care, was convicted and sentenced to prison. In an official statement, the board of the KNMG expressed its concern not over his killings but over the fact that conviction of the doctor could cause insecurity among doctors and discourage them from helping patients to die. A higher court overturned the conviction on the grounds that evidence against him had been improperly seized. Finally a civil court awarded him $150,000 in damages. See Fenigsen, "Case Against Dutch Euthanasia," 25.

20. "Doctor Unpunished for Dutch Suicide," *New York Times,* June 22, 1994, A10.

21. W. Nolen, W. A. van Dyk, E. Sutorius, and W. J. Schudel, "De Zaak van de Vasthoudende Inspecteur" [The case of the overzealous inspector], *Mgv,* August 7, 1993, 738–49.

22. E. Borst-Eilers, "Euthanasia in the Netherlands: Brief Historical Review and Present Situation," in *Euthanasia: The Good of the Patient, the Good of the Society,* ed. R. I. Misbin (Frederick, Md.: University Publishing Group, 1992).

23. "Nonvoluntary euthanasia" is a problematic term. Is one not justified in assuming a desire to live unless there is evidence to the contrary? Could one murder a demented stranger and plead as an extenuating circumstance that we did not know if the victim wanted to keep on living? Nonvoluntary euthanasia is particularly disturbing when applied to partially competent patients whose consent is not sought but who often can be quite clear about whether they want to live or die. Surely competent patients put to death without their consent are clear cases of involuntary euthanasia.

24. Van der Maas et al., *Euthanasia and Other Medical Decisions,* 64, table 6.7.

25. L. Pijnenborg, P. J. van der Maas, J. J. M. van Delden, and C. W. N. Loonan, "Life-Terminating Acts Without Explicit Consent of the Patients," *Lancet,* 1993, 341:1196–1200.

26. H. Ten Have et al., "Euthanasia: Normal Medical Practice?" *Hastings Center Report,* 1992, 22, 2:34–38.

27. Van der Maas et al., *Euthanasia and Other Medical Decisions,* 58, table 6.1.

28. Ibid., 133.

29. Ibid., 134.

30. Ibid., 75, table 7.7, and 87. The figure of 5,000 is based on the physician interview part of the study. The figure based on death certificates, also used in the study (p. 133, table 13.5), is about 3,500. The figure based on the interviews is considered more credible, although even the lower figure is alarming.

31. Ibid., 134, table 13.5.

32. The Hague Editor, "Netherlands the Only Country," 1.

33. J. Keown, "The Law and Practice of Euthanasia in the Netherlands," *Law Quarterly Review,* 1992, Winter:51–78.
34. Pijnenborg et al., "Life-Terminating Acts."
35. Joint Report of KNMG and Commission on Life-Terminating Decisions, April 1993.
36. "Borst voor medisch onderzoek op dementen" [Borst favors medical research on people with dementia], *De Telegraaf* (Amsterdam), October 4, 1995.
37. Joint Report of KNMG and Commission.
38. B. E. Chabot, letter to author dated August 18, 1994.
39. G. van der Waal and R. J. M. Dillmann, "Euthanasia in the Netherlands," *British Medical Journal,* 1994, 308:1346–1349.
40. Pijnenborg et al., "Life-Terminating Acts."
41. Van der Maas et al., *Euthanasia and Other Medical Decisions.*
42. Van der Maas, letter to author dated August 4, 1994.
43. H. W. Hilhorst, *Euthanasie in het Ziekenhuis* [Euthanasia in the hospital] (Lochem: De Tijdstroom, 1983).
44. J. V. M. Welie, "The Medical Exception: Physicians, Euthanasia and the Dutch Criminal Law," *Journal of Medicine and Philosophy,* 1992, 419–37.
45. Ibid., 434.

4: *The Politics of Euthanasia*

1. R. Diekstra, "Assisted Suicide and Euthanasia: Experience from the Netherlands," *Annals of Medicine,* 1993, 25:5.
2. Ibid., 7.
3. R. Fenigsen, "A Case Against Dutch Euthanasia," *Hastings Center Report,* Special Supplement, 1989, 19, 1:22–30.
4. J. G. M. Aartsen et al., letter to editor, *Hastings Center Report,* 1989, 19, 6:47.
5. B. E. Chabot, *Zelf Beschikt* [Chosen death] (Amsterdam: Balans, 1993).
6. Koerselman's clinical view of the Netty Boomsma case is similar to mine. He sees Netty as having suffered from a personality disorder as well as depression. F. Koerselman, "Balanssuicide Als Mythe: Over *Zelf Beschikt,* door B. E. Chabot" [Balanced suicide

as a myth: on *Chosen Death* by B. E. Chabot], *Mgv,* 1994, 5:515–527.

7. H. Achterhuis, J. Goud, F. Koerselman, W. J. Otten, and T. Schalken, *Als de Dood Voor Het Leven: Over Professionele Hulp Bij Zelf-moord* [Scared to death of living: on physician-assisted suicide] (Amsterdam: Uitgeverij G. A. van Oorschot, 1995).

8. "Psychiater Berispt na Hulp bij Zelfdoding" [Psychiatrist reprimanded for help with assisted suicide], *De Volkskrant* (Amsterdam), March 31, 1995; Report of Amsterdam Medical Tribunal, Boudewijn Elise Chabot, March 1995.

9. "Berisping Chabot Zaait Verwarring" [Reprimand to Chabot creates confusion], *Algemeens Dagblad* (Rotterdam), March 31, 1995; "Straf en tucht zijn voor Chabot te veel" [Punishment and discipline are too much for Chabot], *Het Parool* (Amsterdam), April 1, 1995.

10. "Euthanasia: No Reason to Tighten Up Prosecution Policy," *Netherlands News Monitor,* April 25, 1995.

11. C. I. Dessaur and C. J. C. Rutenfrans, "The Present Day Practice of Euthanasia," *Issues in Law and Medicine,* 1988, 3:4, reprinted from C. I. Dessaur and C. J. C. Rutenfrans, *Mag de dokter doden?* [May the doctor kill?] (Amsterdam: E. M. Querido, 1986).

12. C. J. C. Rutenfrans, "Vrijwillige Euthanasie" [Voluntary euthanasia], *Trouw* (Amsterdam), October 7, 1986; C. J. C. Rutenfrans, personal communication with author, January 22, 1996.

13. Richard Fenigsen, personal communication with author, January 21, 1996.

14. C. Gomez, *Regulating Death: Euthanasia and the Case of the Netherlands* (New York: Free Press, 1991).

15. Ibid., 133.

16. J. Keown, "The Law and Practice of Euthanasia in the Netherlands," *Law Quarterly Review,* 1992, 108:51–78; J. Keown, "Euthanasia in the Netherlands: Sliding down the Slippery Slope?" in *Euthanasia Examined: Ethical, Legal, and Clinical Perspectives,* ed. J. Keown (New York: Cambridge University Press, 1995).

17. Keown, "Euthanasia in the Netherlands," 265.

18. A. Capron, "Euthanasia in the Netherlands: American Observations," *Hastings Center Report,* 1992, 22, 2:30–33.

19. Keown, "Euthanasia in the Netherlands," 265.

20. "Inspectie wil proefproces bij tuchtcollege. Bij euthanasie moet arts doorverwijzen" [Inspector wants test trial with disciplinary college. Euthanasia calls for referrals by physician], *Reformatorisch Dagblad* (Apeldoorn), August 22, 1994; "Blokkeren euthanasie niet gepast, Borst: 'Arts moet tijdig waarschuwen,' " [Blocking euthanasia not appropriate, Borst: "Physician should give early warning"], *Het Parool* (Amsterdam), September 15, 1994.

21. "Inspectie: Actie tegen euthanasie op afroep" [Inquiry: action against euthanasia on call], *Reformatorisch Dagblad* (Apeldoorn), August 11, 1994, 3.

22. "Opheldering over uitspraak Van Dinter: SGP wil aanpak euthanasie artsen" [Explanation of Van Dinter's statement: SGP wants defined approach for euthanasia physicians], *Reformatorisch Dagblad* (Appeldoorn), August 5, 1994; "Onderzoek PG's Naar Euthanasie Artsen" [Prosecutor-general's investigation into euthanasia physicians], *Reformatorisch Dagblad* (Apeldoorn), August 12, 1994, 3.

23. Central Medical Tribunal, Pub. 126, June 16, 1994.

24. On December 5, 1995, the Dutch Supreme Court affirmed both the conviction and the appellate court's reduction of the sentence. Case No. 100400.

25. F. Abrahams, "Euthanasie-arts Wine Mulder-Meiss. 'Ik heb vaak genoeg mensen levensmoed ingesproken' " [Euthanasia Physician Wine Mulder-Meiss: "Often enough I have persuaded people to have the courage to live"], *NRC Handelsblad* (Rotterdam), Saturday Section, September 10, 1994, 5.

26. *Death on Request,* Ikon television network. First aired October 20, 1994.

27. *Death on Request,* excerpt, *Prime Time Live,* December 8, 1994.

28. S. Hawking, *A Brief History of Time: From the Big Bang to Black Holes* (New York: Bantam Books, 1988), 25; *A Brief History of Time* (Triton Pictures, 1992).

29. Ward op den Brouw, "Wereldwijde aandacht euthanasie-uitzending" [Worldwide attention for euthanasia documentary], *NRC Handelsblad* (Rotterdam), October 22, 1994.

30. C. Verbraak, "Beelden van een Zelfgekozen dood; Documentairefilmer Nederhorst over 'Dood op Verzoek' " [Images of a self-chosen death; documentary filmmaker Nederhorst on "Death on Request"], *Vrij Nederland,* October 8, 1994, 42.

31. Ibid.

32. Ibid.

33. G. van der Wal and P. J. van der Maas. *Euthanasie en Andere Medische Beslissingen rond het Levenseinde* (The Hague: Staatsuitgeverij, 1996).

34. P. J. van der Maas, G. van der Wal, I. Haverkate I et al., "Euthanasia, Physician-Assisted Suicide, and Other Medical Practices Involving the End of Life in the Netherlands, 1990–1995," *New England Journal of Medicine,* 1996, 335:1,609–1,705; G. van der Wal, P. J. van der Maas, J. M. Bosma et al., "Evaluation of the Notification Procedure for Physician-Assisted Death in the Netherlands," *New England Journal of Medicine* 1996, 335:1,706–1,711.

35. K. Gunning, "Euthanasia," *Lancet,* 1991, 338:1,010; J. Walton, "The House of Lords on Issues of Life and Death," *Journal of the Royal College of Physicians and Surgeons of London,* 1994, 28:235–236.

36. C. Gomez, *Regulating Death: Euthanasia and the Case of the Netherlands* (New York: Free Press, 1991); J. Keown, "Euthanasia in the Netherlands: Sliding Down the Slippery Slope?" in *Euthanasia Examined: Ethical, Legal, and Clinical Perspectives,* ed. J. Keown (New York: Cambridge University Press, 1995).

37. Van der Maas et al., "Medical Practices Involving the End of Life in the Netherlands," 1,703.

38. C. Gomez, *Regulating Death.*

39. H. Hendin, Z. Zylicz, and C. Rutenfrans, "Physician-Assisted Suicide and Euthanasia in the Netherlands: Lessons from the Dutch," *Journal of the American Medical Association,* 1997, 277:1,720–1,722.

40. Van der Wal et al., "Notification Procedure for Physician-Assisted Death," 1,708.

41. Ibid., 1,708.

42. P. J. van der Maas, J. J. M. van Delden, and L. Pijnenborg, *Euthanasia and Other Medical Decisions Concerning the End of Life* (New York: Elsevier, 1992); van der Wal et al., "Notification Procedure for Physician-Assisted Death," 1,710.

43. Van der Maas et al., "Medical Practices Involving the End of Life in the Netherlands," 1,704.

44. Van der Maas et al., *Euthanasia and Other Medical Decisions,* 58.

45. Ibid., 73; Keown, "Euthanasia in the Netherlands," 270.

46. Van der Maas et al., "Medical Practices Involving the End of Life in the Netherlands," 1,700.

47. Ibid., 1,704.

48. Ibid.

49. Ibid., 1,700, 1,704; van der Maas et al., *Euthanasia and Other Medical Decisions,* 75.

50. Van der Maas et al., "Medical Practices Involving the End of Life in the Netherlands," 1,704.

51. R. Twycross, "Where There Is Hope, There Is Life: A View from the Hospice," in *Euthanasia Examined: Ethical, Legal, and Clinical Perspectives,* ed. J. Keown (New York: Cambridge University Press, 1995), 161.

52. H. Ten Have and G. Kimsma, *Geneeskunde: Tussen Droom en Drama* [Medical science: between dream and drama] (Kampen: Kok Agora, 1985).

53. K. L. Dorrepaal et al., "Pain Experience and Pain Management Among Hospitalized Cancer Patients," *Cancer,* 1989, 63:593–598; Z. Zylicz, "The Story Behind the Blank Spot," *American Journal of Hospice & Palliative Care,* July/August 1993, 30–32.

54. Z. Zylicz, "Euthanasia," *Lancet,* 1991, 338:1,150.

55. D. Callahan and M. White, "The Legalization of Physician-Assisted Suicide: Creating a Regulatory Potemkin Village," *University of Richmond Law Review,* 1996, 30:1–83.

56. Dorrepaal et al., "Pain Experience and Management"; Zylicz, "Euthanasia"; British Medical Association Working Party on Euthanasia, *Euthanasia* (London: British Medical Association, 1988), 49.

57. L. Pijnenborg, P. J. van der Maas, J. J. M. van Delden, and C. W. N. Loonan, "Life-Terminating Acts Without Explicit Consent of the Patients," *Lancet,* 1993, 341:1196–1200.

58. L. Pijnenborg, *End-of-Life Decisions in Dutch Medical Practice* (The Hague: CIP-Gegevens Koninklijke Bibliotheek, 1995), 119–32.

59. Ibid., 135–51.

60. KNMG Guidelines on Assisted Suicide and Euthanasia, August 1995.

61. M. Simons, "Dutch Doctors to Tighten Rules on Mercy Killings," *New York Times,* September 11, 1995, A3.

62. Ibid.

63. Ibid.
64. Ibid.

5: A Cure for Suicide

1. H. Hendin, "Assisted Suicide, Euthanasia and Suicide Prevention: The Implications of the Dutch Experience," *Suicide and Life-Threatening Behavior,* 1995, 25:193–203.
2. J. H. Groenwoud, P.J. van der Maas, G. van der Waal et al., "Physician-Assisted Death in Psychiatric Practice in the Netherlands," *New England Journal of Medicine,* 1997, 336:1800.
3. Ibid.
4. Ibid.
5. Ibid.
6. L. Ganzini and M. A. Lee, "Psychiatry and Assisted Suicide in the United States," *New England Journal of Medicine,* 1997, 336:1824–1826.
7. P. Admiraal, "A Physician's Responsibility to Help a Patient Die," in *The Good of the Patient, The Good of Society,* ed. R. I. Misbin (Frederick, Md.: University Publishing Group, 1992), 80.
8. P. Admiraal, "Voluntary Euthanasia: The Dutch Way," paper given at the Fifth International Congress on Medicine at the Imperial College, London, September 2, 1993, 9.
9. K. Foley, personal communication, September 1996; Z. Zylicz, personal communication, August 1996.
10. H. Hendin, *Suicide in America* (New York: Norton, 1995).
11. S. Asch, "Suicide and the Hidden Executioner," *International Review of Psychoanalysis,* 1980, 7:51–60.
12. H. Hendin, "Suicide and the Request for Assisted Suicide: Meaning and Motivation," *Duquesne Law Review,* 1996, 35:285–310.
13. H. Hendin, "Suicide, Assisted Suicide, and Medical Illness," *Primary Psychiatry,* 1997, 4:22–25.
14. H. Hendin, "A Psychiatric Perspective on Physician-Assisted Suicide," *American Journal of Forensic Psychiatry,* 1998, in press.
15. S. Klagsbrun, "Case in Favor of Physician-Assisted Suicide," presentation at the American Academy of Forensic Sciences, New York City, February 21, 1997.

16. S. Block and J. A. Billings, "Patient Requests for Euthanasia and Assisted Suicide in Terminal Illness: The Role of the Psychiatrist," *Psychosomatics,* 1995, 36:445–457.
17. H. Hendin, "A Psychiatric Perspective."
18. E. H. Moskowitz, "Difficulties Involved in Identifying the Legal Incapacity to Consent to Physician-Assisted Suicide," *American Journal of Forensic Psychiatry,* 1998, in press.

6: Why the Netherlands? Why the United States?

1. T. H. C. Bueller, "The Historical and Religious Framework for Euthanasia in the Netherlands," in *The Good of the Patient, The Good of Society,* ed. R. I. Misbin (Frederick, Md.: University Publishing Group, 1992).
2. Ibid., 186.
3. Ibid., 186.
4. D. Phillips, *De Naakte Nederlander* [The Dutch exposed] (Amsterdam: Uitgeverij Bert Bakker, 1985).
5. J. A. van Doorn, "Welfare State and Welfare Society: The Dutch Experience," *Netherlands Journal of Sociology,* 1978, 14:1–18.
6. J. H. Huizinga, *Dutch Civilization in the Seventeenth Century and Other Essays* (New York: Harper Torchbooks, 1969), 59–60.
7. Ibid., 48, 53.
8. Ibid., 49, 53; K. H. D. Haley, *The Dutch in the Seventeenth Century* (London: Thames and Hudson; New York: Harcourt Brace Jovanovich, 1972), 85.
9. S. Schama, *The Embarrassment of Riches* (New York: Knopf, 1987).
10. J. H. Huizinga, *Dutch Civilization,* 112.
11. D. Defoe, *A Plan of the English Common* (1728), 192, cited in C. Wilson, *The Dutch Republic and the Civilization of the Seventeenth Century* (New York: McGraw-Hill, 1968), 22.
12. A. Hauser, *The Social History of Art* (New York: Knopf, 1952), 1:461.
13. B. Haak, *The Golden Age: Dutch Painting of the Seventeenth Century* (New York: Abrams, 1984).
14. Schama, *Embarrassment of Riches,* 44.
15. Ibid., 28–34 Schama considers Willem Ysbrantzoon Bontekoe's

References

The Memorable Account of the Voyage of the Nieuw Hoorn, first published in 1686 and reprinted seventy times by 1800, as the prototypical and most enduring tale of Dutch triumph over disaster at sea. The tone of such works contrasts sharply with the recurrent vision in English and American literature of the sea as a symbol for what is unchanging and uncontrollable, expressed in works ranging from Matthew Arnold's "Dover Beach" to Herman Melville's *Moby Dick.*

16. Schama, *Embarrassment of Riches,* 45.
17. Huizinga, *Dutch Civilization,* 114.
18. B. van Heerikhuizen, "What Is Typically Dutch?" *Netherlands Journal of Sociology,* 1982, 18:103–125.
19. Huizinga, *Dutch Civilization,* 122.
20. Ibid., 114.
21. Ibid., 121.
22. D. Phillips, letter to author dated April 26, 1995.
23. D. de Baena, *The Dutch Puzzle* (The Hague: L. J. C. Boucher, 1966), 6.
24. Phillips, letter.
25. Ibid.
26. C. Gomez, *Regulating Death: Euthanasia and the Case of the Netherlands* (New York: Free Press, 1991), 95; D. Callahan, "When Self-Determination Runs Amok," *Hastings Center Report,* 1992, 22, 2:52–55.
27. *The Encyclopedia of Philosophy* (New York: Macmillan, 1972), 2:9.
28. Bueller, "Historical and Religious Framework."
29. Gomez, *Regulating Death,* 95.
30. Phillips, letter.
31. Bueller, "Historical and Religious Framework."
32. M. P. Battin, "Should We Copy the Dutch? The Netherlands' Practice of Voluntary Active Euthanasia as a Model for the United States," in *The Good of the Patient, The Good of Society,* ed. R. I. Misbin, (Frederick, Md.: University Publishing Group, 1992), 95–103.
33. Bueller, "Historical and Religious Framework."
34. Conversation with Ernst Hirsch-Ballin, August 25, 1994.
35. Huizinga, *Dutch Civilization.*

36. H. Y. Vanderpool, "Death and Dying: Euthanasia and Sustaining Life. Historical Aspects," in *Encyclopedia of Bioethics,* ed. W. T. Reich (New York: The Free Press, 1995).

37. Ibid.

38. D. M. Pappas, "Recent Historical Perspectives Regarding Medical Euthanasia and Physician–Assisted Suicide," *British Medical Bulletin,* 1996, 52:386–393.

39. Ibid.

40. R. J. Lifton, *Medical Killing and the Psychology of Genocide* (New York: Basic Books, 1986).

41. R. Lifton and E. Olson, *Living and Dying* (New York: Praeger, 1974).

42. Ibid.

43. Ibid., 36.

44. P. Ariès, *The Hour of Our Death,* trans. Helen Weaver (New York: Knopf, 1981).

45. P. Marzuk, "Increased Risk of Suicide in Persons with AIDS," *Journal of the American Medical Association,* 1988, 259:1333–137.

46. A. Beckett and D. Shenson, "Suicide Risk in Patients with Human Immunodeficiency Virus Infection and Acquired Immunodeficiency Syndrome," *Harvard Review of Psychiatry,* 1993, 1:27–35; W. Breithart, B. D. Rosenfeld, and S. O. Pasik, "Interest in Physician-Assisted Suicide Among Ambulatory HIV Infected Patients," *American Journal of Psychiatry,* 153:238–242.

43. C. Lasch, *The Culture of Narcissism* (New York: Norton, 1979).

44. H. Kohut, *The Restoration of the Self* (Madison, Conn.: International Universities Press, 1977), 267–312.

45. A. de Tocqueville, *Democracy in America,* trans. F. Bowen (New York: Random House, 1994).

7: *Theory and Practice*

1. F. Nietzsche, *Human, All-Too-Human,* trans. H. Zimmern (Edinburgh: Foulis, 1909), 88.

2. T. Marzen et al., "Suicide: A Constitutional Right?" *Duquesne Law Review,* 1985, 24:1–241.

3. H. Hendin, *Suicide in America* (New York: Norton, 1995).

4. T. Szasz, *The Myth of Mental Illness: Formulations of a Theory of Personal Conduct* (New York: Harper & Row, 1974); T. Szasz, "The Essence of Suicide," *Antioch Review,* 1974, 31:7–17.

5. D. Wasserman, "Passive Euthanasia in Response to Attempted Suicide: One Form of Aggression by Relatives," *Acta Psychiatrica Scandinavica,* 1989, 79:460–67.

6. R. Dworkin, *Life's Dominion: An Argument About Abortion, Euthanasia and Individual Freedom* (New York: Vintage Books, 1994).

7. D. Callahan, "Can We Return Death to Disease?" *Hastings Center Report,* 1989, Special Supplement, 19, 1:4–6.

8. D. Brock, "Voluntary Active Euthanasia," *Hastings Center Report,* 1992, 22, 2:10–22.

9. D. Callahan, "When Self-Determination Runs Amok," *Hastings Center Report,* 1992, 22, 2:52–55.

10. T. Preston, "Killing Pain, Ending Life," *New York Times,* Op-Ed, November 1, 1994, A27.

11. C. E. Koop, "The Challenge of Definition," *Hastings Center Report,* 1989, Special Supplement, 19, 1:2–3.

12. K. Praeger, "Legal Euthanasia Imperils Medical Integrity," *New York Times,* letter to the editor, November 7, 1994, A17.

13. R. Doerflinger, "Evading the Guidelines," *New York Times,* letter to the editor, November 7, 1994, A17.

14. G. R. Scofield, "Exposing Some Myths About Physician Assisted Suicide," in *Seattle University Law Review Symposium on Assisted Suicide,* July 17, 1995, 477.

15. D. J. Bakker, "Active Euthanasia: Is Mercy Killing the Killing of Mercy?" in *Euthanasia: The Good of the Patient, the Good of Society,* ed. R. I. Misbin (Frederick, Md.: University Publishing Group, 1992), 92.

16. L. Kass, "Neither for Love nor Money: Why Doctors Must Not Kill," *Public Interest,* 1989, Winter:25–46.

17. E. Pellegrino, "Doctors Must Not Kill," in *Euthanasia: The Good of the Patient, The Good of Society,* ed. R. I. Misbin (Frederick, Md., 1992), 27–41.

18. Ibid., 33.

19. Ibid., 34.

20. E. Borst-Eilers, "Euthanasia in the Netherlands: Brief Historical

Review and Present Situation," in *Euthanasia: The Good of the Patient, The Good of Society,* ed. R. I. Misbin (Frederick, Md., 1992), 68.

21. A. Capron, "Euthanasia in the Netherlands: American Observations," *Hastings Center Report,* 1992, 22, 2:30–33.

22. E. Slater, "Choosing the Time to Die," in *Suicide: The Philosophical Issues,* ed. M. P. Battin and D. Mayo (New York: St. Martin's Press, 1980), 199–204.

23. *Compassion in Dying v. Washington.* U. S. Court of Appeals for the Ninth Circuit. opinion by Judge John T. Noonan, March 9, 1995, Lexis 4589: 3–11.

24. Y. Kamisar, "Are Laws Against Assisted Suicide Unconstitutional?" *Hastings Center Report,* 1993, 23, 3:32–41.

25. *Compassion in Dying v Washington,* 6.

26. "Court Voids a Law Barring Help in Suicide," *New York Times,* March 7, 1996.

27. *Compassion in Dying v State of Washington.* U. S. Court of Appeals for the Ninth Circuit, opinion by Judge Stephen Reinhardt, March 6, 1996, 3,132.

28. Ibid., 3,176.

29. Ibid., 3,168.

30. *Quill et al. v Vacco et al.,* No. 95-7028, U. S. Court of Appeals for the Second Circuit, opinion by Judges Roger Miner, Milton Pollack, and Guido Calabresi, April 2, 1996.

31. Y. Kamisar, "The Right to Assisted Suicide," *Legal Times*, March 23, 1996, 23–24.

32. Y. Kamisar, "Are Laws Against Assisted Suicide Unconstitutional?" 34.

33. Supreme Court of the United States. *Quill v. Vacco.* Argued January 8, 1997. Decision reported June 26, 1997; Supreme Court of the United States. *Washington et al. v. Glucksberg et al.* Argued January 8, 1997. Decision reported June 26, 1997.

34. *Quill v Vacco,* Sup. Ct., 13.

35. *Gary Lee et al. v State of Oregon*, U. S. District Court for the State of Oregon, opinion by Judge Michael Hogan, August 3, 1995.

36. Ibid.

37. Ibid., 8–9.

38. Ibid., 8.
39. Ibid., 11–12. Studies have shown that treating physicians are not qualified to make psychiatric judgments.
40. Ibid., 13.
41. Ibid., 14–15.
42. Ibid., 17.
43. Ibid., 18.
44. Ibid., 18.
45. G. J. Annas, "Death by Prescription: The Oregon Initiative," *New England Journal of Medicine,* 1994, 331:1,240–1,243.
46. L. Kass, "Death by Ballot in Oregon," *Wall Street Journal,* November 2, 1994, A14.
47. Y. Kamisar, personal communication with author, February 7, 1995.
48. *Compassion in Dying v Washington,* 3,186.
50. F. G. Miller, T. E. Quill, H. Brody, J. C. Fletcher, L. D. Gostin, and D. E. Meier, "Regulating Physician-Assisted Death," *New England Journal of Medicine,* 1994, 4,331:119–122.
51. P. Admiraal, from remarks made at International Conference on Palliative Care, Montreal, Canada, 1989.
52. C. Gomez, *Regulating Death: Euthanasia and the Case of the Netherlands* (New York: Free Press, 1991).
53. T. Quill, C. K. Cassell, and D. Meier, "Case of the Hopelessly Ill: Proposed Clinical Criteria for Physician Assisted Suicide," *New England Journal of Medicine,* 1992, 327:1,380–1,384.
54. F. Miller and D. Meier, "Voluntary Death: A Comparison of Terminal Dehydration and Physician-Assisted Suicide," *Annals of Internal Medicine,* in press.
55. G. D. Meier, personal communication, July 21, 1997.
56. G. van der Wal, P. J. van der Maas, J. M. Bosma, et al. "Evaluation of the Notification Procedure for Physician-Assisted Death in the Netherlands," *New England Journal of Medicine* 1996, 335:1706–1711; Gomez, *Regulating Death.*
57. D. Callahan and M. White, "The Legalization of Physician-Assisted Suicide: Creating a Regulatory Potemkin Village," *University of Richmond Law Review,* 1996, 30:1–83.
58. New York State Task Force on Life and the Law, *When Death Is Sought: Assisted Suicide and Euthanasia in the Medical Context* (May 1994), 120.

59. *A Survey of Voter Attitudes in the United States,* the Tarrance Group, Houston, Texas, September 25–28, 1994.
60. M. P. Battin, "Manipulated Suicide," in *Suicide: The Philosophical Issues,* ed. M. P. Battin and D. Mayo (New York: St. Martin's Press, 1980), 179.
61. Kamisar, "Are Laws Against Assisted Suicide Unconstitutional?" 37.
62. Bakker, "Active Euthanasia," 92.
63. Pellegrino, "Doctors Must Not Kill," 30.

8: Who Should Decide? Coma and Dementia

1. K. Praeger, "When Medical Treatment Is Futile," *Wall Street Journal,* June 29, 1995, A16.
2. G. R. Scofield, "Exposing Some Myths About Physician Assisted Suicide," in *Seattle University Law Review Symposium on Assisted Suicide,* July 17, 1995, 473–493.
3. A. Capron, "Abandoning a Waning Life," *Hastings Center Report,* 1995; 25, 4:24–26.
4. Multi-Society Task Force on PVS, "Medical Aspects of the Persistent Vegetative State," *New England Journal of Medicine,* 1994, 330:1,499–1,508.
5. R. Truog, A. Brett, and J. Frader, "The Problem with Futility," *New England Journal of Medicine,* 1992, 326:1,560–1,564.
6. M. Danis, S. L. Jarr, M. S. Gerritt, L. I. Southerland, and D. L. Patrick, "A Comparison of Patient, Family, and Nurse Evaluations of the Usefulness of Intensive Care," *Journal of the American Medical Association,* 1987, 15:138–143; M. Danis, D. L. Patrick, L. I. Southerland, and M. L. Guere, "Patients' and Families' Preferences for Intensive Medical Care," *Journal of the American Medical Association,* 1988, 260:797–802.
7. Truog et al., "Problem with Futility."
8. Ibid., 1,563.
9. S. B. Nuland, *How We Die* (New York: Knopf, 1994), 103.
10. R. Dworkin, *Life's Dominion: An Argument About Abortion, Euthanasia and Individual Freedom* (New York: Vintage Books, 1994).

9: Caring Beyond Cure

1. "California Natural Death Act," California Health Safety Code, Section 7186-5, West Supplement, 1996.
2. "California Durable Power of Attorney Health Care Act," California Probate Code, Section 4771, West Supplement, 1996.
3. M. Callanan and P. Kelley, *Final Gifts: Understanding the Special Awareness, Needs, and Communications of the Dying* (New York: Poseidon Press, 1992).
4. T. Quill, *Death and Dignity: Making Choices and Taking Charge* (New York: Norton, 1993).
5. N. I. Cherny, N. Coyle, and K. Foley, "The Treatment of Suffering When Patients Request Elective Death," *Journal of Palliative Care,* 1994, 10:71–79.
6. E. J. Cassell, "The Nature of Suffering and the Goals of Medicine," *New England Journal of Medicine,* 1982, 306:639–645.
7. Ibid., 641.
8. Ibid., 642.
9. C. Gomez, case presented at workshop on the "Care of Patients Who Are Terminally Ill" held in Bellagio, Italy, in August 1996.
10. Cherny et al., "Treatment of Suffering," 76.
11. D. Wasserman, "Passive Euthanasia in Response to Attempted Suicide: One Form of Aggression by Relatives," *Acta Psychiatrica Scandinavica,* 1989, 79:460–467.
12. N. Cousins, *The Anatomy of an Illness as Perceived by the Patient: Reflections on Healing and Regeneration* (New York: Norton, 1979).
13. P. Marzuk, "Increased Risk of Suicide in Persons with AIDS," *Journal of the American Medical Association,* 1988, 259:1,333–1,337.
14. W. Breitbart and S. D. Passik, "Psychiatric Aspects of Palliative Care," in *Oxford Textbook of Palliative Medicine,* ed. D. Doyle, G. W. Hanks, and M. MacDonald (Oxford: Oxford University Press, 1993); J. Holland, "Psychological Aspects of Cancer," in *Cancer Medicine,* ed. J. Holland and E. Frei (Philadelphia: Lea & Febiger, 1982); G. R. Brown, J. R. Rundell, S. E. McManis, S. N. Kendal, R. Zachary, and L. Temoshok, "Prevalence of Psychiatric Disor-

der in Early Stages of HIV Illness," *Psychosomatic Medicine,* 1992, 54:588–601.

15. H. M. Chochinov, K. G. Wilson, M. Enns, N. Mowchun, S. Lander, M. Levitt, and J. J. Clinch, "Desire for Death in the Terminally Ill," *American Journal of Psychiatry,* 1995, 8:1,185–1,191.

16. Ibid.

17. K. Foley, "The Relationship of Pain and Symptom Management to Patient Requests for Physician-Assisted Suicide," *Journal of Pain and Symptom Management,* 1991, 6:289–297.

18. K. Foley, case presented at workshop on the "Care of Patients Who Are Terminally Ill" held in Bellagio, Italy, in August 1996.

19. A comprehensive study found that seriously ill hospitalized patients were often given aggressive treatment that is unwanted and ineffective. In a second phase of the project, specially trained nurses informed patients and families of their options, encouraged them to express their wishes, and gave physicians reports of the discussions. Neither patient nor physician behavior was significantly changed by the intervention. Patients did not communicate their wishes to doctors in any greater numbers despite being encouraged to do so. Doctors appeared to ignore the nurses' reports. Although the project investigators are now pessimistic about the possibility that improving patient-doctor communication will change treatment outcomes, one could conclude that the intervention through intermediaries was faulty and that what is needed is direct communication between physicians and patients. One cannot quarrel, however, with the authors' suggestion that social and medical guidelines are needed to make such communication more fruitful. See "A Controlled Trial to Improve Care for Seriously Ill Hospitalized Patients: The Study to Understand Prognoses and Preferences for Outcomes and Risks of Treatment (SUPPORT)," *Journal of the American Medical Association,* 1995, 20:1,591–1,598. The more than 100 principal investigators are listed at the end of the article.

20. J. Lynn, letter to the editor, *New England Journal of Medicine,* 1989, 321:119.

21. B. Shaw, preface to *Getting Married,* in *Complete Plays with Prefaces* (New York: Dodd, Mead, 1963), 4:335.

22. D. Callahan, "When Self-Determination Runs Amok," *Hastings Center Report,* 1992, 22, 2:52–55.

23. J. C. McCue, "The Naturalness of Dying," *Journal of the American Medical Association,* 1995, 273:1,039–1,043.

24. P. Ariès, *The Hour of Our Death* (New York: Vintage Books, 1981).

25. B. Zylicz, "Euthanasia," *Lancet,* 1991, 338:1,150; K. L. Dorrepaal, N. K. Aaronson, and F. van Dam, "Pain Experience and Pain Management Among Hospitalized Cancer Patients," *Cancer,* 1989, 63:593–598; K. M. Foley, "Pain, Physician-Assisted Suicide, and Euthanasia," *Pain Forum,* 1995, 4:163–178.

26. K. M. Foley, "Pain and America's Culture of Death," *Wilson Quarterly,* 1994, Autumn: 20–21.

27. Ibid.

28. Even this figure may be high, since when polled people are inclined to claim they have done what they only intend to do.

29. New York State Task Force on Life and the Law, *When Death Is Sought: Assisted Suicide and Euthanasia in the Medical Context* (May 1994).

30. *A Survey of Voter Attitudes in the United States,* the Tarrance Group, Houston, Texas, September 25–28, 1994.

31. *A Survey of Voter Attitudes in the United States,* the Tarrance Group, Houston, Texas, July 18–20, 1995.

32. R. K. Portenoy, N. Coyle, K. M. Kash, F. Brescia, C. Scanlon, D. O'Hare, R. I. Misbin, J. Holland, and K. M. Foley, "Determinants of the Willingness to Endorse Assisted Suicide: A Survey of Physicians, Nurses and Social Workers," *Psychosomatics,* 1997, 38:277–287.

33. C. Gomez, *Regulating Death: Euthanasia and the Case of the Netherlands* (New York: Free Press, 1991); H. Hendin, "Seduced by Death: Doctors, Patients and the Dutch Cure," *Issues in Law and Medicine,* 1994, 10:123–168.

34. A. Trollope, *The Fixed Period* (New York: Oxford University Press, 1993), 163–64.

35. A. Solomon, "A Death of One's Own," *New Yorker,* May 22, 1995, 54–69.

36. Ibid., 66.

37. Ibid., 62.

38. Ibid., 69.
39. Ibid., 64.
40. Ibid., 69.
41. Ibid., 68.
42. Ibid.

Afterword: The Culture of Euthanasia

1. M. Angell, "Euthanasia in the Netherlands: Good News or Bad?" *New England Journal of Medicine,* 1996, 335:1,675–1678.
2. D. Humphry, "Lethal Drugs for Assisted Suicide: How the Public Sees It," and G. Kimsma, "Euthanasia and Euthanizing Drugs in the Netherlands," both in *Drug Use in Assisted Suicide and Euthanasia,* ed. M. Battin and A. G. Lipman (New York: Hawthorn Press, 1996).
3. T. Quill, *A Midwife Through the Dying Process* (Baltimore: Johns Hopkins University Press, 1996).
4. B. Keizer, *Dancing with Mister D: Notes on Life and Death* (New York: Doubleday, 1996).

INDEX

abortion, 113, 119, 176, 194, 195
Abraham, God challenged by, 62
Achterhuis, Hans, 117
Adkins, Janet, 44
Admiraal, Pieter, 156–57, 163, 193, 207, 240
advance directives, *see* health care proxies; living wills
advance requests, for euthanasia, 98, 125, 221–22
adversarial judicial systems, 87, 88, 149
African-Americans, 212
age groups, suicide rates and, 152–55
aging process, death and, 245–46
AIDS, 181, 236–38, 239, 240, 242, 251
   see also HIV-positive patients
Alzheimer's disease, 44, 98, 221, 222, 223
   of author's mother, 224–27
American Foundation for Suicide Prevention, 24, 255
American Medical Association (AMA), 232, 242, 263
American Thoracic Society, 219
Amsterdam, 165
Amsterdam medical tribunal, 117–19
amyotropic lateral sclerosis, 128, 132, 142
analgesic medicine, 177, 235, 241
anesthetics, 177
Angell, Marcia, 259–60
"angels of death," 124–27, 146, 205
Anglican Church, 166
Annas, George, 202
antibiotics, 97, 105, 224, 225

antidepressants, 118, 158, 223, 237
anxiety about death, 32–33, 47, 207, 239–40
   cultural management of, 179–82
   displacement of, 32
   suicidal thoughts and, 153–55
Appointment with Death, An, 69–71
Ariès, Philippe, 246
arthritis, 206
Assen case, 63–64, 112, 153, 160, 210, 243, 244
   absence of bereavement therapy in, 80–81, 84, 86
   berisping (reprimand), 117
   Chabot-patient relationship in, 77–83, 85–87, 100–103, 118
   Chabot's acquittal in, 63, 76, 83–84
   consultation in, 80–81, 84, 88, 89, 117
   criticisms of, 75–76, 88–89, 112, 115–17
   deaths of patient's sons in, 77, 78, 86, 102, 118
   deciding on assisted suicide in, 78, 80–81
   force majeure as criterion in, 63, 88, 102–3, 124
   higher court rulings on, 84–85
   legal precedent set by, 76, 84, 88, 119, 148
   medication used in, 81
   patient's death in, 81–83
   patient's marriage in, 78–79
   patient's pseudonym in, 77
   prosecutor's reluctance in, 88, 90–91
atheists, 172
authority, Dutch attitudes toward, 11

Index

autonomy, of patients, 71, 74, 105, 122, 186–87, 190–92, 221, 244, 247–48, 251–52

Baena, Duke de, 170
Bakker, D. J., 21, 120–21, 191, 214
barbiturates, 51, 78, 81, 158, 234
  Hemlock Society's recommendation of, 41, 261
Baron, Charles, 204
Battin, Margaret, 213
Belkin, Lisa, 50, 53, 54, 55–56, 60
bereavement therapy, Assen case and, 80–81, 84, 86
Betzold, Michael, 45
bilanz Selbstmord ("balanced suicide"), 36
bioethics, 220
"Boomsma, Netty," *see* Assen case, patient's pseudonym in
Borst-Eilers, Els, 98, 106, 118, 124, 147, 192
bourgeois society, Dutch, 166–67, 169
brain death, 218–19
Brett, Allan, 219–20
Breyer, Stephen G., 14–15
Brock, Dan, 188
Brody, Howard, 206
But What If She Wants to Die? (Delury), 58

California, 49, 179, 229, 230, 231–32
California Declaration, 230
Callahan, Daniel, 171, 186–87, 188, 210–11, 245
Callanan, Maggie, 233
Calvin, John, 166
Calvinism, 164–66, 167, 168, 171–72
cancer, 65, 70, 74–75, 77, 99, 105, 177, 220, 221, 235, 240–41, 247, 254, 259
capital punishment, 176, 186, 191
Capron, Alexander, 123, 192, 217, 218
cardiopulmonary resuscitation (CPR), 217
"Case of the Overzealous Inspector, The" (Schudel, Sutorius, et al.), 89–90
Cassell, Eric, 234–35
Catholics, 163, 164, 165, 171, 172
causality vs. culpability, in death, 188
Central Medical Tribunal, 125
cerebral vascular failure, 221
Chabot, Boudewijn, 114, 148, 153
  background and career of, 76
  celebrity status of, 116
  criticisms directed against, 75–76, 88, 112, 115–17
  medical tribunal's reprimand of, 117–18
  see also Assen case
chemotherapy, 40, 79, 220

children, death anxieties of, 179
"children of the Netherlands," God's covenant with, 168
Choice in Dying, 229–30
Choosing Death, 61
Christian Democratic party, 106, 111, 148, 174
Christian Institute of Medical Ethics, 120
chronically ill patients, euthanasia for, 64, 206–7
class structure, 174–75, 211–12
closure, 241
Cohen, Herbert, 76, 100, 106–7, 114, 118, 160, 173, 212
  as "angel of death," 127
  on death, 176
  as euthanasia practitioner and consultant, 65–69, 122, 174, 207
  notification procedure opposed by, 98–99
  on physician-assisted suicide vs. euthanasia, 146–47
  professional position, 65–66
comas:
  brain death and, 218–19
  Cruzan case, 193, 195–96, 218
  Gilgunn case, 216, 217–18, 219
  physician vs. family decisions for, 215–20
  Quinlan case, 218
compassion, 56–57, 147
Compassion in Dying, 15–16, 50, 52, 53, 55–56, 189, 252
competent patients, 199, 200
  see also dementia
concentration camps, 67, 112, 118
conformity, 170, 171
consensus, as basis of Dutch judicial system, 87
Constitution, U.S., 195, 196, 197
consultation (second opinions), 109
  in Assen case, 80–81, 84, 88, 89, 117
  by Cohen, 66, 68, 126–27, 207–8
  in Dutch guidelines, 64, 75, 121, 138–39, 146, 147
  Groen-Prakken on, 99–100
  Measure 16 and, 33, 199
  palliative care and, 207–8
  by psychiatrists, 115–16
  in von Wendel case, 129
Cornelisse-Claassen, Martine, 71
corticosteroids, 237, 238
Court of Appeals, U.S., 193–95
Cousins, Norman, 239
criminals, Kevorkian's proposed medical experiments on, 46
Cruzan, Nancy Beth, 193, 196, 218

culpability vs. causality, in death, 188
Curren, Judith, 44–45

Dancing with Mister D (Keizer), 264
Daniel Den Hoed Clinic, 66
death:
    acceptance of, 238
    aging process and, 245–46
    causality vs. culpability in, 188
    Cohen on, 176
    determination of, 219
    with dignity, 32, 49, 61, 131, 134, 178,
        240
    at home, 174, 181
    intimacy and, 254
    "medicalization" of, 246
    see also anxiety about death
Death and Dignity (Quill), 39–40, 42
death certificates, in Dutch euthanasia cases,
    65
death clinics, 46
Death on Request, 145
    consultation in, 130
    patient's death in, 130–31
    patient-wife relationship in, 128–33
    physician-patient relationship in, 128–33
    U.S. broadcast of, 128, 134
death row inmates, Kevorkian's suggested
    medical experiments on, 46
Defoe, Daniel, 166–67
Delury, George, 58–60, 260, 261–62
dementia, 221–28
    advance euthanasia requests and, 221–22
    of author's mother, 224–27
    causes of, 221
    involuntary euthanasia for, 95–100, 125
Denmark, 176
depression, 15, 32, 40, 200, 205–6
    Assen case and, 85, 148, 157
    patient's rigidity and, 36, 41
    suicide and, 34–36, 157–60, 213, 222–23,
        246, 260
Dessaur, Caterina, 119
diabetes, 206
Diane, Quill's assisted suicide of, 39–43, 86,
    160
Diekstra, René, 76–77, 85, 86, 100, 144, 175,
    212
    academic positions held by, 72
    on Assen case, 75–76, 112
    Nicholas and René Speijer's suicides and,
        74–76
    on nontreatment of pneumonia, 97
    on physician-assisted suicide and
        euthanasia, 72–76, 112

public vs. private stances taken by, 112
dignity, death with, 32, 49, 61, 131, 134, 178,
    240
dikes, 168
Dillman, Robert, 97, 100, 106, 107, 111,
    112, 114, 123, 125, 144, 173
    on Assen case, 102–3
    on consultation, 147
    on physicians' burden, 146
doctors, *see* physician-assisted suicide;
    physicians
"doctors must not kill" principle, 191
Doerflinger, Richard, 189–90
Donaldson, Sam, 128
Double Exit (Wickett), 48
drugs, 165
    see also medication
due process, 195
Durable Power of Attorney for Health Care,
    231
Dutch art, 166, 167
Dutch Civilization in the Seventeenth Century
    (Huizinga), 166
Dutch East India Company, 168
Dutch engineering, 167
Dutch land reclamation, 167–68
Dutch Patients' Association, 113
Dutch Physicians' Association, 112–13
Dutch Reformed Church, 165
Dutch Voluntary Euthanasia Society (NVVE),
    66, 69, 97, 99, 124, 135, 171–72, 248
    "angels of death" and, 126–27
    Death on Request and, 127, 132
    euthanasia "passports" of, 71
    euthanasia policy of, 71, 107, 119–20, 135
    involuntary euthanasia supported by, 120
    membership and budget of, 71
    politics and, 111
Dworkin, Ronald, 186, 221–22
"dying phase," 104, 105

elderly:
    as future target of euthanasia, 15, 193,
        211–12
    health care costs for, 192
    suicide rates of, 153–55
    U.S. attitudes toward, 180, 181
electroconvulsive therapy, 115, 118
"empowerment," 61
engineering, 167
England, 165, 166, 168
equal protection, 195, 197, 200, 202
Erasmus University, 65
eugenics, 192
Europe, 193

Europe (*continued*)
  anti-euthanasia opinions voiced in, 111,
    163
euthanasia:
  advance requests for, 98, 125, 221–22
  and advent of modern hospital, 177
  advocates' marketing of, 49–50, 62
  "angels of death" and, 124–27, 146
  arguments for and against, 183–214
  for chronically ill patients, 64, 206–7
  comas and, 215–20
  culture of, 257–68
  death certificates in Dutch cases of, 65
  Dutch consensus on, 173–77
  Dutch critics of, 114–21
  Dutch definition of, 91, 97–98, 122
  Dutch governmental report on, *see*
    Remmelink Report
  Dutch legal guidelines for, 64–65, 71, 94,
    96, 98, 106–7, 121, 123–24, 125, 146,
    148, 173
  Dutch legal status of, 63–64, 94, 106,
    148–49
  Dutch national characteristics and, 163–73,
    174, 177
  Dutch political issues and, 111–49
  Dutch politicization of research on,
    134–44, 145
  Dutch practitioners of, 65–76, 161, 264–68
  Dutch rates of, 136–37
  Dutch support of physicians in cases of,
    88–91, 106
  Dutch suppression of criticism made
    against, 19, 111–21, 134–35
  Dutch television film on, 128–33
  early U.S. support for, 177–78
  estimated annual Dutch cases of, 65
  ethical argument for, 187–90
  euphemism for, 36
  family pressure and, 16, 20, 49–50, 54, 55,
    57, 61, 97, 108, 128–34, 142, 185,
    211, 213
  frequency of performance by practitioners
    of, 131–32, 207
  future prospects in Netherlands for, 18,
    144–49
  Gomez study on, 121–22, 210
  health care organizations opposed to, 263
  impossibility of control of, 252–56
  international frequency of, 145
  international opinion on, 74, 111, 121–24,
    145, 163, 175–76
  legal argument for, 193–211
  lethal dose for, 261–62
  medical argument for, 189–93

most vulnerable potential targets for,
    211–14
  in Nazi Germany, 178
  palliative care affected by, 15, 18–19,
    143–44, 244–45, 255
  patient competence and, 161–62
  patient's vs. doctor's needs and, 69–70, 146
  physician-assisted suicide as first step to,
    49–50, 63–64, 135, 162
  physician-assisted suicide compared with,
    68–69, 71–72, 146–47
  physician-patient relationship and, 69,
    71–75, 141–42, 209
  physician's initiation of discussion of, 68,
    136, 185
  physicians opposed to, 263
  physicians' power enhanced by, 37, 115,
    174, 214, 244, 258
  physicians' refusals to perform, 147
  physicians troubled by performance of,
    160–61
  for psychologically distressed patients, 36,
    64, 72, 135, 155–56
  religious opposition to, 112, 120, 124, 164,
    263
  reporting deaths due to, 64–65, 83, 138–41
  social argument for, 184–87
  social implications of, 31–32
  social policy and, 245–56
  for terminally ill patients, 12, 36, 63–64,
    135
  U.S. physicians on, 251–52
  U.S. proponents of, 261, 262–64
  violations of Dutch guidelines for, 75, 121,
    136–44, 171, 174, 210, 252, 258
  withdrawal of life support compared with,
    187–90, 196, 242–45
  see also involuntary euthanasia; physician-
    assisted suicide
euthanasia "passports," 71

families, 120
  alienation from, 181
  of comatose patients, 215–20
  in Dutch vs. U.S. medical decisions, 96
  emotional suffering of, 239
  as health care proxies, 231
  at physician-assisted suicides, 43
  pressure exerted by, 16, 20, 49–50, 54, 55,
    57, 61, 97, 108, 128–34, 142, 185,
    211, 213
  suicide and, 239
family doctors, 213
fatalism, 172
Feber, Herman, 88–89

Index

Feiger, Geoffrey, 44, 47
Fenigsen, Richard, 113–14, 120
Final Exit (Humphry), 47
Fixed Period, The (Trollope), 253
Fletcher, John, 206
Foley, Kathleen, 240, 247
force majeure, 175
  as criterion in Assen case, 63, 88, 102–3, 124
  criticism of, 123, 124
  definition and Dutch legal status of, 63, 64, 109, 117, 123
  in Remmelink Report, 94
Fourteenth Amendment, 194, 196, 198
Frader, Joel, 219–20
France, 168
free thinkers, 163
futile treatment, 219–20, 247

Ganzini, Linda, 155
Giel, Robert, 83
Gilgunn coma case, 216, 217–18, 219
God:
  Abraham's challenge of, 62
  covenant between Dutch and, 168
Gomez, Carlos, 121–22, 171–72, 208, 210, 236, 239, 242, 251
"good faith," 201, 202
Gostin, Lawrence, 206
Goud, Johan, 117
Great Britain, 179, 233
Groen-Prakken, Johanna, 99–100, 173
guilt vs. shame, 170–71
Gunning, Karl, 112–13, 120, 137

Hague medical tribunal, 125
Hastings Center Report, 113
Hauser, Arnold, 167
Hawking, Stephen, 132–33
health care, 163, 192–93, 211–12, 249–50
health care proxies, 215, 227, 229, 231–33, 243, 248
Health Department, Dutch, 89
Hemlock Society, 41, 43, 47, 60, 179, 254, 261
Hilhorst, H. W., 108
Hirsch-Ballin, Ernst, 174–76
HIV-positive patients, 34, 70, 107–8, 244
  see also AIDS
Hogan, Michael, 199–203, 204
Holocaust, 113
  see also concentration camps
home, death at, 174, 181
hospice care, 14, 233–34, 243
hospitals, "safe," 113

"house doctors" (*huisarts*), 174, 213
Huizinga, Johan, 166, 169, 176
human nature, 166
Humphry, Derek, 43, 47–48, 58, 160

Ikon television network, 133
"incurable debilitating disease," 206–7
individualism, 170
infectious diseases, demented patients and, 96–97
integrated self, 221
"intent of the heart," 189
interdisciplinary teams, 109
involuntary euthanasia, 14, 64–65, 72, 91–100, 113–14, 120, 258
  borderline cases of, 92
  definition of, 91, 104–5
  dementia and, 96–100, 125
  Dutch physicians' support of, 91
  estimated number of cases of, 91, 92, 104, 122–23, 137, 139–41
  notification procedure and, 94, 98, 103, 104, 107
  "passports for life" and, 113
  physician as decision-maker in cases of, 19, 95–100, 104–10, 139
  rationale given for, 64, 91, 93–95, 105, 123, 140
Issues in Law and Medicine, 114
IV feeding, 96
  see also life support

Jannink-Kapelle, Lide, 69, 71, 97, 107–8
Jean's Way (Humphry), 47
Jews, 163, 178
Journal of Forensic Psychiatry, 60
judiciary, Dutch, 71, 149, 171
  consensus as basis of decisions made by, 87, 173
  judicial panels used in, 83, 173
  reluctant prosecutorial approach of, 116, 149
juries, Dutch judicial system and, 83

Kamisar, Yale, 194, 195–96, 214
Kass, Leon, 191
Keizer, Bert, 264–68
Kelley, Patricia, 233
Keown, John, 122–23
Kevorkian, Jack, 17, 43–47, 56, 62, 66, 160, 252
  medical experiments on criminals proposed by, 46
  "obitiatry" and "medicide" proposals of, 45–46

Index

Kevorkian (*continued*)
    physician-assisted suicides attended by,
        43–44
    and suspension of license, 47
killing, justifications for, 186–87
KNMG, *see* Royal Dutch Medical
    Association
Koerselman, Frank, 115–17, 119
Kohut, Heinz, 181
Koop, C. Everett, 189

law, as solution to societal problems, 182,
    212–13
Lebov, Myrna, 58–60
Lee, Melinda, 155
Leeuwarden, appeals court in, 84, 116
Leiden, siege of, 167–68
Leiden, University of, 72, 76
leukemia, 31, 40–41, 162
"liberty interests," 196
life support:
    comatose patients and, 215–20
    dementia and, 221–28
    discontinuing of, 65, 187–90, 196, 216–18
    presidential commission on, 217–18
    prolonging of, 179
    withholding of, 65, 91, 96–97, 122,
        242–45
Lifton, Robert, 179
living wills, 229–33, 248
Louise, physician-assisted suicide of, 16,
    50–57, 160, 262
lung cancer, 220
Lynn, Joanne, 244–45

Macbeth (Shakespeare), 57
malpractice, 124
managed care, 249–50
Marks, Isaac, 76
marriage, Shaw on, 245
Massachusetts General Hospital, 216
"meaningful survival," 219
Measure 16 (Oregon physician-assisted suicide
    law), 11, 16, 33, 49, 179, 199–204,
        228, 261, 262, 263
    enactment of, 199
    overturning of, 199–203
    reaffirmed, 204
media, Dutch, 116, 118, 125, 175
medical decision at the end of life (MDEL),
    65, 92
Medic Alert Foundation, 232
medical experiments, on criminals, 46
"medical help in dying," 104–5
"medicalization of death," 246

medical school, 247
medical tribunals, Dutch, 89, 90, 117–18,
    123, 125, 208
medication, 115, 118, 158
    analgesic, 235, 241
    hastening of death through use of, 65, 69,
        81, 92, 130, 146–47, 189, 234
"medicide," 45
Meier, Diane, 206, 209–10
Memorial Sloan-Kettering Cancer Center,
    239, 240
"mental duress," 94
Mero, Ralph, Louise's assisted suicide and,
    16, 50–57
Michigan, 43, 44, 47, 193
Michigan Supreme Court, 47, 195
Miller, Franklin, 206, 207, 208, 209
ministers, 71
Ministry of Justice, Dutch, 19, 84, 88, 107
Mittendorf, Carlo, 81
morality, in Dutch national character, 169–72
morphine, 189, 237, 241
Mulder-Meiss, Wine, 125–26
multiple sclerosis, 45, 67–68
Multi-Society Task Force on PVS, 218
myelocytic leukemia, 26, 31, 162

narcissism, culture of, 182–83
Nederhorst, Maarten, 127, 132–34
Netherlands, 62, 63–177
    as commercial power, 166, 168
    consensus on euthanasia in, 173–77
    18th-century decline of, 168–69
    estimated annual number of euthanasia
        cases in, 65
    future prospects for euthanasia in, 18,
        144–49
    guideline violations for physician-assisted
        suicide and euthanasia in, 75–76, 121,
            136–44, 171, 174, 210, 252
    land reclamation in, 167–68
    legal status and guidelines for physician-
        assisted suicide and euthanasia in,
            63–65, 71, 75, 96, 98–99, 106–7, 121,
            123–24, 125–26, 134–44, 146,
            148–49
    as maritime power, 163–64, 167–68
    national characteristics of, 163–73, 174,
        177
    palliative care in, 15, 18–19, 134, 176, 244
    politics of euthanasia in, 19, 111–49
    public opinion polls taken in, 112
    religion in, 163–66, 167, 168, 170–72
    social and moral attitudes in, 169–73
    suicide rates in, 151–55, 176

tolerance and intolerance in, 163–64, 169
see also judiciary, Dutch
New England Journal of Medicine, 19, 39, 135,
    206, 259
New Yorker, 253–54
New York State, 11–17, 193, 195, 196–98,
    226, 232, 249
New York State Task Force on Life and the
    Law, 211–12, 249
New York Times, 146
New York Times Magazine, 16, 50, 55
Nietzsche, Friedrich, 183, 185
Ninth Circuit Court of Appeals, U.S., 14, 15,
    193–95, 198, 203–4
nonmedical volunteers, 127
Noonan, John T., 193, 244
Norton, W. W., & Company, 114
Norway, 176, 180–81
notification procedure, for involuntary
    euthanasia, 94, 98, 103, 104, 107
nursing homes, 231, 248
NVVE, *see* Dutch Voluntary Euthanasia
    Society

Oakland County Circuit Court, 44
"obitiatry," 45, 46
Oregon, physician-assisted suicide law in, *see*
    Measure 16
Oslo, 180
Otten, Willem Jan, 117

pain, 31–32, 156, 189, 240, 256
    control of, *see* palliative care, pain control
        through
    involuntary euthanasia performed for relief
        of, 91, 95, 104
    subjectivity of, 105, 122, 192, 244
palliative care, 16–17, 66, 122, 134, 176,
    233–42, 243, 247, 251, 263
    AIDS and, 236–38, 239
    as casualty of euthanasia, 15, 18–19,
        143–44, 244–45, 255
    consultation and, 207–8
    euthanasia wishes reversed through, 240–43
    hospice programs and, 14, 233–34
    managed care and, 249–50
    pain control through, 17, 234–35, 259
    settings for, 233–34
papal authority, 171
"passports":
    for euthanasia, 71
    for life, 113
patient-physician relationships, 71–76
    in Assen case, 77–83, 85–86, 100–103, 118
    limitations of, 115

and nonphysical aspects of personhood, 235
    physician as decision-maker in, 95–100
    and physician's need for inclusion in
        patient's death, 86
    psychological blackmail in, 85, 126, 159
    Quill on, 209
    reunion fantasies in, 42, 86
    trust in, 191
    in van Wendel case, 128–34, 142
patients:
    advance directives made by, *see* health care
        proxies; living wills
    advance requests for euthanasia made by, 98
    ambivalence of, 16, 45, 54, 119, 121,
        172–73, 184–85
    autonomy of, 71, 74, 105, 122, 192, 221,
        244, 247–48
    chronically ill, 12, 64, 206–7
    comatose, *see* comas
    demented, *see* dementia
    HIV-positive, 34, 70, 107–8, 244
    protection of, 173, 203, 213, 229–56
    see also psychologically-distressed patients;
        terminally-ill patients
Pellegrino, Edmund, 191–92, 214
persistent vegetative state (PVS), *see* comas
Phillips, Derek, 164, 170, 172
physician-assisted suicide:
    advocates' marketing of, 49–50, 62, 260
    ambivalence in patients' requests for, 54,
        119, 121, 172–73, 184–85
    of Diane, 39–43, 86, 160
    Dutch critics of U.S. legalization of,
        212–13
    Dutch government's commissioned report
        on, 135–44
    Dutch legal guidelines for, 64–65, 75, 94,
        134–44
    Dutch legal status of, 63–64, 94, 106,
        148–49
    Dutch support of physicians in cases of,
        89–91
    effects of legitimization of, 103
    estimated annual Dutch cases of, 65,
        136–37
    euthanasia compared with, 68–69, 71–72
    family presence at, 43
    family pressure and, 16, 20, 49, 54, 55, 57,
        61, 97, 108, 128–34, 160, 185, 211,
        213
    as first step to euthanasia, 49, 64, 135, 162
    of Louise, 16, 50–57
    New York case and, 11–17, 196–98
    Oregon legalization of, 11, 33, 49, 179,
        199–204, 228, 261, 262

physician-assisted suicide (*continued*)
  patient competence and, 161–62
  physician-exerted pressure and, 15–16, 20,
    57–58, 61
  physicians' power enhanced by, 37, 115,
    174, 214, 244, 258
  psychological distress as grounds for, 12,
    15, 36, 64, 72–73, 84, 90, 115, 135,
    155–56
  reunion fantasies and, 42
  right to withdraw from treatment vs.,
    12–13
  social implications of, 31–32
  U.S. model proposals for, 204–10
  violations of Dutch guidelines for, 75,
    136–41, 262
  Washington case and, 196, 198–99
  withdrawal of treatment vs., 12–13, 258
  see also Assen case; euthanasia; involuntary
    euthanasia
physicians:
  as "angels of death," 124–27, 146
  anti-euthanasia stances of, 111, 112–21
  as authority figures, 171–72, 174
  comatose patients and, 215–20
  as decision-makers in involuntary
    euthanasia cases, 19, 95–100, 104–10,
    139–41
  Dutch euthanasia practitioners, 65–76,
    264–68
  Dutch support for rights of, 89–91,
    106
  euthanasia discussions initiated by, 68, 136,
    185, 258
  "house doctors" (*huisarts*), 174, 213
  Measure 16 responsibilities of, 199–202
  opposition of, to euthanasia, 263
  palliative care by, 16–17, 233–42, 243, 247,
    259
  percentage of Dutch euthanasia
    practitioners among, 65, 131–32
  physician-assisted suicide and euthanasia as
    enhancing power of, 37, 115, 174,
    214, 244
  pressure on patients by, 16, 57–58, 61, 160
  recommended training for, 246–48
  terminally-ill patients as difficult for, 37,
    69–71, 155–56, 240
  as troubled by performance of euthanasia,
    160–61
  as uninformed about end-of-life issues,
    258–59
  U.S., euthanasia views of, 252
  see also consultation; patient-physician
    relationships

Pijnenborg, Loes, 92, 144–45
Planned Parenthood v. Casey, 194, 198
plastic bags, suffocation with, 48, 126, 261–62
pneumonia, 96, 97, 220, 224, 225, 236
political parties, Dutch, 164
poverty, 211–12
Praeger, Kenneth, 21, 189, 216–17, 219
Preston, Thomas, 189
Prime Time Live, 128, 134
privacy, right to, 196
"profoundly fatigued family," 239
prostitution, 165
Protestants, 113, 164
  see also Calvinism
proxies, health care, 215, 227, 229, 231–33,
  243, 248
psychiatrists, 40, 60, 80–81, 89, 115–16, 148,
  155–56, 157, 159–62, 181, 199, 243
psychologically-distressed patients:
  physician-assisted suicide or euthanasia for,
    12, 36, 64, 72–73, 84, 90, 115, 135,
    155–56
  see also anxiety about death; Assen case;
    depression; *force majeure*
public opinion polls:
  Dutch, 112
  U.S. 250–51
PVS (persistent vegetative state), *see* comas

"quality assurance," 109
quality of life, 91, 97
Quill, Timothy, 47, 58, 206, 252, 260
  academic position of, 40
  criticism against, 40–41
  Diane's assisted suicide and, 39–43, 86, 160
  Jane's assisted suicide and, 261
  on physician-patient relationships, 209
Quinlan, Karen, 218

race, 211, 212
"rational suicide," 36
Reding, George, 45
"regulating physician-assisted death," 206–9
Rehnquist, William, 15, 196, 197
Reinhardt, Stephen, 194, 196, 203
religion:
  in Netherlands, 163–66, 167, 168, 170–72
  in opposition to euthanasia, 112, 120, 124,
    164
Rembrandt van Rijn, 167
Remmelink, Jan, 65
Remmelink Commission, 65, 94, 104–5, 106,
  107, 108, 123
Remmelink Report, 108, 112, 121, 122, 135
  absence of recommendations in, 93

Index

collegial relationship between interviewers and physicians in, 106
estimated annual number of euthanasia cases in, 65
on involuntary euthanasia, 91–94, 104, 111, 113–14
on notification procedure, 94
on physicians' initiation of euthanasia, 93
Remmelink Commission's supplement to, 94, 104–5
respirators, 220, 225, 227, 236
reunion fantasies, 42, 86, 159
"right to die," 12, 185, 190–91, 193–204
Roe v. Wade, 195
Roose, William, 171–72
Rotterdam, 66
Royal Dutch Association for the Advancement of Pharmacy, 81
Royal Dutch Medical Association (KNMG), 93, 95, 105, 107
"angels of death" and, 126–27
Committee on Ethics of, 80, 120
on involuntary euthanasia for demented patients, 98
membership of, 113
on notification procedure for involuntary euthanasia, 94, 103–4
physician-assisted suicide and euthanasia guidelines established by, 64–65, 71, 96–97, 134–44, 146, 148, 173
politics and, 111
splinter group formed from, 112–13
rules, Dutch faith in, 172
Rutenfrans, Chris, 19, 119–20

"safe" hospitals, 113
Sanctuary Foundation, 113
Scandinavia, 176, 180–81
Schalken, Tom, 117
Schama, Simon, 166–68
schoon, 169
Schudel, Joost, 89, 114
on Assen case, 80, 88
on involuntary euthanasia, 95–96
Scofield, Giles, 190–91, 217
Scotland, 166
second opinion, *see* consultation
sedation, 259, 264
sex, suicide rates related to, 152, 154
Shakespeare, William, 57
shame vs. guilt, 170–71
Shaw, George Bernard, 245
Slater, Eliot, 192–93
Sodom, 62
Solomon, Andrew, 253–55, 260

"Son of Sam," law, 60
Sorgdrager, Winnie, 118
Spain, 166, 167–68
Speijer, René, 74–75
"Spirit of the Netherlands, The" (Huizinga), 169
"spiritual and physical decay," 156–57
suffering, 234
see also pain; unbearable suffering, in Dutch guidelines
suicide, 33, 151–62
depression and, 34–36, 157–60, 213, 222–23, 246, 259–60
Dutch rates of, 151–55, 176
family response to, 239
Hemlock Society's recommended methods, 41, 48
making conditions and, 36
of Nicholas and René Speijer, 74–75
patients' threats of, 159
physical illness and, 33–36, 259–60
rationality and, 36–37
right to, 183–87
U.S. rates of, 176
see also physician-assisted suicide
Suicide in America (Hendin), 114
"suicide machine," 44
Supreme Court, Dutch, 84, 103, 117, 118, 123
Supreme Court, U.S., 193, 194–96, 204, 263–64
New York case (*Vacco v. Quill*), 11–17, 196–98
Washington case (*Washington v. Glucksberg*) in, 196, 198–99
surrogates, 226
Sutorius, Eugene, 89–90, 97
background of, 87–88
as Chabot's attorney in Assen case, 83, 87–88
euthanasia critics suppressed by, 119–20
involuntary euthanasia supported by, 95
Sweden, 176
Szasz, Thomas, 184, 185

terminally-ill patients, 12, 50, 135, 162, 206, 246–48
depression in, 35
equal protection and, 195, 199–200, 202
euthanasia for, 64, 214
last days of, 32–33
as legal "person," 195
physicians' difficulties with, 37, 69–71, 155–56, 240
psychiatrists and, 157

terminally-ill patients (*continued*)
    reversal of euthanasia requests made by,
        240–42
    state commissions on care of, 248–49
    suicidal thoughts as initial response of, 32,
        36–37
"termination of the patient without explicit
    request," 91–95
Thomas, Lewis, 37
Tocqueville, Alexis de, 182
Toynbee, Arnold, 180
traveling physicians ("angels of death"),
        124–27, 146
Tribe, Lawrence, 11, 13–14
Trollope, Anthony, 253
Truog, Robert, 219–20
Twycross, Robert, 33

unbearable suffering, in Dutch guidelines, 64,
        75, 121
United States:
    Dutch critics of legalization of physician-
        assisted suicide in, 212–13
    early support for euthanasia in, 178
    legal arguments over euthanasia in,
        193–204
    reasons for support of physician-assisted
        suicide and euthanasia in, 163, 176,
        177–82
    western expansion of, 168
"unnatural causes," in Dutch euthanasia cases,
        64–65, 83, 138
U.S. News & World Report, 46

Vacco, Dennis, 249
values, societal breakdown of, 177
van Dantzig, Dries, 83

van der Maas, Paul, 100, 114
    involuntary euthanasia study led by, 92–94,
        106
    on patients in "dying phase," 104
    private vs. public stances taken by, 94–95,
        144
van der Sluis, Isaac, 119
van Dinter, G. J., 124
van Oijen, Wilfred, 128–34, 142
van Ree, Frank, 81, 84
van Wendel, Antoinette, 128–33,
        160
van Wendel, Cees:
    Dutch television film about physician-
        assisted suicide of, 128–33, 160
Verhoef, J., 124–25, 147
voluntariness, in Dutch guidelines, 64, 75,
        136
voluntary euthanasia societies, 165

Wantz, Marjorie, 44
Washington state, 11, 49, 179, 193–95, 196,
        198–99
Wasserman, Danuta, 239
Welie, Jos, 109
Wesley, Patricia, 40–41
White, Margot, 210–11
Wickett, Ann, 47, 48, 160
witches, 166
withdrawal of treatment, physician-assisted
        suicide vs., 12–13, 258
women:
    Dutch euthanasia case law and, 66
    Dutch suicide rates of, 152, 154
World War II, 179

Zylicz, Zbigniew, 18–19